MARK BREND

DOWN RIVER

IN SEARCH OF DAVID ACKLES

DOWN RIVER
IN SEARCH OF DAVID ACKLES
MARK BREND

A Jawbone book
First edition 2025
Published in the UK and the USA by
Jawbone Press
7 Orlando Road
London SW4 0LE
England
www.jawbonepress.com
books@jawbonepress.com

ISBN 978-1-916829-22-0

Printed by Short Run Press, Exeter, Devon
1 2 3 4 5 29 28 27 26 25

CONTENTS

PROLOGUE

SOURCE

“

Shall we gather at the river?

ROBERT LOWRY

”

In January 1985, I moved to a flat in Highgate, North London, with Matt Gale and Geoff Smith. The three of us were three-quarters of a band, The Palace Of Light, that went on to release an obscure album in 1987. The flat was in a 60s low-rise block on an affluent, leafy residential street off the Archway Road. It was unfurnished, and we lived there with little more than mattresses to sleep on, our guitars and amps, our record players and our records. We were all signing on for unemployment benefit, though not, I think, on the same day, as you were allocated a slot based on the first letter of your surname. I don't recall where we had to go to sign on, exactly, but it involved a walk down the Archway Road, under what was known as suicide bridge, and then a left turn. Somewhere on that route, on a side street, was a shop that sold second-hand records. Memory tells me that it didn't just sell records—maybe books and clothes too. But I can't be sure. I went into that shop after signing on one day. It was there that I saw for the first time a copy of the debut David Ackles album.

At that point I had never heard of David Ackles. I was attracted by the sleeve. A murky, out-of-focus, browny-maroon photo of a room seen through a cracked window. A man stands to the right of the image at an angle to the camera, hands in pockets. He looks over his shoulder straight at you, as if the photographer has called his name. Although his gaze is direct, the man's features are all but obscured by shadow.

In The Palace Of Light we were getting interested in singer-songwriters from the 1960s. Starting with Dylan and Cohen, we had already branched out to Tim Hardin and Tim Buckley. This album, I thought, looked like it might be that sort of thing. I noted that it was on Elektra Records. 1968. I knew enough by then to know that an album on Elektra Records from that period was a safe bet. It was worth a try. It would have been a few pounds. No more. I didn't have the money to splash out on expensive records, let alone speculative purchases.

When I got the album home, I sat down and listened to both sides straight through, the way you listened to records in those days. I have listened to it straight through many times since. I loved it then and I still do. It is the soundtrack to my personal mythology of our months in that bare flat in Highgate. Matt and Geoff loved it, too. I recall Matt taping it and rewinding the cassette to play 'His Name Is Andrew' over and over again, working out the chord changes. I was right in a sense with my singer-songwriter hunch. Ackles was a member of Elektra's stable of literate, serious, intense singer-songwriters—alongside Buckley, Fred Neil, David Blue, Tom Rush, and more. Yet he was different. For a start, he was a piano player, not an acoustic guitar picker. And he didn't seem to have folkie roots in the way the others did. Even on his debut, the most conventional of his albums, he sounded like a man apart.

We spent the first few months of that year writing songs and recording demos at a studio in Brixton called Cold Storage, where our drummer, Charlie Llewellin, was a partner. We then embarked on a wearisome and dispiriting round of sending demo tapes to any record company that might possibly be interested. Most weren't, but eventually we got an offer from a small independent label, Bam Caruso. When we met Phil Smee, who owned the label, we told him we were David Ackles fans. He was astonished.*

* Phil gave us a cassette of songs he thought we might consider covering, including 'Postcards', by Ackles. We never attempted it, though we did cover two songs on the cassette: 'Bright Islands' by Cyrus Faryar and 'Wish I Was' by Mickey Newbury (both recording for Elektra at the same time as Ackles).

About ten years older than us, Phil had bought Ackles's albums as they were released in the late 60s and early 70s and revered them as much as we did. But the thing is that by then, the mid-1980s, not much more than ten years since his recording career had quietly drawn to a close, Ackles was forgotten. None of his albums had sold well. A few people like Phil, who had bought them at the time, knew of him. Nobody else did. Ackles was not a revered cult figure, in the way that Nick Drake—a near contemporary—already was. He was not a name to drop. He was just forgotten.

After buying that first album I found out soon enough that Ackles released three more. The second, *Subway To The Country*, and the third, *American Gothic*, both on Elektra, were easy to find in the bargain bins of the Camden and Notting Hill second-hand record shops where I later worked. The fourth, *Five & Dime*, was harder to locate—in the UK, at least—as it had never been released over here. It was a decade or more before I found it.

For years, decades, Ackles's third album, *American Gothic*, was the one I listened to the least. I admired it more than I liked it. I don't think I was alone in that. Though his first two albums are an acquired taste, on them Ackles tempers his intense idiosyncrasies with enough just-about-mainstream rock and country gestures to place him on the periphery of the singer-songwriter circle. By *American Gothic*, Ackles was out on his own. That's not to say he was *sui generis*. All music bears the marks of its influences, and Ackles was no exception. It's just that his particular mingling of influences, interests, and abilities led him to a style and aesthetic out of step with almost everything else that was happening then. And since.

Although its title suggests otherwise, *American Gothic* owes much of its distinct character to England. In September 1971, Ackles moved from California to England, ending up in a riverside cottage in Wargrave, Berkshire, to prepare the album which he'd been planning for more than a year already. He said that he needed the distance to get a clear perspective, and in this small town on the Thames, which features in Jerome K. Jerome's *Three Men In A Boat*, he pieced together *American Gothic*'s lavish orchestrations. Musicians from the London Symphony Orchestra and the Salvation Army choir and band, under the guiding hand of producer Bernie Taupin and conductor Robert Kirby, then joined Ackles to make the record at IBC studios in London. Ackles travelled to the sessions like any other commuter from the home counties—by train and tube.

If Ackles's first two albums retained some tenuous connection with rock convention, on *American Gothic* he fashioned a sort of baroque musical theatre style all his own. With scarcely a guitar to be heard, and Ackles's sometimes austere, rumbling enunciations over brass, woodwind, and piano, it's a record that defies easy classification. With hindsight and close attention, you might locate the album's more accessible songs in remote, previously unexplored territory somewhere between Randy Newman, Harry Nilsson, early Tom Waits, and Scott Walker. The rest—about half the album—sounds like nothing recorded before or since.

Elektra spent a lot of money on *American Gothic* and released it with a flurry of full-page press ads declaring it the album of the year. For the most part, the press agreed. Yet the album, like its two predecessors, didn't sell. The world wasn't ready for it, and maybe it still isn't. At the time of writing, *American Gothic* lives on only in the streaming netherworld.

A critical triumph but a commercial under-achiever, *American Gothic* marked the end of Ackles's tenure at Elektra. He moved to Columbia for the more understated *Five & Dime* in 1973, and then nothing. Volume 2 of the *NME Encyclopedia Of Rock*, published in 1976, signed off a short entry about Ackles with the words, 'Ackles is a writer and performer of remarkable power, perhaps doomed to remain under-rated. Elektra dropped him in 1972; one Columbia album followed, but he is currently without a contract.'

He never had one again.

In the years following my own introduction to Ackles, I would, when talking to fellow music enthusiasts, look for ways of bringing him into the conversation. Almost always, the few people who had heard of him loved the music as much as I did. There seems to be no middle ground. You've either never heard of David Ackles or you love him. That puzzled me, and I came to wonder if there is something integral in the music that excludes

Ackles from a big audience. Is his music just too strange, or might his time yet come?

My first published writing about music was a 'Buried Treasure' article in *Mojo* magazine, published in August 1998. This was just before the time when it became easy to contact people by email. If you wanted to pitch an idea to a magazine, you had to phone up. It was advisable to avoid the days when the publication was about to go to print. All of this was nerve-wracking for a beginner. But after much rehearsal I phoned *Mojo*'s office and said I had an idea for an article. The man on the phone—I don't recall who it was—told me to be quick, because the next issue was going to print and everyone was busy. I said I'd like to do a 'Buried Treasure' article about David Ackles. There was a moment's silence, and the man said, 'That's incredible, I've literally just been talking to somebody about David Ackles.' He went on to explain that he'd been listening to Gastr Del Sol's album *Camoufleur*, released earlier that year and that he'd been telling somebody how it reminded him of Ackles. I went out and bought *Camoufleur* right after that phone call. I really like it, though to these ears it sounds nothing like David Ackles.* The *Mojo* editor told me that a fanzine, *Ptolemaic Terrascope*, had published an interview with Ackles in 1994. I was dispatched with the contact details for *Ptolemaic Terrascope*'s editor, Phil McMullen, and the suggestion that *Mojo* might run something if I spoke to Ackles myself.

I phoned Phil, who in turn put me in touch with Kenny MacDonald, who had conducted the *Terrascope* Ackles interview. Kenny passed on Ackles's address and phone number. I think—though I'm not certain—that I wrote to Ackles asking if he would be willing to do a telephone interview. If I did, I didn't get a reply. I clearly recall, though, phoning him up on April 24, 1998. It was early evening in London, mid-morning in Los Angeles. A woman answered the phone and sounded uncertain when I introduced myself. But she passed me over to Ackles. He started off by explaining that

* Just as I was coming to the end of writing this book, I heard a podcast in which Jim O'Rourke, one half of Gastr Del Sol, spoke about his favourite music. He started with a David Ackles song.

he was being treated for lung cancer, and his wife was screening his calls. He was friendly, gracious, cheerful, and modest. Immediately after putting the phone down, I called Phil Smee of Bam Caruso and said, 'I've just spoken to David Ackles.' Phil said that Ackles was a musical genius, and I agreed.

Drawing on that short phone call with Ackles as source material, I wrote my article for *Mojo*, which was duly published—my factual errors escaping the notice of the subeditors, who added a few more. I sent a copy of the magazine to Ackles, and we exchanged occasional emails until February 1999, as I prepared a much longer Ackles profile for *Ptolemaic Terrascope*. By then I had made friends with Brian Mathieson, who ran an Ackles website. For years it was pretty much the only decent source of online information about Ackles. I remember Brian emailing me to say that he'd heard that Ackles was close to death, and a few days later he left this life, on March 2, 1999, shortly after his sixty-second birthday. When I heard he'd gone I played 'Out On The Road', from *Subway To The Country*, at full volume, and shed a tear or two.

My *Terrascope* Ackles profile appeared that summer. It wasn't planned as a posthumous tribute, but that's what it became. Ever since then, I've wanted to write a book about Ackles. Until now, the closest I've come is a chapter in my first book, *American Troubadours* (2001). In 2022, I thought, almost on a whim, that I'd put a pitch together to see what came of it. Nothing ventured etc. My agent Matthew Hamilton was intrigued, partly on account of having his ear bent by a friend who is an Ackles fanatic. Matthew sent the pitch to Tom Seabrook at Jawbone Press, who made an offer. I was both pleased and anxious. Would anybody read a book about Ackles—a long-dead artist, an acquired taste who was hardly a household name in his time and is now so obscure that he doesn't even qualify as a cult figure? I'm about to find out.

Down River goes in search of David Ackles and tells the story of the writing and recording of *American Gothic*, the last lost classic of the 70s, the two albums that preceded it, and the one that followed. Just as David Ackles didn't really make rock'n'roll music, it is not a rock'n'roll story. Ackles didn't die shockingly young or join a commune or end up homeless with a drug problem. His career as a recording artist, which had started at the relatively late age of thirty-one, lasted just six years. There was no comeback. No undignified clamouring for attention and clinging to former glories. Just the four peerless albums and then silence.

It's a hunt for an artist that disappeared. Not a pretty-good, I-wonder-what-happened-to sort of talent, but a man revered by peers and critics as one of the true greats.

As much as it is a biography of Ackles, *Down River* is a book about the process of searching for him. Or, more accurately, information about him. This—I have found—has been no easy task. Telling the story of the man and his brief musical career involved piecing together personal recollections from people who were around at the time, contemporaneous press accounts, and archive material. The internet has come on a long way since I first started researching Ackles in the late 1990s, and I turned up hundreds of items of press coverage. Far more than I was expecting, given Ackles's lack of commercial success. Satisfyingly, these included many interviews with Ackles—some probably not read by anybody since they were published in the late 60s and early 70s. I could hear him speaking about his career as it unfolded.

Personal recollections were harder to come by. Ackles stopped recording in 1973 and died in 1999. Many of his contemporaries—the people who worked with him, his friends—are gone. Most of those left are old, and memories fade. For example, in addition to Ackles, twenty-two musicians are credited on his second album *Subway To The Country*. By the time I started serious research for this book, toward the end of 2022, fifteen were dead. One—drummer Jim Gordon—was incarcerated for murdering his mother. He died in 2023. Of the remaining six musicians who were—as far as I could tell—still alive, I traced three. Of those, one (Louie Shelton) could remember no details about the sessions. Another (Doug Hastings) had no recollection of being involved and did not even know he was credited on the album. The third, drummer Craig Woodson, did remember doing a single session for the album and playing on one song.

Sometimes I got lucky with archives. Other times they remained inaccessible. On February 6, 2022, I emailed the New York Public Library, whose catalogue database indicated it had some Ackles material in its archive, and the American Federation Of Musicians (AFM), asking about the possibility of locating Ackles session records. The New York Public Library replied within four hours, directing me to a form I could fill in. Two days later I received a 140-page PDF, at no charge, including the complete script of an Ackles musical play previously unknown to me, and associated correspondence. The AFM responded within twenty-four hours. A few months later, for a small fee, they sent me multiple session records, which illuminated my attempts to understand how Ackles's four albums were put together. Encouraged by the helpful response from the AFM, I contacted several musicians' organisations in England, to see if I could locate any records pertaining to the recording of *American Gothic*. Most didn't reply. One said they did retain an archive for that year which I was welcome to look at, though what was in it they couldn't say. But as it was in Scotland, five hundred miles from me, was not digitised, and there was no knowing whether there would be anything at all in the archive relevant to my research, I declined.

Despite the frustrations, I did accumulate a lot of research material, but I make no claims that this book is comprehensive. This must be the case for all biographers. You can go a certain way, but the picture will always be incomplete. You can't always tie up the loose ends. The dead ends remain dead. Sometimes I found that credible, plausible interviewees had recollections of events that flatly contradicted the recollections of other equally credible, plausible interviewees. There is nothing strange in this. We would all struggle to recall accurately events of decades ago that maybe didn't seem that important at the time. Other times the trail just went cold. Nobody could remember. The archives had nothing to say. Ackles gave no interviews for a few months. That means this story has gaps in it. I decided early on to try to resist the temptation to fill those gaps with too much conjecture. For the most part I've kept to that, though I've given myself slack to speculate a little. When I do that, I point out that it's speculation, using words like maybe and possibly. Where accounts of events contradict each other, I've tried to represent all accounts equally, while sometimes indicating which I think might be the most accurate.

Down River is not intended as a 'life' in the biographical sense. Ackles's career as a recording artist lasted about six years. A tenth of his life. I've concentrated on those years.

In writing this book, I set out to understand the disconnect between Ackles's obvious gifts, the esteem in which he is held by a few, and his relative commercial failure. It considers why some artists get first overlooked, then forgotten. It wonders about the fickleness of fame and cult status. How does the process of retrospective recognition work? Who qualifies and who doesn't? Is the whole game really nothing much to do with music? And what do the answers to those questions say about the mythmaking of the music industry—and us, the audience?

Quite early on in my research, I came to the view that the reasons—musical and personal—why Ackles didn't fit into the rock music industry in which he was briefly active are much the same as the reasons why he has not yet been granted retrospective cult adulation. He was not a rock musician, and his story is not typical. If you're looking for the classic rock cult narrative of mystery and tragedy you won't find it. Read no further. It's just the story of an unusually talented man who made four great records and then stopped.

As I sign off and prepare to send this manuscript to the publisher, I realise it's forty years almost to the day since I first came across David Ackles's debut album in that shop in North London. That album and the three that followed have given me great joy through all those years. If nothing else, I hope this book encourages a few more people to listen to them.

MARK BREND

DEVON, JANUARY 20, 2025

CHAPTER ONE

FAMILY BAND

EARLY YEARS • THE ACKLES TWINS • *RUSTY* • MUSIC HALLS AND CHURCH THEATRE PRODUCTIONS • UNIVERSITY OF SOUTHERN CALIFORNIA • A CREATIVE APPRENTICESHIP

“

Pickin' up a little bit of steam.

'ROCK ISLAND LINE'

”

A slim twelve-year-old boy walks into a room. It's a black-and-white film, so you can't tell if his dark sweater and wide dark trousers are navy blue or black. He is the second youngest of four boys following an older boy called Danny. They are looking for Danny's dog, Rusty, who has gone missing. The boys are greeted by Danny's father. Then Danny's mother appears with a tray of drinks and cookies...

This is a scene from *Rusty's Birthday*, released in November 1949, the last of an eight-film series of second features for children. The boy in dark clothes is David Ackles, who had uncredited roles in six of the Rusty films (first as Peanuts, then as Tuck Worden).

Though his Hollywood acting career never went any further than this, when David Ackles died in 1999, some obituarists called him a former child star. 'Seasoned child performer' is more accurate. By the time he hit his teens, Ackles was already a veteran of film, stage, and television, as an actor and dancer. But he wasn't famous. It was an unusual start to life, yet at the same time Ackles had an ordinary childhood. His mother and father provided him with a loving, conventional, comfortable, churchgoing family life and a good education, while simultaneously encouraging his drive to perform and create. There's a danger in superimposing convenient shapes in hindsight when trying to understand a life, and in doing so reducing the person to a neat construct that bears little relation to who they were. With that caveat, though, you can see in Ackles a pattern. A restless, creative urge to write and perform running alongside stability, constancy, and faith. It started in childhood and persisted throughout life.

—

David Thomas Ackles was born in Rock Island, Illinois, on February 20, 1937, the second child of Thomas Howard Ackles (1910–1997) and Queenie Ackles (née Rolfe 1911–2006). Their first daughter, Sally, had been born in 1935. Another daughter, Kim, arrived sixteen years after David. The 1940 census records the family living at 1830 11th Street, Rock Island—less than a mile from the Mississippi River.

DAVID ACKLES I always felt a strong connection to the traditions of the river, both north and south. Also, it was the terminus of the Rock Island Line, a railroad made famous in song and legend. Not a bad place for an incipient songwriter to get a start.[1]

Thomas Ackles was a businessman who owned a used car dealership, which provided the family with a comfortable life. According to his friend Steve Spellman, as a teenager, David liked to imply, mysteriously, that his father was wealthy and owned substantial property, with the car dealership being more of a hobby.[2] This might have been an overactive adolescent imagination. Thomas was also an amateur musician, playing bass and viola. Queenie Ackles was born in Andover, England. She emigrated with her mother and sister first to Australia and from there to America, arriving in 1920. Her father, Arthur Rolfe, had preceded the rest of the family and was already living in America. When David became a performer, he was following in the footsteps of several generations on his mother's side. Everyone, he said, was in the theatre on that side of the family.

People who knew David's mother recall her as a formidable, engaging, energetic woman with wide interests. Though she lived in America for eighty-six of her ninety-five years, she retained an English accent until the end. Showbusiness was in her blood. Her mother, David's grandmother, was born Frances Annie Buckley. She appeared in music hall in Scotland and England under the name Queenie Clyde, and, like a lot of music hall performers, she had several strings to her bow. When appearing at the Operetta House in Edinburgh, she was described as a 'comedienne and instrumentalist', contributing 'many variety items'.[3] In December 1908, theatre trade papers—describing Clyde as a 'speciality act'—reported her marriage to Arthur Rolfe, a baker from Andover, England.[4] It seems Queenie Clyde stopped performing in music hall thereafter and—as Frances Rolfe—helped in the family business. Later, though, she played movie-house piano for silent films in America. Like her daughter, Frances Annie Rolfe (Queenie Clyde) had a long life and lived to witness her grandson's recording career. She died in her late eighties in 1973, in Los Angeles.

Frances's father was a Frank Buckley. Buckley was French and changed his name when he took to the stage in England. There was more than one Frank Buckley performing in English theatres in the late nineteenth and early twentieth centuries. Most likely, Frances's father was the one who worked first as a solo comedian, then as an actors' manager, and was married to Alice Jennings ('comedienne and chamber maid').[5]

Though there are references that indicate she acted a little in early life, Queenie Ackles was not a career stage entertainer like her grandparents, or her mother until she married. Even so, she carried on the performing tradition. In Rock Island, Queenie presented a one-hour radio show called *The Story Hour Lady*, and later, in Los Angeles, she formed a church theatre group, which she ran for decades. She passed on to her children a love of music and the stage, a love that took enduring root in David. He later recalled creating a musical called *The Fabulous Story Of Three Little Pigs* while at kindergarten, and he continued writing musicals throughout his life.[6] Maybe Queenie was living out her ambitions vicariously through him. Sally and David performed as The Ackles Twins, a vaudeville song-and-dance act, doing USO shows for forces personnel in Chicago and elsewhere.* A photo of the duo shows David striking a pose in top hat and tails. He must have been about five years old.

In 1945, the Ackles family moved to Los Angeles. Thomas relocated the car dealership, and Queenie encouraged Sally and David to continue performing. In a 1973 interview, David implied that the family's move to California was in response to an approach from the movie producer and director William Castle, who offered him a film part when The Ackles Twins were doing a USO tour in California. Castle turned out a run of B-movies from the 1930s to the 1970s and is best remembered now for producing *Rosemary's Baby* (1968). In 1946, David appeared as a character

---

* United Service Organizations Inc. (USO) is an American non-profit charitable corporation that provides live entertainment to members of the armed forces and their families.

called Peanuts in *The Return Of Rusty* (1946), directed by Castle. This was the second film in a Columbia Pictures franchise about Rusty, a German Shepherd dog, that ran to eight entries. Ackles appeared in five more of the films as Tuck Worden, one of a group of children who share Rusty's adventures.* In the same interview, David talked about being well paid for the *Rusty* films and acting in television shortly after, at a time when television was almost exclusively live.†

Aimed at children, the *Rusty* films are around an hour long—moralistic, gently liberal, low-budget B-movies with a message. They took about ten days to shoot. *Rusty Leads The Way* (1948) is typical. Lead child character Danny Mitchell (played by Ted Donaldson) makes friends with a girl called Penny Waters (Sharyn Moffett). Penny, it turns out, lost her sight in an accident two years previously. When the authorities decide that she must go to the State Institution For The Blind, Danny and Rusty intervene. The dog helps persuade an initially reluctant Penny that a guide dog is the solution. Penny teams up with her own dog at a guide dog school and—after the obligatory trials and tribulations—gains her independence.

David Ackles was no more than a supporting player in the Rusty films. In *Rusty Leads The Way*, Ackles has a few lines in some early scenes—a dark-haired, dark-eyed, cherubic little boy rushing around with the rest of the gang, mostly older than him. After those early scenes he doesn't appear for the rest of the film. Even so, by the time the series ended in 1949, he was an old hand in front of the camera and, still performing at military bases with his sister, on stage.

---

* *The Son Of Rusty* (1947), *My Dog Rusty* (1948), *Rusty Leads The Way* (1948), *Rusty Saves A Life* (1949), *Rusty's Birthday* (1949).

† In 1973, British rock journalists John Tobler and Pete Frame spent some weeks in the USA, interviewing many American performers, including Ackles. The Ackles interview was published in parts in *Melody Maker*, *Fat Angel*, and *Hot Wacks* between 1973 and 1980, usually credited to Tobler alone. These articles make up the most detailed published accounts Ackles gave of his early life and recording career. Nuno Robles owns the original typewritten transcript of the whole interview and kindly sent me a reference copy. References to this interview are credited as 'Tobler 1973 (via Robles)'.

If the drive to perform came more from his mother, it was balanced by a conventional approach to life attributable more, perhaps, to his father, whom Ackles described as 'conservative'. David observed that his childhood was secure and stable. He went to regular schools, except for the couple of weeks it took to shoot each *Rusty* film.

—

This mingling of eclectic creativity and stability characterised Ackles's teenage years. The left-handed, piano-playing, budding actor, singer, writer, and dancer's life revolved around family, school, church, and various artistic endeavours. In 1950, while attending John Burroughs Junior High, Ackles won the junior high school first prize in that year's California Federation Of Chaparral Poets awards. In 1951, Queenie Ackles—described as a 'drama teacher who has acted in New York'—wrote and directed a play called *Island Holiday*, performed at the First Presbyterian Church Of Hollywood, which Ackles attended as a child. Her children David and Sally were in the cast.* Twenty-two years later, Ackles played a solo show at a coffeehouse run by the same church.

Church theatre productions like *Island Holidays* loomed large in the Ackles family for many years.

DAVID ACKLES I come from a very strong, almost doctrinaire Christian background, having been raised—God help me—a Presbyterian. How I managed to survive that, I've no idea. What it has resulted in of course is a

* The play was reported in *Citizen News*, May 5, 1951. While a member of Hollywood Presbyterian, Ackles was recognised by the Sunday School director for memorizing scripture. Tim McAlmont, who later ran the Salt Company coffeehouse (associated with the church) where Ackles performed, says, 'We had a program where each child in the Sunday School was invited to memorize certain assigned passages of verses in the Old and New Testaments each year and would get credits for all he/she could commit to memory. Each Sunday we would come to church and sit down with one of a team of older ladies to whom we would recite the assigned biblical text for which we would receive credit and a badge we would place on a shield. That would have been the program David was a part of.' (Email to author January 13, 2025)

lot of questioning of the whole area of values as interpreted by those who think themselves in the know in positions of power in the church. And I'm still fascinated by it. I think it's an area that certainly deserves a lot more attention than it normally gets.[7]

The questioning surfaced in Ackles's songs from his first album and remained a dominant theme in his last big creative project toward the end of his life.* Faith took root, though, albeit in a less strict form. Ackles was a lifelong churchgoer, as his wife recalls:

JANICE VOGEL ACKLES David was a very spiritual person . . . going to church, thinking of things spiritually, and having a close relationship with God was very important to him. He was always a religious person, but not fanatically; he didn't have a religious conversion. Because of all this, when he was in the recording business he didn't really get into the lifestyle, and I think it made him suspect to some degree.[8]

It was in church settings that Ackles got much of his early performing experience. In 1958, Queenie formed a troupe called The Geneva Players, based at Immanuel Presbyterian Church, Wilshire Boulevard. From then into the 1970s she directed many plays, using amateur and professional actors drawn from the congregation and beyond. David, Sally, and Kim all appeared, and David sometimes wrote the plays and designed and built the sets. As late as 1971, by which time Ackles was two albums into his recording career, The Geneva Players put on what was billed as 'a new Easter play by David Ackles' called *The Second Disciples*.

It was presumably the Geneva Players connection that led David to an acting job in front of a far bigger live audience. In 1955, he had a prominent role as the French Ambassador in a dramatisation by the General Assembly Of The Presbyterian Church, USA of the life of Scottish

* This was a musical, *Sister Aimee*, about the American evangelist Aimee Semple McPherson.

theologian John Knox. Ackles was one of a cast of a hundred, backed with a two-hundred-voice choir, that performed the play to an audience of around twenty thousand at the Hollywood Bowl.[9]

Through the 1950s, the Ackles family lived in a large house at Keniston Avenue. It was a few blocks from Los Angeles High School, which Ackles attended after leaving John Burroughs Junior High. The actor Dustin Hoffman was an exact contemporary.

Alongside church productions, David took an enthusiastic part in school plays. He was something of a teenage renaissance man—writing, acting, directing, singing, dancing, making scenery. He was still a teenager when rock'n'roll broke, exactly the right age. Elvis, Little Richard, and Jerry Lee Lewis seem to have made little impact on him, though.

STEVE SPELLMAN I don't recall any affinity for rock'n'roll … he and his … friends were very attached to Broadway musicals. I still remember him playing his recordings of *The Desert Song* and *Kismet* for me. … He kept up with Broadway shows all through our youth. I can also recall him and some of his friends singing madrigals. I think it was stuff they did at school but enjoyed so much, they did it for fun outside of school.[10]

Broadway musicals and madrigals in the age of Elvis. Already, Ackles was out of step with the music industry into which he later drifted. For most musicians of Ackles's age and a little younger who ended up in the rock world, in the broadest possible sense, how they interacted with first-generation rock'n'roll is a foundational part of the story. In most cases they were inspired by it. But for Ackles, it wasn't a big deal.

Ackles and Spellman met in 1952 or '53 at Beverly Vista Community Church. Queenie had been hired to lead the church's youth group, and David accompanied her to help and play the piano. Spellman didn't stay long at the youth group, but his friendship with Ackles endured. He remembers the fifteen or sixteen-year-old Ackles as 'arty'.

STEVE SPELLMAN He sometimes used an English accent. He dressed differently. He knew he was perceived as odd, but he did it anyway. I don't think that's *who he really was*. I think it was a persona he was trying out and was interested in reactions to it. ... He wasn't sporty. But he was a dancer and was physical in that sense ... an introvert/extrovert distinction doesn't really fit. He was more self-contained.[11]

Up to this point, Ackles was more actor and dancer than musician. Eventually, the balance shifted, but not for a while yet. He did have some musical training, but he did not go on to study music formally in a conservatoire or music school setting. A 1976 article recounting the career of a Miss Englin, a former vaudeville star, records that she taught Ackles piano while he still lived at Rock Island.* Ackles later spoke of having six months of piano lessons when he was twelve years old.[12]

In 1955, Ackles enrolled at the University Of Southern California (USC) in Los Angeles to study English. Ackles later said he wished he'd studied music more than he did. His extracurricular activities did put him in touch with the music department, though. Singing in the USC choir meant he could sit in on some classes and take part in concerts. His involvement in the choir gave rise to a myth that outlived him.

The first significant press interview Ackles gave as a recording artist led to enduring confusion. Wayne Warga was a friend of Ackles's who had studied at USC and, by 1968, was working as a journalist for the *Los Angeles Times*. In an attention-grabbing interview feature published on August 22, titled 'Ackles Reached Bottom Before Reaching Top', Warga wrote that Ackles had been jailed five times for theft—one of several colourful vignettes from a supposedly wild youth. Warga explained that Ackles had then found God and was now volunteering for Immanuel Presbyterian Church. All of this was in the context of a review of Ackles's debut, which

* The article, in the *Quad City Times,* dated May 9, 1976, made the claim that Ackles was, then, 'as big as the Beatles' in England.

was presented as another example of the thirty-one-year-old's reformation. The whole piece was riddled with exaggerations and inaccuracies. Ackles later said that as far as he was concerned, the interview had been an extended joke—the sort of banter friends might engage in—and that when he spoke of 'going to jail' he was talking about performing in jail as a member of the USC choir. Warga, it seems, didn't get the joke. Though Ackles explained the misunderstanding in later interviews, his comments did not lodge in the *Los Angeles Times*' institutional memory. When Ackles died, the paper's obituary rehashed the adolescent misdemeanour angle, then shortly after had to publish a correction from Kim Ackles, who clarified that her brother had never been incarcerated for a crime in his life.

Ackles spent the 1956–57 academic year in the arts faculty at Edinburgh University, living at 28 Polwarth Terrace, a large suburban villa built in 1896.*

DAVID ACKLES I was studying West Saxon, the origins of the English language. If you know of any gathering which requires to hear the Lord's Prayer recited in West Saxon, I'm their man.[13]

He also mentioned learning Spanish during the year in Scotland.[14] After this he did a further two years at USC, graduating in the summer of 1959. He returned for postgraduate studies later. Contemporaries and friends at USC included David Anderle (in the drama department) and Fred Myrow (USC Thornton School Of Music). Both would feature in Ackles's later recording career.

—

In Spellman's opinion, he and Ackles were an unlikely pair. Ackles was an artist, whereas Spellman considered the arts frivolous. But they became best friend as teenagers.

* The house is listed category C by Historic Scotland.

In the spring of 1959, coming to the end of his university career, Ackles told Spellman he planned to go to New York to break into theatre after graduating. He asked Spellman to accompany him. Spellman, still at university, havered and then agreed to take a semester break. In August 1959, the two friends travelled to New York and found what Spellman describes as a 'squalid little apartment'.*

Spellman had just $700 dollars and had to find a job. Through a family contact, he found himself a role as a page with NBC-TV. In those days, TV was mostly broadcast live in front of studio audiences. The pages—wearing blue uniforms with gold braid and buttons—kept the audiences in line, answered their questions, and made sure they were where they were meant to be.

Ackles was supported to some extent by his family, and at first he spent all his time going to auditions and making contacts. But before long he had to find a job, too. An NBC-TV page role would have suited him, but the only work Ackles could find was clerking in the office of a rubber wholesaler. Which he hated. In what spare time he had left to him he continued to seek out opportunities in the theatre. But it came to nothing.

Come Christmas, Spellman returned home in readiness to resume his studies in January 1960. Ackles soldiered on alone in New York for the first few weeks of the new decade. Before long, though, the grind of doing menial work while chasing a dream wore him down, as it has so many budding artists before and since. He returned to Los Angeles, probably in February 1960, out of money, disappointed, and dispirited. By all accounts, though, Ackles was an optimistic character. Not the sort to spend much time reflecting on failure.

In March 1960, he rekindled his dancing partnership with his sister Sally (now married), with the duo doing a 'straw hat and dance routine' in a variety show.[15] It was an early entry in a bewilderingly varied litany of low-key creative projects that occupied him through his twenties until

* The details of this episode come from a short unpublished memoir by Steve Spellman.

he signed with Elektra Records in 1967. Little tangible evidence of this work survives, but a paper trail of adverts and short reviews in Los Angeles newspapers builds up a fragmented timeline. Though this work was juvenilia, the scale and range give a sense of the breadth of Ackles's abilities and interests. And, maybe, of a young man not quite sure what he wanted to do. The writing, the acting, the dancing, and the set building all carried on, alongside which Ackles began to emerge as a musician and composer.

In the early 1960s, the folk revival, which gave birth to the singer-songwriter movement with which Ackles was later associated, was in full flow. He joined in for a while. There are press mentions of Ackles performing in 1962 in a duo with a Sharon White. In a 1968 interview, he indicated that he and his sister performed as a duo, singing 'the most obscure folksongs we could find. The more obscure they were, the more people liked them.'[16]

Taken in the context of all his other activities, this folk-song period seems more like an opportunistic dalliance than a serious interest. Just another chance to get on stage. Other musical work was more in character. In 1963, children in a community arts facility were studying an Ackles musical, *Stage 21*. In 1964, the 'accomplished musician and composer' conducted his own music for another play, *Children On Their Birthdays*, at a Roman Catholic college.[17] Also in 1964, Ackles appeared as a talking head on local TV, discussing the challenges of adapting short stories for the stage. He was described as a composer in the TV listings pages.[18]

Ackles's involvement with his mother's church theatre group, The Geneva Players, continued throughout this period, too. He starred in the troupe's Christmas play, *This Is Christmas* (December 1960), with younger sister Kim in the cast; designed the set for their production of Daphne Du Maurier's *Rebecca* (November 1962); played a British aircraftman stranded behind enemy lines in France in *The River Line*, by British playwright Charles Morgan (November 1963); and wrote the Easter play *A Few Coins* (April 1965). In June 1967, just before Ackles signed to Elektra, he was acting in The Geneva Players' production of John Dos Passos's *USA* (June 1967), with the *Los Angeles Times* noting, 'Director Queenie Ackles has assembled eleven fine actors, both amateur and professional, from the congregation and from outside sources alike.'[19]

In the midst of this, Ackles reconnected with USC, returning for graduate studies in communications. He didn't complete his Masters, partly on account of the death of his supervisor. In August 1962, he was acting in a USC drama department production of an 'enjoyably naughty' Georges Feydeau farce for which his friend David Anderle designed an 'imaginative' set.[20] In November of that year, both Ackles and Anderle were in the cast of a USC drama department production of *The Visit* by Friedrich Dürrenmatt. In 1965, a review of USC's department of cinema's 1964–65 showcase mentions Ackles starring in a spoof musical, *Make It Move*.[21]

There was much more of this sort of thing. In interviews in the 1970s, Ackles was given to rattling off lists of past activities. Commissions to write ballet scores. Touring South America with a circus. Working as a carpenter with a theatre group in Sacramento. Failed musical comedies in New York. Dubbing spaghetti westerns in Rome. Studying at the University Of Madrid and wintering in Cadiz. More generally, bumming around Europe.

Ackles worked as an assistant for a writer on the TV shows *The Many Loves Of Dobie Gillis* (which ran from 1959 to 1963) and *The Ann Sothern Show* (1958–61). The lead role in Dobie Gillis was played by Dwayne Hickman, who had been a supporting cast player in the Rusty films, along with Ackles. In 1966, Ackles landed another minor film role, as a carousel operator in a creaking, low-budget horror B-movie, *Blood Bath*. He also said he worked on *The Girl In Daddy's Bikini*, one of the last of the beach party films.* Somewhere in all this there was a very brief first marriage,

* Also known as *It's A Bikini World*, this low-budget music comedy was shot in 1965 but not released until 1967. Bobby 'Boris' Pickett, of 'Monster Mash' fame, was in the cast, and artists including The Animals and The Castaways performed in the obligatory party scenes. Ackles isn't credited. Perhaps he worked behind the scenes, or as an extra (though I didn't spot him). Ackles had another oblique connection with teen beach movies—when living at Pacific Palisades in the 1970s, a neighbour was Kathy Zuckerman, who was the model for *Gidget*, written by her father, Frederick Kohner. The original 1959 *Gidget* film spawned many sequels and the whole beach movie genre.

too, about which Ackles sometimes joked in interviews once his recording career began.

In 1961, the Ackles family moved to a smaller house on North Beachwood Drive, near the famous Hollywood sign. Shortly after that, Queenie became a realtor, as did Thomas some years later. Both worked until they were close to eighty. In 1961, Kim was the only child still at home, but David returned to live in the family home in 1964, staying for several years—a sign that, for all his busyness, he probably wasn't making much money, which is why the creative work was punctuated by short-term coffer-boosting side jobs. Ackles's 1968 debut album came with a press release claiming that he had worked as a security guard at a toilet paper factory and a private detective. Both claims were true.

Ackles turned thirty in February 1967. The cherubic little boy had grown into a handsome, open-faced young man with a winning smile, about five foot eight inches tall. He looked set for a varied, low-key creative life: teaching, provincial theatre, a little writing, composing for the stage. Indeed, that's much the life he went on to have, eventually. There is almost nothing to suggest, though, that before the year was out he would be recording his debut album for the hippest of US record labels.

CHAPTER TWO

WHAT A HAPPY DAY

SIGNING TO ELEKTRA • DAVID ANDERLE, RUSS MILLER, JAC HOLZMAN • THE WRECKING CREW • THE MEN WHO BECAME RHINOCEROS • RECORDING *DAVID ACKLES*

"

I thought myself lucky to be among them, such a truly gifted bunch—Tim Buckley, Tom Rush, Tom Paxton, and numerous others who came and went during my tenure there. It certainly motivated me to want to do my best.

DAVID ACKLES

"

January 11, 1968. It's two o'clock in the afternoon. David Ackles is sitting at the piano in Columbia Studios on Sunset Boulevard, Los Angeles. Though the former CBS radio studio was converted to a recording studio just seven years earlier, hundreds of hit records have been made here. In the storied room with him are musicians who have played on many of those hit records. Drummer Hal Blaine. Guitarist Al Casey, who later that year loaned his red Hagström guitar to Elvis Presley for what became known as the '68 Comeback Special. Several others. Leading them is Don Randi, just five days younger than Ackles. Randi's career as a session musician and bandleader began more than ten years earlier. He has already played on hundreds of sessions, as has everyone else in the room. Except for Ackles. He is a studio neophyte. He's never even made a record, let alone had a hit. The band start playing his song 'Road To Cairo'...

In the 1960s, most American rock musicians tended to serve their apprenticeships in one or more of a few time-honoured ways. Maybe you paid your dues in a garage band, making a few singles on local labels. Or you made your way as a folk singer on the coffeehouse circuit. If you happened to live in one of the urban centres of music making, with recording studios and record companies, you might have picked up session work or touted your songs around the music publishers. Ackles never played in a garage band, and his folk duo days were a brief diversion. He didn't play sessions, either—at least not in the rock'n'roll sense. Nor is there any evidence that he hawked his songs, trying to get other artists to record them. He was writing songs, but in a different context entirely. In later interviews he talks of writing throughout his twenties. He seems to be referring to songs for musical theatre. Songs for shows.

Ackles served a long and varied creative apprenticeship that did little to prepare him for the rock music industry. By the time he turned thirty, he had written, composed, acted, danced, sung, designed, and built—for film, theatre, television, and education. But he had never played live as a solo performer, and most likely he had never been in a recording studio. He did, though, live in Los Angeles, where a good proportion of the

American music business was based. And this proximity led to an entirely unexpected and unsought-for opportunity.

Jac Holzman formed Elektra Records in 1950 and for the first decade or so released mainly folk and blues music, and a sequence of sound effects albums, while operating out of New York. By the mid-60s, Holzman, still only in his mid-thirties, saw that many young folk musicians were moving into rock, and took the label in the same direction. At the same time, the West Coast music industry was expanding, with acts including The Byrds, The Beach Boys, and Sonny & Cher having huge international success. After a false start in 1962, Holzman set up an Elektra Los Angeles base in 1965 and signed local artists Love, The Doors, and Tim Buckley. By 1967, Elektra was flourishing commercially. The Doors were selling millions of records around the world. But it still felt like a small label and retained an aura of underground credibility, reflecting Holzman's eclectic interests.

While Elektra was getting established on the West Coast, Ackles's friend and contemporary from USC days, David Anderle, was progressing through the early stages of an illustrious and eclectic career in music management and A&R. When Anderle died in 2014, obituarists had him heading up Elektra's West Coast outpost from 1968. Most likely, this is incorrect. Speaking in Holzman's oral history of Elektra, *Follow The Music*, Anderle says his connection with the label began shortly after the Monterey Pop Festival (June 1967), at the suggestion of Judy Collins.[1] Anderle came to the label with impeccable credentials. He had, according to *Rolling Stone*, been MGM's 'company freak' for a while.[2] Tall, lean, and moustachioed, he was equal parts music industry scenester and aspiring painter, with a sound business head. In 1965, he had persuaded Verve to sign The Mothers Of Invention. Shortly after, while managing Van Dyke Parks, Anderle got to know Brian Wilson. He ran The Beach Boys' label, Brother, from October 1966 to spring 1967. 'He defined hip LA, laid-back and cool,' said Holzman.[3]

Mild confusion and contradictions feature in accounts of how Ackles came to sign for Elektra. Speaking just six years after the event, Ackles himself considered that the story had already passed into a sort of hazy creation myth. Maybe so, but he, Anderle, and others all gave more or less correlating accounts of an outline sequence of events. It's establishing the detail and mapping those events onto dates that's sometimes problematic.

At some point, probably in 1967, Ackles ran into Anderle. The two had not seen each other for a few years. Anderle was now working for Elektra. Ackles played Anderle some songs. Anderle, impressed, signed Ackles to a songwriting deal. He later said Ackles was his first ever signing for Elektra. Ackles recorded some demos of his songs for other artists to consider. These demos came to the attention of Jac Holzman. Holzman suggested Ackles record the songs himself. Anderle, working with Russ Miller, then assembled musicians for the sessions that produced *David Ackles*.

A more detailed version of this story can be assembled by piecing together comments from Ackles himself, and the people around him at the time.

Speaking in 1973, Ackles said he wrote several songs about the Watts Riots of August 1965.* One of these was about a white woman pregnant by a black man, which became 'Blue Ribbons'. Later, Ackles was working in a musical show in Portland—he wasn't specific about what this show was—and happened to play the song for the show's arranger, who was also arranging for Sonny & Cher at the time. The arranger liked the song and said he thought Cher could do a good version of it. This arranger presented the song to Cher, who was initially interested but then turned it down. Ackles speculated that this decision was related to Cher having a miscarriage, making a song about pregnancy too painful a prospect.† Although it came to nothing, Ackles was enthused by Cher's interest and started playing the song to friends. One of the friends was a woman who knew David Anderle, with whom Ackles had lost touch. Ackles agreed to go and play the song for Anderle as an opportunity to renew contact,

* The Watts Riots were nearly a week of social unrest, which took place between August 11 and 16, 1965, motivated in part by the Los Angeles Police Department's racist and abusive conduct.

† Speaking to *Vanity Fair* in November 2024, Cher said she had three miscarriages by the time she turned twenty-one in 1967.

without realising that Anderle had—in the intervening years since they were last in touch—become established in the music business.

DAVID ACKLES Last time I'd seen him was several years before in a paint-spattered outfit leaving a set—he was a set designer at USC.... So, I played the song for him ... and he liked it a lot. He said, 'Yeah. I really like that, and I want you to write some more.' And I said, 'Why?' And that's when he divulged the truth: 'I am with Elektra!' ... so I immediately ran home and whipped out twenty songs and came back, and then he introduced me to Russ [Miller], who was at the house that day. I played the songs for both of them, and that's when they signed me.[4]

In September 1968, on his first promotional visit to the UK as an Elektra artist, Ackles explained that he'd written some songs and made some demo recordings to show how they went, which prompted Elektra to suggest he record them himself.[5]

He'd said much the same thing in a *Los Angeles Times* interview a month earlier. And when I spoke to him thirty years later:

DAVID ACKLES Did I always hope and plan to be a songwriter? Yes, from earliest childhood, that was one of my ambitions. I had others, of course, but songwriting was the dominant goal. But a recording artist? Not on your life! My intention was to have lots of other, much better singers record my songs. Alas, it was not to be. I believe the truth is that Jac Holzman couldn't interest any other singers on his label in recording my stuff, so was forced into offering that chance to me. I had an album released before I had ever performed solo in public.[6]

JANICE VOGEL ACKLES I remember David telling me that once he submitted the material, *he* didn't think he was going to record it. He thought that they were going to farm it out to other people, so it came as a big surprise to him.[7]

DAVID ANDERLE I believe Russ Miller and I took him into the studio and cut some demos with him. . . . We played the demos for Jac, and Jac certainly gave the okay to proceed [with the album].[8]

JAC HOLZMAN Ackles was very sweet, considerate—the kind of guy who wouldn't swat a mosquito. A gentle soul, an extremely gentle soul. Introspective. He lived a lot within himself and within his music. Ackles came to us through David Anderle, he had been kicking around and was a high school buddy of Anderle's. And Anderle brought him to Russ Miller who was an A&R guy who was on the outside, in the beginning, didn't do a lot of production. They produced the first Ackles album together.[9]

Holzman thought that Miller had good taste and was sensitive to acoustic music. Which, as piano and vocal renditions, is what Ackles's music was when Miller first encountered it. Miller immediately engaged with the songs and recorded demos with Ackles, which he played to Holzman. Miller's enthusiasm rubbed off on Holzman, who loved the demos for their gentle introspection. He was intrigued by the theatrical bent in the writing and thought the songs probably wouldn't sell. And, crucially, that Ackles should sing them himself.

Miller himself added some detail to the story. He's quoted in Elektra's UK newsletter in 1968, just before Ackles's promotional visit to Europe, that it took three visits to persuade Ackles to sing his own songs.

Though aspects of the journey remain elusive, the destination isn't in dispute. Ackles found himself recording an album for Elektra, produced by Anderle and Miller. If Anderle was an interesting character, his co-producer, Miller, something of a spiritual seeker, could have stepped out of one of Ackles's songs. As a youth he had been a tent evangelist and singer, and then later a recording artist and producer. After leaving the music business, he became a motivational speaker and was then ordained as a Religious Science minister.

In 1969, Miller was appointed Elektra vice president and head of the West Coast division. In 1967, though, he was running Elektra's affiliated publishing company, Paradox Music Group, to which Ackles signed on November 10, 1967. The transition from staff songwriter to debut recording artist must have happened within a few weeks. There are American Federation Of Musicians records showing that Ackles was recording in January 1968, so almost certainly the decision to do so would have been made before the end of the previous year.

When Ackles turned thirty in February 1967, he most likely would have had no thought of signing a record deal before the year was out. Yet here he was, recording his debut album under the watchful eye of a paradigm of LA cool and a one-time youth evangelist. On the surface, it seemed like an unimaginable turn of events. But that wasn't quite the case.

In 1967, Ackles didn't appear quite as unusual as he does now. By the time he recorded his third album in 1972, he'd carved out a musical niche entirely his own. And, looking back, you can see in his first album clear hints of that mature style. The theatrical, the hymnal. In 1967, though, with his style still emerging, it was possible to place him alongside a new generation of literate, intelligent artists. Leonard Cohen. Labelmates Fred Neil, Tim Buckley, Judy Collins, Tom Paxton and Tom Rush. Some even played piano, not guitar. Randy Newman, Laura Nyro, Harry Nilsson. Newman, Nyro, Nilsson, and Cohen all wrote songs that demonstrated an awareness of forms beyond the normal rock idioms of the time. As did Ackles. Indeed, reviews of Ackles's debut album often mentioned one or more of those artists as a comparator to help orientate the reader. It was not a scene, hardly even a trend, but there was something happening, and Ackles seemed to be skirting the fringes of it. But he didn't really fit.

Buckley, Neil, Newman, Nyro, Nilsson, Paxton, and Rush had come up through versions of one of the established routes into the music business. Ackles hadn't. As he put it, 'I came in the back way.'[10] Fred Neil had been writing songs and making obscure singles since the late 1950s. Randy Newman had been writing songs for other artists since 1961 and had recorded a flop single himself in 1962. The prodigiously gifted Laura

Nyro had landed a record deal and recorded her debut album while still a teenager. So had Tim Buckley. By 1967, Tom Rush had been playing the folk circuit for years and was already five albums into his career. Tom Paxton, the same age as Ackles, was already hanging around the Greenwich Village folk clubs when Ackles was in New York trying to break into theatre. He had released four albums by 1967. Harry Nilsson started out singing songwriting demos and writing for other artists. Only Leonard Cohen had no previous music industry form, but his provenance as a poet and experimental novelist gave him countercultural credentials in a way that Ackles's history of acting, church theatre productions, and writing for television didn't. It's as if, launching himself on a different trajectory some time earlier, his idiosyncratic journey intersected with a well-travelled path in 1967. For a while, it looked as if his career might shape up in similar ways to some of his contemporaries—that he might continue that well-worn path. But the intersection was an accident. The further Ackles went on his journey, the harder it became to relate him to anyone else and fit him into what was happening.

If it's possible to see how people imagined Ackles might find a niche then, it's possible, too, to see how events played out in his favour. Ackles and Anderle were old friends. And Anderle was working for probably the only label with the vision to see the potential in Ackles, and the nerve to sign him. And this at a time when the music business was booming in Ackles's hometown. Though that's not to imply Elektra's signing policy was profligate. Holzman, speaking about the company's expansion, said, 'One song in 1,000 tapes are eventually recorded.'[11] There was happenstance and opportunism in Ackles's arrival at Elektra, but it wasn't just being in the right place at the right time. Anderle's association with Van Dyke Parks and Brian Wilson marked him out as a man with an ear for songwriters pushing at the established boundaries of pop. Holzman, a born risk-taking entrepreneur, combined hard-nosed business acumen with a true love and deep knowledge of music. Under his guiding hand, Elektra was becoming a rock label, but it didn't start out as one. Holzman was always open to other forms of music. Miller was also a seasoned music industry insider with—as his career demonstrates—an unconventional streak. These were the men—successful, powerful, and unusual, always looking for the next thing, not just bean counters—who saw something special in Ackles and his strange songs. Songs of originality and daring, and yet songs, too, that you could have just about imagined then as hits. Songs that almost were hits, in some cases.

—

Coming to his eponymous debut album without any context, you'd be forgiven for thinking that Ackles was a seasoned campaigner given to recording live in the studio with a familiar group of musicians. The raw and brooding intensity of the vocal performances and the loose-limbed, apparently semi-improvised playing give the impression of a man at ease with what he was doing, leading a band who knew him well enough to follow his every move.

None of this is true. For a start, Ackles had no previous recording experience. His first session for Elektra, whenever that was, was almost certainly the first time he had ever set foot in a recording studio. And he had not become properly acquainted with the musicians before the sessions started, let alone played with them. It's possible, too, that some of the sessions involved musicians playing to recordings of Ackles singing and playing his piano, with the man himself not even present.

About eight months elapsed between Ackles signing to Elektra and the album's release. As with the period leading up to his signing, a precise timeline of events through those months is elusive. Furthermore, accounts of how the album was recorded sometimes appear at odds with each other, and with surviving documentary evidence. Ackles himself talked about recording the album twice. A first attempt with an arranger failed, then Ackles was introduced to the musicians credited on the album, and it all came together easily after that. Producer David Anderle referred to a meticulous assembling of final mixes involving musicians overdubbing accompaniment to existing recordings of Ackles's piano and voice. The recollections of surviving contributors don't neatly tally with either of those accounts. A piecing together of recollections and documentation of the sessions does not provide a coherent narrative. It indicates, though, that most likely the album's creation was a series of false starts, multiple sessions involving different combinations of musicians, and much fixing-it-in-the-mix editing to put together the final track list.

In addition to Ackles, five musicians are credited on the album: Danny Weis (guitar), Doug Hastings (guitar), Jerry Penrod (bass guitar), Michael Fonfara (organ), and Jon Keliehor (percussion). All were much younger than Ackles and far more experienced. And all, by September 1967, were looking for work. The oldest of them, Jon Keliehor (b. 1941), had been a member of The Daily Flash, a folk-rock band that hailed from Seattle and then moved to Los Angeles. Though well-regarded, The Daily Flash never quite broke through, hampered by a lack of original material. Doug Hastings (b. 1946) was a member, too. He left in late May 1967 to replace a briefly absent Neil Young in Buffalo Springfield—a short-lived berth, as Young re-joined in August. Keliehor, meanwhile, was sacked from the Daily Flash in June, shortly after Hastings's departure: 'I was dismissed from the band because I wanted to take a weekend to learn transcendental meditation in Los Angeles, which happened to clash with a semi-important, last-minute scheduled performance in Las Vegas.'[12] Danny Weis (b. 1948) was the youngest musician on Ackles's album, still a teenager. Even so, he had previous form, as a founder member of Iron Butterfly. Jerry 'The Bear' Penrod (b. 1946) was a fellow Iron Butterfly founder. He left just after Weis, in the summer of 1967, following the recording of Iron Butterfly's debut, *Heavy*. Canadian Michael Fonfara (1946–2021) was a member of Toronto-based Jon and Lee & The Checkmates, who managed one single before splitting in September 1967.

Given that Hastings, Weis, Penrod, and Fonfara all ended up in the first line-up of Rhinoceros, and that Keliehor had been present at early auditions for that band, the Ackles album looks like an early run-out for the Elektra supergroup. But if Keliehor's recollections and timeline are correct, it wasn't quite like that. In the summer of 1967, after leaving The Daily Flash, he was sharing a house in Laurel Canyon with Kerry Magness, a bass player who had recently departed garage rock primitives The Kingsmen. While pondering their next moves, the pair discovered that Elektra producer Paul Rothschild lived less than a quarter of a mile away. They introduced themselves in the hope that Rothschild would present some opportunities. Which in time he did, inviting Magness to play on a Doors session and both Magness and Keliehor to audition for the project that would become Rhinoceros. It was through this contact with Rothschild that Keliehor and his former Daily Flash comrade Doug Hastings found themselves at a meeting with Ackles, discussing arrangements for the singer's debut album.

JON KELIEHOR I didn't know what to expect. He was really rather welcoming at first . . . but he was very reserved . . . I thought maybe he was engrossed in his expectations around producing an album. You could sense—and this is a guess—that for the first time he was opening his songs to others.[13]

Keliehor places this meeting in New York, in mid-September 1967. A single recording session followed, probably within twenty-four hours, at which Keliehor thinks only he and Hastings were present along with Ackles. Not any of the other musicians credited on the album. Keliehor and Danny Weis had met recently in Los Angeles when they and Kerry Magness backed singer-songwriter Pamela Polland on a demo. But Keliehor is certain Weis wasn't present at the Ackles session he played on. He thinks, too, that he met the other credited musicians—Michael Fonfara and Jerry Penrod—for the first time at the auditions for Rhinoceros, in early November 1967.

DAVID ANDERLE David didn't know any of these people. These weren't like cats that he hung around with. He hung around with nobody in this scene.[14]

This New York date seems anomalous. Was it the first session for Ackles's debut album? Was it even an album session at all? Maybe there was no New York session. Ackles signed to Elektra's publishing arm in November 1967, so possibly the New York date that Keliehor recalls was an Elektra-funded demo, a try-out to see if Ackles might pass muster. Whatever it was, Doug Hastings has no recollection of recording with Ackles in New York, though he accepts it might well have happened. He also has no recollection of appearing on Ackles's second album, *Subway To The Country*, on which he is credited.* He remembers, though, several short Ackles sessions over a few days in Los Angeles, in late October and early November 1967. In other words, around when the first Rhinoceros auditions took place. Ackles, Hastings says, was 'not weird, not wild ... an adult in the room'.[15] He thinks that there were only a few musicians at a time on these sessions, not the whole band, and that they were playing to existing recordings of Ackles's piano and vocals. Keliehor does not recall taking part in these sessions.

Assuming that Keliehor's and Hasting's memories are credible, if understandably incomplete, they could fit with producer David Anderle's recollections.

DAVID ANDERLE I remember what a bitch it was, making that first album . . . we used him and his piano as a bed and added instruments afterwards. I'm not even sure if he cut anything with a band. We might have cut some of the things with the boys playing, but I remember working really hard matching stuff up after the fact. It was a lot of overdubbing, making stuff fit in, and it gave it a really interesting feel. It didn't sound like anything else.[16]

Ackles's own recollections, dating from 1973, were quite different. He

---

* AFM records show that Hastings was present at several sessions for *Subway To The Country*, sometimes as session leader.

talked of presenting Russ Miller with twenty-five to thirty songs in the early days of his publishing deal, at a rate of two or three a week. 'I made occasional tapes playing them, so they would know how they sounded.' It was one of these tapes that prompted Jac Holzman to decide that Ackles should record his own album. The first formal album sessions were with an arranger. They didn't work out. After a two-week break, Ackles, Miller, and Anderle agreed to start again with the musicians credited on the finished album.

DAVID ACKLES They were not yet Rhinoceros, they were just a group of musicians Elektra wanted to encourage, to make into a supergroup. And I went up and met them ... we sat around, and I played the songs, and they filled in, and we just had such a good time. We knew that was the right thing to do, so we just did it.[17]

There were some vocals that we went back and added later—it was a combination of both live and overdubbing—but all of the instrumentation you hear from the group was done at the moment.[18]

It's clear from all of this that no single account of the recording of *David Ackles* captures exactly what happened. Probably, there's something in all the versions. People remembering some events and attributing the whole story to those events.

The available documentary evidence confirms that there were indeed multiple sessions for the album, though the dates of these sessions don't always correspond to participants' recollections.* Three pieces of evidence point to recording in the second week of January 1968, which seem likely to be the aborted sessions with the 'arranger' that Ackles mentioned.

The first is tape reels from Columbia Studios located by researcher and producer Andy Zax when preparing what ended up as an unreleased

---

* This does not necessarily mean that participants are incorrect in their recollections. I have no way of knowing if the documented sessions I have discovered are the only sessions that took place. There might have been others of which no records remain.

collection of Ackles's Elektra recordings, *There Is A River*. From this source there's an alternate, instrumental version of 'Down River', one of the songs that appeared on the album but with a different arrangement. Alongside are incomplete versions of other songs that were never released. Three don't have vocals ('It's Me, It's Me', 'In The Morning', 'We Are Not Ready') and one does: 'Old Shoes'. The songs without singing feature piano, two guitars, vibes, bass, and drums. 'Old Shoes', a simple bluesy shuffle, has Ackles on piano and vocals, with drums and acoustic guitar.* The names Don and Harvey can be heard in the talkback chat. And there's an English accent among the American ones.† Ackles discarded most of these songs by the time he started playing live later in 1968, though he performed 'In The Morning' at least once, introducing it as an antidote to his more serious, intense, downbeat songs.‡

Second, AFM records log David Ackles sessions on January 11, 12, and 16 at Columbia, led by a Don (Randi), who—along with Roy Caton—is listed as 'arranger'. There is also a Harvey (bassist Harvey Newmark). A host of Wrecking Crew stalwarts contributed across the three sessions.§ These recordings yielded versions of familiar album songs 'The Road To Cairo', 'The Lotus Song' (probably 'Lotus Man'), 'Down River', 'What A Happy Day', and 'Lazzies Faires' (sic). Also listed are the four titles Zax located ('In The Morning', 'It's Me, It's Me', 'Old Shoes', 'We Are Not Ready') and one other, 'Happy Birthday World'.

Third, a tape reel in Anderle's archive, dated '1.11.68', includes 'Cairo', 'In The Morning', 'Happy Birthday World', and 'Lotus Man'. This must surely be the same session recorded in the AFM log for that day, which in

---

* 'Old Shoes' was later included in the aborted box set *There Is A River*.

† Conceivably this belongs to one of two engineers credited on the finished album, Brian Ross-Myring. Ross-Myring (1931–1992) was born in Kent, England, but by the mid-1950s was working as a sound engineer in the USA. The other engineer was Bruce Botnick (b. 1945), already a veteran of Love and Doors albums, though still in his early twenties.

‡ See Appendix 1, *The Canterbury House Recording*.

§ Hal Blaine, Alvin Casey, John Carl Clauder, Norman Jeffries, Gerald James McGee, Lou Morell, Joe Osborn.

turn is probably the source of the material Zax located, though there are anomalies. The Anderle tape box lists an extra song ('In The Morning') not listed in the AFM session for January 11 (though it is listed for the following day). The line-up on the Anderle reel is listed as 'drums, bass, guitars, perc, piano and sitar', whereas the AFM records nine musicians taking part. And the Anderle reels list sitar, but there is no sitar audible on the tracks Zax discovered.* Inconsistencies aside, if these were the first, unsuccessful sessions with the 'arranger' that Ackles referred to, and which he was critical of, you have to admire his nerve. A studio debutante rejecting the work of crack session musicians who'd already played on dozens of hit records. It's an early indication of the singularity of his musical vision, which co-existed alongside his amenable temperament and modesty.

There was more activity in February. According to David Anderle, there were sessions on February 6 and 8, 1968, at Columbia Studio D.[19] Not quite correlating with this is another reel in the Anderle archive, dated February 3, 1968, which lists 'Road To Cairo', 'The Grave Of God', 'Step Out In The Morning', 'Blue Ribbons', 'Lotus Man', 'When Love Is Gone', 'Old Shoes', 'Sonny Come Home', and 'Les Se Fair' (sic).

The AFM also records a double session on February 8, followed by another on February 15. These are not listed as Ackles sessions, but the musicians—Douglas Hastings, Jerry Penrod, Danny Weis, Jon Keliehor—are the album's backing musicians, minus organist Michael Fonfara. If these indeed were sessions for *David Ackles*, they could be the ones that Hastings recalls as taking place late in 1967. Or what Anderle was referring to when he talked of overdubbing musicians onto recordings of Ackles's voice and piano.

Whatever sessions took place, and whatever the process for piecing together the finished mix, the album was finished and ready to go by the early summer of 1968.

---

* I have not listened to the Anderle tape reel, as the owner of the archive had not digitised it at the time of writing, so I was unable to confirm definitively if the versions discovered by Zax are the same as the ones on the Anderle tape.

David Ackles was released on June 15, 1968, in the USA, in stereo and mono vinyl versions, and on eight-track cartridge. Two months earlier, fellow Elektra artist Tom Rush had released *The Circle Game*, the album sometimes marked as heralding the singer-songwriter movement with which Ackles became associated. *David Ackles* came sandwiched between two British artists in the Elektra schedule—preceded by *The Hangman's Beautiful Daughter* by The Incredible String Band and followed by an eponymous album by Eclection. On September 3, 1968, it was released in the UK. A French edition on Disques Vogue appeared at about the same time. In Portugal, an EP with the album cover image was released, comprising 'Down River', 'Laissez-Faire', 'Sonny Come Home', and 'When Love Is Gone'.

That year, popular music was pulling in multiple directions. Easy-listening bandleader Paul Mauriat & His Orchestra topped the *Billboard* charts for a long run in the spring, followed from late May until the end of July by Simon & Garfunkel's *Bookends* and *The Graduate* soundtrack albums. Later, Herb Alpert, The Doors, The Rascals, Big Brother & The Holding Company, The Jimi Hendrix Experience, and Glen Campbell all had chart-topping albums, as did British acts The Beatles and Cream. In the UK, big-selling acts through the summer of 1968 included Tom Jones, Engelbert Humperdinck, Pink Floyd, The Seekers, and Aretha Franklin. Underground scenes were thriving in both countries. In principle at least, the prevailing eclecticism indicated an open-mindedness of which, as a hard-to-categorise artist, Ackles might have been the beneficiary. As the year went on, it was the British underground scene that offered the warmest welcome to the thirty-one-year-old new boy.

CHAPTER THREE

What a Groovy Morning

DEBUT ALBUM RELEASE • THE *LOS ANGELES TIMES* MISUNDERSTANDING • PROMOTIONAL VISIT TO EUROPE • BBC RADIO AND TELEVISION • JULIE DRISCOLL AND BRIAN AUGER

“

That’s really great.

JOHN PEEL

”

August 24, 1968. In a few days' time, David Ackles is flying to Europe to begin a promotional tour in support of his debut album. But now, at 7pm, he is starting work on its follow-up, in studio B at Elektra's newly opened Los Angeles recording studio. He looks around at the assembled musicians. There are some familiar faces. Bassist Jerry Penrod and guitarist Doug Hastings both played on Ackles's first album. There are new faces too. Some brass players from Don Ellis's band. The jazz trumpeter, drummer, composer, and bandleader Ellis is leading the session, having arranged two new Ackles songs with Al Kooper. This is the first attempt to record the second of those songs. Guitarist James Burton is joining in today, lending his Telecaster chops to a country ballad called 'Cabin On The Mountain'. Ellis counts in, and the musicians play fast and loud in waltz time...

David Ackles's arresting front cover has an out-of-focus Ackles staring through a cracked windowpane. It's the work of Elektra art director William (Bill) S. Harvey, using a photo by Joel Brodsky. It's not that clear, but Ackles's hair is straightened and swept back. For much of his recording career and in many other known photos, it's a thick, curly, unruly mop.

Harvey (1920–1993) was a year older than Jac Holzman, and at six foot two, just a little shorter. His first job for Elektra was in 1953, when he was already father to three children. He freelanced for the label for a while, alongside work for many other clients, before Holzman brought him into the fold permanently. The two men bickered constantly but creatively for almost twenty years. By the time Elektra emerged as a hip rock label in the mid-60s, Harvey was a jacket-and-tie man in his late forties. Yet despite the generation gap he managed to capture the mood of the age, producing multiple classic album covers for The Doors, Judy Collins, Love, Tim Buckley, and many others, along with several iterations of the Elektra logo.

The much younger Brodsky (1939–2007) was just beginning to get established. The previous year his photographs had adorned the first two Doors albums. The hazy, pastoral image of Van Morrison on *Astral Weeks*, released just after *David Ackles*, is Brodsky's work, too. In 1969, *David*

Ackles was reissued as *Road To Cairo*, after one of its better-known near-hit songs. The retitled album featured a more traditional portrait photograph on the cover.

The Williams/Brodsky *David Ackles* cover was a mysterious image, apt for the music it represented. And, given Ackles's later drift into obscurity, prophetic. But that was all in the future. In 1968, Elektra was launching an unusual new artist. That the label put considerable effort into promoting the album indicates the high hopes they had for Ackles. New to the game though not young by the standards of the time, Ackles must have had high hopes, too.

Musically, this first album is the most immediately accessible and conventional of Ackles's records, albeit with some clear signals of a highly original future direction. Lyrically, Ackles's style was fully formed from the start. He wrote as a dramatist or an author, creating songs like one-act plays or short stories. Not surprising, as up to this point Ackles was more actor and playwright than singer-songwriter. Often, though not always, he wrote in character, in the first person. It would be a mistake, however, to assume that these first-person songs are necessarily telling stories from Ackles's life.

DAVID ACKLES The songs are autobiographical to the extent that any writer has to draw on the experience of his or her own life. Certainly emotionally they are. In the particulars, no. I draw the line at that. There are some things that I could tell you are true, and some are not, and I don't care to make the distinction.[1]

Elsewhere, he talked of writers having the privilege of translating their feelings into different settings.[2] So, for example, in 'Down River', which starts side two of the album, the narrator who has just been released from prison and runs into his one-time girlfriend is not Ackles in any literal sense. Ackles did not go to prison. But he was drawing on an experience of running into a former love.

'Down River' was one of several songs that became familiar in the UK through airplay and cover versions by established artists, but which fell short of being hits. Another was 'Road To Cairo', which opens side one. Written in the first person, it tells the story of a drifter hitching a lift to Cairo. Presumably Cairo, Illinois, about four hundred miles south of Ackles's birthplace, Rock Island. As with 'Down River' and many other Ackles songs written in the first person, what we hear is one side of a conversation—a familiar Ackles strategy to draw the listener in and hint at the character of the speaker. The narrative unfolds on two levels, with an outer voice of casual, macho braggadocio at odds with an inner voice of fear and vulnerability—both coming from the same man. In the end, the inner voice prevails, and the drifter asks to be dropped off short of his destination on the pretext of buying some gifts for his wife and children. This character—an outwardly tough travelling man consumed by despair, regret, and loss—is an Ackles archetype. We meet versions of him throughout this first album, and on two of the three that follow. In his youth, he sets out for a life of adventure. He works dead-end jobs. He never settles down. He travels on the cheap, on buses and hitch-hiking. He sits in bars. He is no longer young, yet not old. His dreams have almost died, but not quite. This man isn't Ackles. Though, as noted, he shares some of Ackles's experiences: the sequence of going-nowhere jobs, for example, and they're roughly the same age.

Though it was the first David Ackles song that most people heard, 'Road To Cairo' did not prove at all representative of what followed. A slow, bluesy ballad structured around an ominous descending pattern, it tapped into that moment when rock was just getting heavy. Ackles leads on piano, and the other musicians fall in behind through the first verse—a rhythm guitar, melodic bass, lead guitar, drums, and organ—building to a crescendo of churning organ and anguished vocals.

Musically, the album's second song, 'When Love Is Gone', is an entirely different prospect. Ackles sings quietly over bass guitar with electric guitar interjections: jazzy, heavy on reverb, a little like Lee Underwood's playing on Tim Buckley's early albums. After a while, a subdued organ joins in, and then—quietly—Ackles's piano picks up the 3/4 time signature. Ackles sings again in the first person, sombre and world-weary, ruminating on a failed, hollowed-out relationship. Verse, chorus, verse, chorus, and a fade out.

'Sonny Come Home' changes tack again. It's the first outing for Ackles's unique musical theatre style—the one that came to define him. A song of shifting time signatures divided into sections, punctuated by dynamic swells of carousel organ and sudden pauses, as percussion joins in and then abruptly stops. Listening to it, you can imagine Ackles declaiming from the dark stage of a theatre, rather than singing in a rock venue or a recording studio. Once again using the first person, he tells an impressionistic, fragmented story of a man (or boy) trying to return to a home that is no longer there. Or, if it is there, that has become strange to him. After Ackles died, Jonathan Romney, writing in the *Guardian* in 1999, described the theme and atmosphere of the song as 'uncannily close' to Burt Lancaster's film *The Swimmer*.*

Next up is 'Blue Ribbons', the song that Ackles tried to sell to Cher, which led to him signing for Elektra. With an expansive melody worthy of Jimmy Webb, Ackles sings it well, but it's a big enough tune for a Sinatra or a Streisand.

Carried along by Penrod's bubbling bass and Fonfara's sweeping organ, 'Blue Ribbons' is a topical song about racial prejudice, but hardly a protest song.

DAVID ACKLES I never was in that protest thing. I admire Pete Seeger and Malvina Reynolds, but the great danger about a lot of protest songs is that they only hit the converted. That's okay, I suppose, but there are a lot of good people those songs don't reach, who might see things straighter if it was explained to them more gently.[3]

* The movie was released just a month before Ackles's album, so the similarity must be coincidental, though Ackles might have known the John Cheever short story from 1964, on which the film is based.

Though he was not a protest singer like—for example—Phil Ochs, Ackles engaged with contemporary issues. His way of addressing them was to create characters and tell their stories. Ackles was in Los Angeles during the Watts riots and responded not with a polemic, but a drama about a pregnant white woman mourning the loss of her black lover, though not in any sloganeering sense. Instead, Ackles delivers an impressionistic lyric of ravens and shining wings of song.

DAVID ACKLES Well—there are various reasons why you write songs. This particular one I wrote because of the race riots in California and Detroit—any place in the United States, I guess, last year at this time—it's pretty frustrating. You feel you can't do anything to help personally. You can't hit people over the head and say, 'Change your mind,' so instead you write a song and hope that maybe some people will change their minds.[4]

Side one closes with 'What A Happy Day', one of the album's two apparent swipes at solipsistic, self-indulgent hippie culture. It's a solo Ackles performance, which could indicate that this is one of the demos Ackles recorded when he first signed to Elektra. The prettiness of the piano part offsets the sarcasm of the lyrics.

DAVID ACKLES Then there's upsetting things happening with the hippie society. All the really beautiful people who were in the Haight three years ago have gone, and there's only phonies left—all the plastic weekend hippies.[5]

Side two opens with 'Down River', one of Ackles's best songs, and one of the most covered. An ex-con runs into a former girlfriend and finds out she's married to an old friend of his. The ex-con is resigned, calm, stoic, and sad. A fine, narrative ballad, it retains a musical restraint matching the narrator's demeanour, until the drums and lead guitar join in for an extended fade out.

DAVID ACKLES Yes, this is intensely personal, I guess . . . it involves something of the heart, and while it isn't specifically my situation, I would admit it's autobiographical in its feeling, and so consequently it's terrifically personal.[6]

Some reviews of *David Ackles* picked up on a Brecht/Weill influence on 'Laissez-Faire', the second song on side two. Musical theatre was Ackles's first love, and his songs took on ever more pronounced stagey characteristics as his recording career progressed.

JANICE VOGEL ACKLES His ultimate goal when he was younger was to write, produce, direct, design the sets, do the music, and star in his work [in musical theatre]. And he could have done it. That's where his heart was.[7]

Understanding something of that world, and particularly the songs of Brecht and Weill, and how they related—or didn't—to rock audiences in the 60s and 70s, is key to gaining any depth of insight into Ackles's music.

Poet and playwright Bertolt Brecht (1898–1956) and composer Kurt Weill (1900–1950) were active during the Weimar years before both leaving Germany in 1933 to escape Nazi persecution. Brecht was a communist with a strongly political, socially realist agenda. Weill was a prolific, classically trained composer who turned out songs, orchestral works, chamber music, cantatas, and film scores. As a young man he played piano in a bierkeller to make ends meet, and he often composed for small chamber groups of woodwind, brass, piano, and banjo. Though forever associated with each other in popular memory, their partnership lasted just three years (1927–1930). They produced four major works: *The Threepenny Opera* (1928), *Happy End* (1929), *Rise And Fall Of The City Of Mahagonny* (1930), and *Der Jasager* (1930).

Now, the best-known Brecht/Weill collaboration is *The Threepenny Opera*, though other songs of theirs developed lives beyond the stage.

Brecht created the three-act *Threepenny Opera* by adapting his lover Elisabeth Hauptmann's translation of John Gay's *Beggar's Opera*, which dates from the eighteenth century. Kurt Weill wrote the music, drawing on influences including jazz and German dance music. Brecht translates the action to Victorian London and the life and times of Macheath, a criminal antihero also known as 'Mackie' and 'Mack The Knife'. When he marries Polly Peachum, her angry father machinates to get Macheath hanged—and nearly succeeds. The play ends with a Queen's pardon for Macheath in the nick of time.

The Threepenny Opera opened in Berlin on August 31, 1928, and has since been performed on stage around the world many times and adapted for film and radio. In 1954, Marc Blitzstein's long-running off-Broadway adaptation opened at the Theater De Lys in Greenwich Village. It featured Lotte Lenya, who had once been married to Weill. MGM released a cast recording of this production, which sold well and was reissued in 1959. Ackles almost certainly knew this recording.

The Threepenny Opera is hard to place. Some critics think of it as low-brow opera. Others as high-art musical theatre. Musically, it's unsettling, challenging, angular, and oddly proportioned, and it bears little resemblance to the kind of commercial musical theatre that most audiences might be more familiar with, like Rodgers and Hammerstein. It was a profound influence on Ackles. He was still enthusing about it toward the end of his life when he directed a college production of *The Threepenny Opera*, his last big creative project.

DAVID ACKLES I love the show. It is one of the few shows in the twentieth century which has truly advanced the art of musical theatre because it brings a serious subject matter to what had been frothy entertainment. Now, mind you, I believe that the first obligation of theatre is to entertain, which 'Threepenny' does, but the fact that it chose as its subject the examination of our social value system fascinates me. It changed in many ways the course of musical theatre; we found that we could address serious topics, and thereafter did—not always, but often. It has a great score, intriguing and lively in musical theatre. Very free-form. No rules that say it must be done this way or that way, so that the imagination of the creator is able to rise as much as possible to the imagination of the original creators. Much like Shakespeare.[8]

Some of the songs from *The Threepenny Opera* have been widely covered. Frank Sinatra, Ella Fitzgerald, and Louis Armstrong all recorded 'Mack The Knife', but the definitive version is Bobby Darin's, a big hit in 1959. Before and after Ackles's career, Brecht and Weill were vaguely approved of in rock circles. This might have as much to do with their association with Weimar Republic Germany, a byword for degenerate hedonism, and their tendency to set work in a dark demimonde, as the music itself. The Doors covered a Brecht/Well composition from *Little Mahagonny*, 'Alabama Song' (also known as 'Whisky Bar'), on their debut album. Perhaps the attraction was as much lines like 'Well show me the way, to the next whiskey bar' and a general sense of staggering drunkenness as any deep-rooted appreciation of Brecht/Weill's art. Before The Doors had dipped a toe into Brecht and Weill's dirty river of inspiration, another Elektra artist, Judy Collins, covered 'Pirate Jenny', also from *Threepenny Opera*, on her album *In My Life* (1966). This is a far more sensitive interpretation, and you sense Collins had a deeper understanding of the material she was tackling. It came in a run of albums where she was moving away from folky roots and covering writers like Leonard Cohen and Jacques Brel, and in doing so bringing a European sensibility to her albums. Her 'Pirate Jenny' is like a primer of the Brecht/Weill trademarks that Ackles later assimilated into his own writing and arranging. The staccato, clockwork, one/two rhythms; the abrupt, sometimes harsh declamatory phrasing; time changes; the small chamber group orchestrations; the endings that don't quite resolve, that beg further questions.

All of this meant that by 1968, when Ackles started releasing records, there was some background knowledge of Brecht and Weill's songs among listeners paying close attention to the serious artists of the day. But possibly quite a shallow, superficial knowledge. Identifying a Brecht/Weill influence became almost obligatory in reviews of Ackles's work, but many of those reviewers might only have known 'Pirate Jenny', 'Alabama Song', and 'Mack The Knife'.

'Laissez-Faire' is the most pronounced early indicator of this aspect of Ackles's artistic heritage. Many of his subsequent songs nod in the same direction. It's the shortest song on *David Ackles*—just one minute and thirty-six seconds of oompah bass and drums, organ, and rinky-dink piano. Ackles adopts the persona of a bum concerned with nothing much more than 'money for cigarettes and pennies for wine'. It's a typically oblique, character-driven critique of a system where 'the rich get richer, and the poor get nothing'.

'Lotus Man', a dreamy mid-pace song driven by the interplay between Penrod's virtuoso lead bass and Fonfara's eddying organ, is the album's second critique of hippie shibboleths.

DAVID ACKLES Well, there again, you have a specific situation giving rise to the creation of a song. When I had just come back from Haight–Ashbury in San Francisco … it used to be a very nice place with the real hippies, and I came back very upset and very uptight because the people who were there begging on the streets were not really hippies, not what you'd call the purists, they were simply people who were afraid to face any decisions in life—they could neither be one nor the other—so they just sat around hoping that something would come to them. And nothing comes to him who waits, really. So I wrote the song about them, to say, 'Hey, come on. Don't just sit there. Get up and do something. If you believe in something, tell somebody, vote for somebody, carry a placard, do something, don't just sit there.'[9]

Musically and lyrically, 'His Name Is Andrew' is the album's strangest prospect. Ackles grimly intones a parable of lost faith over six minutes of swirling organ, tolling, bell-like piano, cymbal swells, lead bass, and the gentlest brush of guitar. The titular Andrew is a hapless victim buffeted by authority figures telling him, alternately, that God is love and God is dead. It's an austere, Calvinist song, which, Ackles joked sometimes when playing it live, came from living in Scotland for a while. For the last four lines, Ackles switches to the first person, signing off with a stark 'I choose to wait alone for this life to end'.

An unreleased outtake from the same sessions, 'The Grave Of God', seems like a companion piece to 'His Name Is Andrew'. Singing to electric guitar arpeggios, Ackles tells of a sort of innocent pilgrim who might be Andrew, who endures ridicule as he searches for the Almighty's final resting place. Both songs are taken at a funereal pace and cast an intense gaze into the void that God leaves behind.

The album closes with the keening ballad 'Be My Friend', which became Ackles's regular set closer when he played live. Organist Michael Fonfara excels with a sweeping Hammond solo over the fade-out as the piano and guitar tumble in and out of time. The master recording, without fade out, features the band playing on for two minutes longer. Another aborted take of the song from the same session takes a similar approach—piano, organ and electric guitar apparently playing live and semi-improvised. An indication that this might have been one of the songs Ackles recorded in the studio with some of the credited musicians, without later overdubbing. Not all the musicians, though, as neither the released track nor the outtake include bass and drums. Ackles's explanation of the use of the word Gilead in the song says something about his reference points and his approach to writing:

DAVID ACKLES It's really drawing on the experience of what I had thought was a shared cultural experience of using the term 'a balm in Gilead'—there is a spiritual called 'There Is A Balm In Gilead', and I was drawing on that. I don't like using terribly arcane or confusing references, and I thought that was one that would be universally understood, but it was not.[10]

Elektra put some effort into promoting the album, including sending Ackles over to Europe. The outcome was a critical response ranging from respectful to laudatory, with a few dissenting voices.

DAVID ACKLES Elektra Records were kind enough to put together a promotional tour to various radio stations ... and out of that came some additional airplay and exposure. Of course, all of that helps—it all adds up. But I was so green and new to the business, I just thought, *Well, that's standard, that's the way it's done.* I had no idea that Elektra really was putting itself out in order to make this possible. Now, in retrospect, I think what an ungrateful little asshole I must have been at the time!

[The album] was pretty well received. I got a lot of attention that I was not expecting at all, having never performed in public. I was stunned by the fact that people were actually going out and spending their money on this. Not that I thought it wasn't a product worth spending money on. But I felt that they didn't know who I was from anyone, and I was quite gratified that they were willing to go out and buy it based on very little airplay and, mostly, word of mouth.[11]

Whether they liked the music or not, reviewers struggled to describe it. Folk was a common misnomer. The *Los Angeles Times* thought Ackles 'a male vocalist to match the impact and depth of Judy Collins's and declared him 'one of the most significant composer-vocalists to emerge in the folk field this year'.[12] The *Albuquerque Journal* plumped for 'religiously oriented jazz'.[13] Poetic was the most-used adjective. Comparisons with contemporaries including Nilsson, Laura Nyro, Tom Rush, Tim Buckley, Joni Mitchell, Leonard Cohen, and Bob Dylan were useful in giving the impression of Ackles as a weighty, cultured, adult voice, while not really giving any sense at all of what he sounded like. The *Post-Crescent* compared Ackles unfavourably with Phil Ochs, asking readers to get in touch if they could think of any redeeming features in his music.[14]

In the UK, an interview in *Disc & Music Echo* titled 'The Man Who

Wrote Jools' Next Hit' was revealing on several counts.[15] Ackles mentions family music sessions from his youth, with his father playing bass and his mother drums—memories he later committed to song in 'Family Band', from *American Gothic*. Then there's talk of disillusionment with hippie culture, a theme he explored in two songs on his debut. And there are early signs of an ambivalence about the working musician's life: 'It's all such a hustle! I don't mind the travelling so much, or the actual singing, but it's all the other hustles you get as well that I don't like.'

There was more on this theme in a feature in *Beat Instrumental*, published in November after Ackles had left the UK. 'I don't want to do the endless round of one-nighters, exactly the same thing day after day. I'd much rather stick to a lesser number of concerts that I can really get to grips with. It's the same with recording. I don't want the situation where it's a case of having to have something out by such-and-such a date—I simply can't work that way.... Writing is far more important to me than any other activity—singing, performing, and so on are just a smaller part.'[16]

In that same interview, Ackles said he'd started on a second album, working with Al Kooper and The Don Ellis Orchestra. Ellis was an American jazz trumpeter, drummer, composer, and bandleader with roots in the avant-garde, who later scored *The French Connection*. Ackles, Ellis, and Kooper is an intriguing proposition, but after two trial sessions, nothing came of the collaboration, and it was not mentioned again. Failed attempts to record albums with arrangers, producers, and other collaborators became a recurring theme of Ackles's recording career at Elektra.

As early as November 1968, *Record Week* was reporting that Elektra was reissuing the Ackles debut with a different cover under the title *The Road To Cairo*, featuring a conventional portrait photograph by Guy Webster. This was just five months after the initial US issue, though in the end the reissue didn't appear until 1969. It was an indicator that the label thought Ackles had promise that was—as yet—unrealised. This became a pattern for Ackles's tenure at Elektra. High hopes, a big promotional push, and poor sales. Two singles were pulled from the album for release in the UK. The first of these, 'Down River', had a French-language version of 'Road To Cairo', retitled 'La Route A Chicago', as the B-side.* The British DJ and television personality Kenny Everett, presciently reviewing the single in *Disc & Music Echo*, said, 'This will probably only sell seven copies in the whole country.' A second single paired 'Laissez-Faire' with 'Blue Ribbons'.

What proved to be the most far-reaching of Elektra's promotional efforts was a European promotional tour from August to October 1968. It didn't do much for Ackles's record sales, but it did establish him as something of a favourite—a connoisseurs' choice, particularly among British musicians and a handful of supporters working in TV and radio.

On August 29, Ackles recorded an eighteen-minute sequence for Norwegian television, performing four songs and talking to Harald Are Lund, a DJ, presenter, musician, and producer, and a friend of John Peel's. Wearing a work shirt, waistcoat, jeans, and heavy boots, Ackles lip-syncs to 'Down River', 'Lotus Man', and 'Blue Ribbons', while miming playing piano ('Down River'), standing in front of a backdrop of eclipse images and footage of the sun ('Lotus Man') and sitting at a table ('Blue Ribbons'). Ackles's youthful film and television experience stood him in good stead, as he looks at ease performing to camera, though slightly less so when Lund joins him at the table for an interview in which Ackles explains some of the background to the three songs. He then takes the microphone Lund held during the interview (switched on, as you can hear noise as it passes from one man to the other) and sings live to a backing track of 'His Name Is Andrew'. It's an excellent, controlled performance, with just a few subtle phrasing modifications differentiating it from the album version.

Ackles arrived in England sometime in early September. The Elektra UK newsletter for that month described him as 'one of the most pleasant

* Quite why this was recorded is unclear, as the English version of the single was released in France, backed with 'Be My Friend'.

people in the world'. At about the same time, fellow Elektra artists The Doors and Tim Buckley were in London. The Doors played two nights at the Roundhouse.* The Elektra newsletter exhorted readers to help Buckley by making requests to Radio 1 to play his songs, as he didn't have any new material to promote. Nilsson was also in town.

Ray Connolly picked up on some similarities between Nilsson and Ackles in a feature in the London *Evening Standard*. 'They are what you might call *artists' artists* in that their following is greater inside the popular music business than outside among the general public,' he wrote. 'They are both more songwriter than performer, more storyteller than pop star.'[17]

The *Hartford Courant*, the oldest continuously published newspaper in the United States, tried to develop the connection between Ackles and British singer Julie Driscoll into a morsel of show-business gossip, reporting that Driscoll and Ackles had been carrying on a romance by letter and that she met him when he landed at 'London Airport'.[18] There is no other evidence of romance, but Driscoll and Giorgio Gomelsky (who ran Marmalade Records, the label releasing Driscoll's records) did host a welcome reception for Ackles.[19] This was because Driscoll, with Brian Auger & The Trinity, was about to release a cover of 'Road To Cairo', a fact worthy of front-page billing in *Melody Maker*. 'It must be a smash!' said *Disc & Music Echo*. But it wasn't. Had it been the course of Ackles's career would likely have changed.

In the spring of 1968, Julie Driscoll, Brian Auger & The Trinity had charted strongly with their cover of Bob Dylan's 'This Wheel's On Fire'. With its swirling phase effects, Hammond organ, and Mellotron, the song captured the spirit of the times. And the big-voiced Driscoll, with her cropped hair, was one of the faces of the year. When she and Auger chose

---

* The Doors arrived at Heathrow Airport on September 3. The following day, the band held a press conference at the ICA. On the 6th and 7th, they played at the Roundhouse in Chalk Farm, London, with Jefferson Airplane. The visit was documented in a Granada TV documentary, *The Doors Are Open*.

'Road To Cairo' as their follow-up single, they—and Ackles—had good reason to think they'd have another big hit. The organ and Mellotron were in place, and Driscoll's virtuoso vocals took the melody to places that Ackles couldn't reach. The timing was perfect, too, with the single released in October 1968, while Ackles was on hand in the UK. But the record didn't chart. Ackles commented about the shock value of a woman singing of abandoning her children. Driscoll changed the words from Ackles's 'the life a man should live' to 'the life I chose to leave'. Maybe that's one reason why the record didn't sell. There were comments at the time about a poor-quality pressing or mastering job, leaving the resultant seven-inch single sounding weak and thin.

According to Clive Selwood, who was running Elektra's UK operation at the time, Reg Dwight—who was in the process of becoming Elton John—attended the reception organised by Driscoll and Gomelsky and paid close attention.

CLIVE SELWOOD David played, just sat at the piano and played and was wonderful, and Elton John turned up. David was quite apprehensive about playing but totally engaging, just sat there quietly at the piano and played.[20]

Press accounts of Ackles's visit refer to a press reception. It is likely—though not certain—that this was the Gomelsky and Driscoll event. Assuming it was, it marked the first time Ackles performed live as a singer-songwriter. The reception and subsequent appearances over the next few weeks were also the only time Ackles ever played live with a backing band.

In 1968, John Peel was a rising star at BBC Radio 1, positioning himself as the station's champion of the underground. He admired Ackles and gave him plenty of exposure throughout this promotional visit and in subsequent years. The first public sign of Peel's support was on September 15, when he played 'When Love Is Gone' on *Top Gear*. Three days later, on *Night Ride*, Peel interviewed Ackles:

> **JOHN PEEL** There are a lot of American visitors over at the moment... there's a whole bunch of individual singers coming over, and the first of them is David Ackles, and David's in the studio this evening, and I've just told him I'm probably the worst interviewer, probably in Europe, possibly the world, and he said he was the worst interviewee. One thing you can talk about, though, is your LP, which has just been released in this country... one of the songs on the album is 'Road To Cairo', which has just been recorded by—
>
> **DAVID ACKLES** Julie Driscoll.[21]

The next big event on Ackles's itinerary was an appearance on BBC television. *Colour Me Pop*, broadcast on Friday or Saturday night on BBC2, was the first colour pop music programme in the UK. It ran from June 1968 to August 1969, initially as an adjunct to the contemporary discussion programme *Late Night Line Up*, then as a standalone programme. Most shows featured a single artist performing in the studio, maybe with some filmed inserts. A few shows featured multiple artists. Initially, artists were introduced by a presenter, but by the time Ackles appeared, this had been phased out. The length of episodes varied. This was possible as it was the last show broadcast before BBC2 shut down for the night, so there was no following schedule to disrupt.

Like much British television of its time, *Colour Me Pop* was a low-budget, cobbled-together affair—done on a wing and a prayer. Producer Steve Turner, by his own admission, started work on the show knowing nothing about pop and rock music. His musical experience to that point had been limited to singing in the choir at a church in Leeds until his voice broke. Turner embarked on a steep learning curve that involved visiting clubs most nights to see acts play and listening to records. He had the freedom to choose whoever he fancied for the show but was limited by a £100 artist budget per episode. Acts performed in a small presentation studio. When The Small Faces appeared with Stanley Unwin, who had narrated links between songs in his nonsensical private language on the band's album *Ogdens' Nut Gone Flake*, Unwin was waiting alone in the studio until the band rolled in from the pub three minutes before the live broadcast.

After a few shows had been broadcast, agents and pluggers started to take notice and approach Turner. There was no other opportunity on British television for rock acts to play a twenty-five-to-thirty-minute set. Somebody from Elektra made a call, and Turner sat down to listen to David Ackles's first album, having no idea who he was. Until that point, he'd always insisted on seeing an act live before booking them, even if he liked the record. For Ackles, he made an exception—possibly encouraged by the fact that the unknown American would perform for free.

STEVE TURNER As soon as I heard 'Road To Cairo', I knew I wanted him on the programme. Listening to his tracks now, they almost bring me to tears. He was a brilliant songwriter and performer. After all these years I can see him now, just sitting quietly at the piano, concentrating completely on his playing and singing.[22]

Ackles appeared on episode 12 of *Colour Me Pop*, which aired on September 28. It was a sole-artist edition, with Ackles the first US act on the show. He performed four songs: 'Down River', 'His Name Is Andrew', 'Road To Cairo', and 'Be My Friend'. They were live studio performances—not mimed but pre-recorded between 9pm and 10pm on the day of broadcast. There was one rehearsal run-through, and then the show was recorded in a single take.*

STEVE TURNER He appeared in the studio. He was a lovely person. Perhaps a bit shy. So sincere. We didn't need to put in lots of shots. It was him and the piano. That was enough … I got a feeling of a quiet young man who

* Background information about *Colour Me Pop* comes from emails from Adam James Smith, August 6, 2024.

loved his music, and who I thought was going to go a long, long way. I remember him being very respectful.[23]

The show is now lost, being one of many programmes the BBC wiped at the time so that they could reuse the videotape. However, in 2010, an audio recording of the broadcast emerged, made by BBC engineer Michael Cotton. Ackles was backed by an unknown four-piece band of bass, drums, lead guitar, and Hammond organ, heard but barely seen during the performance—the cameras being fixed on Ackles.* Ackles's performances are almost flawless. His singing is accurate, intense, emotional, powerful, and controlled, his piano playing a steady rhythmic foundation. For the most part, this band reference the album arrangements without slavishly replicating them. 'Down River' and 'Road To Cairo', which fade out on record, have new endings. 'Be My Friend' retains a fade-out, like the album version. The organist and lead guitarist play with more detail and less restraint than their album counterparts, but it still sounds like a band performing the album rather than creating new settings for the songs.

STEVE TURNER 'His Name Is Andrew' was the only song I added to. I was born in Leeds and sang daily services in Leeds Parish Church choir. I remembered the building as being beautiful, with lots of magnificent stained-glass windows, so I took a film crew up a few days before transmission and shot lots of exteriors and interiors and used these over the whole of the number. The results fit beautifully with the music.[24]

On the same day that his *Colour Me Pop* appearance was broadcast, Ackles featured on *Scene & Heard*, a BBC radio programme dedicated to new

* There are references online to these four musicians being members of Glass Menagerie, a band active in Manchester at the time. I have been unable to establish whether that is the case. A short article in *Disc & Music Echo* (October 5, 1968) calls them a 'scratch band' and says that Ackles only had 30 minutes rehearsal with them before his first live performance.

music. The following day, September 29, he played live at Olympop at Fairfield Hall, Croydon, south of London. Olympop was a fundraiser in aid of the British Olympic Appeal, compèred by Peel and running to nearly four hours. It was another opportunity derived from the support of Giorgio Gomelsky, with the concert organised by Paragon Publicity & Public Relations Limited, a company with which Gomelsky was involved. The programme explained the somewhat dubious premise of the concert: Olympians were young, and therefore probably liked pop music, and pop musicians were young and therefore probably played sport on their days off. As well as Ackles, Jethro Tull, Eclection, The Alan Price Set, Spooky Tooth, The Nice, and Julie Driscoll, Brian Auger & The Trinity performed. As Driscoll/Auger's cover of Ackles's 'Road To Cairo' was released shortly after, it probably featured in their set. Jethro Tull, Price, and Driscoll/Auger were filmed for editions of *Colour Me Pop* broadcast in November.

Ackles must have been a late addition to the bill, as he is not featured in the programme. He appeared in the first half of the show, after Jethro Tull and Elektra labelmates Eclection and before Alan Price. An anonymous journalist reviewed the concert for the local newspaper:

> After these two amplified acts, singer/composer David Ackles came as a quiet surprise.
>
> He looks like a gentler, smoother Bob Dylan, with a piano instead of a guitar, and backed by a quartet; but his smoky voice and sad, bitter songs of life and love belong to the longer tradition of French chanson.
>
> He is obviously talented, but Sunday's concert was quite the wrong atmosphere for his act and the audience quickly lost interest. He aggravated the situation by failing to introduce any of his songs, a surprising attitude since one presumes he must be perfectly articulate.[25]

It's a revealing and perceptive account. First, it confirms that Ackles was playing with a backing band through much if not all of this brief UK tour. Second, the reviewer includes another attempt at categorising Ackles's songs, linking them to French chanson. Periodically throughout Ackles's career, critics would pass comment in this way on the perceived European influences in his songwriting. Finally, it points for the first time to an apparent difficulty with playing live in a rock setting, and an inability to hold an audience. In an interview published in November 1968, Ackles expressed ambivalence about live performance, talking of playing a 'very posh' London nightclub and hating it: 'Playing an accompaniment for people to talk to ... it was horrible.'[26]

At first sight, this seems surprising, given Ackles's history as an actor and dancer. But he was used to performing in front of cameras, with no audience or a managed, chaperoned one. He looked quite at ease on Norwegian TV, for example. Or in theatres, where the convention is to sit quietly and pay attention. The act of winning over a distracted, possibly drunk rock audience was alien to him. All the recorded evidence suggests that Ackles could play live to the highest of standards, musically. His singing and playing rarely faltered. But as a performer, he needed to have the attention of the audience and sometimes struggled to win it.

The same day as Olympop, Peel played 'Down River' on *Top Gear*:

> On Tuesday we have two American singers recording for *Top Gear*, Tim Buckley and David Ackles, and we'll be hearing those sessions in a few weeks' time. I'm going to play a Dave Ackles record in just a moment. I got a letter yesterday from Ian Anderson's father—now, Ian Anderson is the singer with Jethro Tull, and I met him at the free concert at Hyde Park yesterday, and he mentioned that yesterday was his mother's birthday, you see, so for Ian Anderson's mother, from Ian Anderson and his dad, here's David Ackles with 'Down River'. Happy birthday Ian Anderson's mum. [*plays record*]

> If you think that's good, you ought to hear the LP. That's David Ackles, that's called 'Down River', which is released as a single. And it's nice that he's going to do *Top Gear*, because he's a very, very nice person and a good singer.[27]

Ackles's sole BBC radio session was recorded on October 1, 1968. Immediately after this, he travelled to Amsterdam for two days, then probably returned to England for a little longer before travelling home. He performed five songs from his debut album for BBC radio, 'Down River', 'Laissez-Faire', 'When Love Is Gone', 'Road To Cairo', and 'Be My Friend'. A surviving recording of 'Be My Friend' from this session indicates that the session—or at least part of it—was almost certainly recorded with the same four musicians who backed Ackles on *Colour Me Pop*. It's reasonable to assume they were also the quartet on stage with him at Olympop.

Peel played the session recordings of 'Down River', 'Laissez-Faire', and 'When Love Is Gone' on *Top Gear* on October 27, 1968.

> There's someone I also rate very highly, almost as highly as Leonard Cohen in fact, and that's on the strength of what he's done for us and his LP, which is excellent. David Ackles—and this is his last number, but he will be back, and you'll undoubtedly hear him on *Top Gear* again.[28]

Peel played 'Down River' and 'Laissez-Faire' again on *Top Gear*, on November 24, 1968, along with the session takes of 'Road To Cairo' and 'Be My Friend'. Ackles left England sometime in October, but through that month and into November, press interviews he'd conducted during the visit were published.

In 1968, the way popular music was marketed and perceived was changing in the UK and the US. A clear divide was emerging between pop (singles, mainstream commercial success, the charts, package tours, a younger audience) and rock (albums, the underground, a more serious, older audience, college gigs). In the UK, an emerging underground press, John Peel, and some parts of the mainstream music press were catering for the rock audience. *Colour Me Pop* was in this camp, too. Pop was the wrong word for the show, really, as it tended toward album-orientated artists. It was to this audience that Elektra marketed Ackles, and where he found considerable favour.

Julie Driscoll and Brian Auger were not the only people who noticed *David Ackles*. Later, Elton John, Bernie Taupin, Phil Collins, and Elvis Costello would all talk of the impression the album made on them. The English folk music community seemed to find a particular affinity with the songs, drawn no doubt by Ackles's storytelling approach. Martin Carthy's desolate rendition of 'His Name Is Andrew', included on *Landfall* (1971), stands out. It somehow positioned the song in the margins of the English folk canon. Traditional singer Dave Burland's stark unaccompanied rendition followed in 1975, on *Songs & Buttered Haycocks*. Then Jon Boden, of Bellowhead, recorded the song in 2010 for *A Folk Song A Day: November*. Boden's version is a voice-and-fiddle interpretation of Carthy's arrangement. It's a testament to the depth and timelessness of Ackles's writing that all these versions sit comfortably amidst the traditional material that forms the bulk of all these artists' repertoires. Boden first heard the song on a cassette of McCarthy's *Landfall*, with no supporting information.

JON BODEN I don't think I worked out where it came from, really … in my mind it felt pre-war. … I don't consider it as a folk song, but I do consider it as tonally sympathetic to folk song … very simple language, but it speaks to a kind of universality of human experience. Certainly 'His Name Is Andrew' has that in spades.[29]

Another English folk stalwart, guitarist, violinist, and singer Barry Dransfield, included a sweet take of 'Be My Friend' on his eponymous

1972 album. His brother, Robin, also performed the song. Two years earlier, The Moths recorded their sole album of what would now be termed acid-folk, closing with a mournful, flute-led take of the same song. Martin Carthy might have introduced Linda Thompson to Ackles's songs; at any rate, he accompanied her on a demo of 'Down River' recorded in the crypt of a London church in December 1970. Thompson's exquisitely poised rendition was released on the rarities collection *Give Me A Sad Song* (2001).

'Down River' caught the attention of plenty of other British musicians beyond the folk community. Spooky Tooth, who had appeared at Olympop with Ackles, slowed it down for a grandiose interpretation on their 1970 album *The Last Puff.** The Hollies tackled the song on their 1972 album *Romany*. Commercially, the band were in a fallow period. Singer Allan Clarke had left, to be replaced by Mikael Rickfors, and the hits had dried up for a while. The Hollies' take on 'Down River' is a heartfelt version that doesn't sound much like a typical Hollies song. Elton John and Elvis Costello drew on this interpretation when performing the song on television, decades later. The Hollies' album featured briefly in the lower regions of the US charts, but it wasn't a UK hit. Before both of these versions, the obscure Scottish singer Alan Trajan recorded 'Down River' on his sole album, *Firm Roots* (1969), with an approximation of Ackles's own arrangement. Trajan drifted into a later life that sounds like something from an Ackles song—playing in pubs, drinking, liver disease, a spell in prison.

The sixteen-year-old Louisa Jane White recorded 'Blue Ribbons' as the B-side of her second single, her powerful voice not unlike Cher's, for whom the song might have been originally intended.

American artists seemed less interested in Ackles. The only roughly contemporaneous US cover of a song from *David Ackles* I can locate is New England singer-songwriter Jaime Brockett's take of 'Down River',

* It was followed in the running order by 'Son Of Your Father' (Elton John/Bernie Taupin).

from *Jaime Brockett 2* (1970). An ardent, elongated acoustic version, it's one of the most original Ackles covers.

—

Was *David Ackles* a success? In immediate commercial terms, no. It didn't sell well and didn't chart anywhere. None of the cover versions of songs from the album were hits, either. The prevailing impression, though—in the UK at least—was that Elektra had found a notable talent. Perhaps not star material, but a serious contender. An artist who would build up an audience over a few albums, whose songs would be widely covered. Label and artist could look ahead with confidence.

As well as establishing a pattern that endured throughout Ackles's career—critical acclaim not matched by commercial success—the songs on *David Ackles* prompted a recurring question. Why did Ackles, who was by most accounts optimistic and cheerful, populate his albums with sorrowful tales of the lost and the lonely? People on the slide, ex-cons, drug addicts, drifters and divorcees, confused spiritual seekers, mourners. There's no easy answer to that.

BRUCE BOTNICK The music may have been intense, but he was a marshmallow: one of the sweetest people. He was obviously conflicted and a complicated person. You don't write about the subjects he engaged with unless it's to deal with demons.[30]

Was Ackles plagued by a secret darkness that seeped out in the songs?

It's an easy and convenient explanation to land on, especially in a business where so many performers are troubled. But the problem with applying this sort of argument to Ackles is that there is nothing much to support the idea. The accounts of people who knew him well and saw the way he led his life don't match that story. He was a thoughtful and intelligent man, with a strong social conscience. He was also slow to judge. He often wrote in character. All these things contributed. Writers don't always write about things from direct personal experience. Ackles wrote a song about the Aberfan mining disaster, but he wasn't there when it happened, and he'd never been a miner or lost a child.

JANICE VOGEL ACKLES He was saddened by the many vagaries and woeful conditions with life that we all have to encounter. And I think, in some cases, they affected him more deeply than others, like with most people. But I think it was hard for him to just kind of put them away and go on.[31]

Ackles was aware of this tension. Recordings of concerts often include him joking about his sad and miserable songs.

CHAPTER FOUR

OUT ON THE ROAD

US LIVE DEBUT • ABORTED SESSIONS WITH AL KOOPER AND DON ELLIS • CANTERBURY HOUSE • FRED MYROW • *SUBWAY TO THE COUNTRY* • HARRY BELAFONTE

“

RUSS MILLER *Fred, it's really fantastic.*
BRUCE BOTNICK *Stupendous.*
RUSS MILLER *Stupendous, as Bruce says.*
FRED MYROW *Fellas—beautiful, sensitive playing. I don't know—it's just blowing my mind. Thank you, all.*
STUDIO CHATTER ON OUTTAKES FROM THE *SUBWAY TO THE COUNTRY* SESSIONS

”

November 22, 1968. David Ackles is in a former print shop in downtown Ann Arbor. It's now a coffeehouse and music venue. The room can hold two hundred at a squeeze. The audience is sitting at small round tables running down two walls of the room and on wooden chairs arranged in loose rows across the middle of the floor. There are coloured glass candle holders on each table. The stage is wide, though not very deep and only about a foot high. But big enough to accommodate Ackles sitting at the piano. The front row of chairs is right up to the stage, so some members of the audience are just a couple of feet from him. The lighting is warm and subdued. To the right of the stage near the rear wall there is a sound booth housing the mixer and lighting controls, and a reel-to-reel tape recorder. Ackles is about to make his US debut as a live performer, and it will be recorded…

In November 1968, after completing his promotional visit to Europe, Ackles returned to Los Angeles, spending some time at his parents' home near the Hollywood sign. Here his thoughts turned again to preparing his second album, *Subway To The Country*, which was released a year later, toward the end of 1969.

The first sessions for the album had been held back in August 1968, shortly before Ackles flew to Europe. This was the collaboration with Al Kooper and Don Ellis, which Ackles mentioned in interviews while in England. American Federation Of Musicians records show that Ackles did two sessions with Kooper and Ellis, on August 23 and 24, 1968, at Elektra Sound Recorders in West Hollywood. The first session saw Ellis and Kooper, both credited as arrangers, lead ten musicians plus Ackles through a version of 'There's No Reason To Cry'—an earlier title for 'That's No Reason To Cry'—taken at a slightly faster pace than the album version. Guitarist Doug Hastings and bassist Jerry Penrod, who played on Ackles's debut, line up alongside drummer Billy Mundi and the horn players from the Don Ellis Orchestra. It's an unusually structured rendition. The core arrangement has a country-soul feel, laden with stabbing, muted horn phrases, as you might expect from Ellis. Ackles attempts some vocal pyrotechnics that don't really come off. An atonal instrumental coda is an abstract of repetitive brass patterns and free-form electronic tones.

The second session saw a similar line-up joined by guitarist James Burton for a version of 'Cabin On The Mountain'. Again, faster than the album version and dominated by Ellis's horn parts. The arrangement evokes Las Vegas Elvis, and Ackles sounds a little uncomfortable trying to keep up. Once again, there's an extended instrumental coda with a similar electronic tone, this time playing a decipherable melody.*

These outtakes, with their swinging horns and electronic flourishes, suggest an attempt to find a more experimental setting for Ackles's songs. They're intriguing, but Ackles doesn't sound at ease. After this abandoned collaboration, Ackles teamed up with a friend from the USC days, the composer Fred Myrow. It was the one occasion he partnered successfully with an arranger.

Once back in the US after the European visit, Ackles began playing live almost immediately, performing regularly throughout the rest of 1968 and through 1969. He avoided the endless round of one-nighters he so dreaded, instead tending to play short residencies or isolated single nights as a solo performer, usually in small folk venues or theatres.

Typical of these was Canterbury House in Ann Arbor, Michigan. Established in the late nineteenth century and still active, Canterbury House is the Episcopal Church's campus ministry at the University Of Michigan. In 1967, the ministry moved to a former print shop, running it as a coffeehouse during the day and a music venue at weekends.† In an effort to engage with the emerging counterculture, a typical Sunday service might include beat poetry, performance art, experimental films, and anti-Vietnam War sermons. This unlikely venue thrived until its closure in 1971, attracting a diverse roll call of esteemed performers including

* This might be an Ondioline, an early French electronic keyboard instrument, as Al Kooper used one at the time.

† Canterbury House, now on a different site, still operates as a music venue, tending to book local acts and experimental musicians.

Odetta, Tim Buckley, MC5, Joni Mitchell, Frank Zappa, Richie Havens, Neil Young, Gordon Lightfoot, and Tom Rush. All watched by audiences of no more than two hundred a show.

Ackles first performed at Canterbury House between November 22 and 24, 1968, shortly after his return home from England. These were his first ever live performances in his home country. Tickets were $1.50, 'eats gratis, shoes optional', according to a November 21 ad in the *Michigan Daily*.* He returned on March 21, 1969, for another three-night stint, 'a spring celebration experience', the prices this time up to $1.75, the food still free. In 1970, he played a third three-night residency at the venue, February 13 to 15. There was likely one more appearance in the spring of 1970 (dates unknown).

In 2018, *Rolling Stone* reported that the Michigan History Project had unearthed a cache of professional soundboard recordings from Canterbury House. The collection had been in private ownership in the past and was thought lost. The tapes, *Rolling Stone* reported, include performances by Neil Young, Joni Mitchell, Tim Buckley, Odetta, and David Ackles.[1] The Ackles recording from this archive is anomalous as it is an undated cassette, whereas the others are reel-to-reel tapes. The tapes and documents associated with the performers' appearances at Canterbury House are now held by Bentley Historical Library.

There is music on both sides of the Ackles Canterbury House cassette, with obvious edits, indicating that the recordings were most likely dubbed from another source and that this is not simply a direct recording of a complete live set as it happened. Ackles is in strong voice throughout, accompanying himself on piano. For the most part, he performs faithful recreations of the familiar recorded versions of the songs, albeit without the additional instrumentation. Occasionally he modifies or adjusts a

* An advert in the same paper from November 23 lists worship services for Sunday 24. This bills Ackles appearing at Canterbury House at 11am, indicating his participation in a service rather than giving a performance. His other appearances that weekend, on Friday, Saturday, and Sunday evenings, were conventional performances to paying audiences.

phrase. Even allowing for the edits, on this evidence Ackles preferred to let the songs speak for themselves. Though there is some between-song banter, Ackles offers little in the way of 'this song is about' introductions. The recording is dominated by songs from *David Ackles* and *Subway To The Country*, indicating that these recordings are most likely taken from Ackles's appearances at Canterbury House in November 1968 and March 1969. The set includes several unreleased songs dating to that period.

In such intimate settings, it was normal for Ackles to speak to and occasionally befriend members of staff at the venues. Jim Friedrich was on a placement at Canterbury House as part of his training for ordination to the Episcopal Church when Ackles performed there in 1969. The two struck up a rapport and remained in touch when Friedrich moved to Los Angeles in May 1970. Later that year, Ackles performed at Friedrich's ordination service.

Friedrich made a copy of the 'official' Canterbury house soundboard recording of Ackles's performance on February 15, 1970. With fewer edits, it is a much more accurate record of an Ackles performance than the Bentley Historical Library cassette. Compared to the earlier recording, Ackles sounds more confident and relaxed. He chats to the audience between songs, cracks jokes, and performs with elan.*

The Main Point in Bryn Mawr, Pennsylvania, was another coffeehouse venue with about the same capacity as Canterbury House. There were rows of wooden chairs, each with a shelf attached to the back that served as a table for the person sitting behind. The Main Point was opened in 1964 by a group of couples including William and Jeanette Campbell. Before long, the other couples dropped out and the Campbells divorced, leaving Mrs Campbell (as she was generally known) to run the place alone until 1981—booking acts, making the food and drinks, and offering bed and board to performers. Like Canterbury House, the Main Point attracted a

* Appendix 1 includes complete set lists of songs and transcriptions of between-song talk on both tapes.

heterogeneous list of acclaimed artists, including Phil Ochs, James Taylor, Bruce Springsteen, Billy Joel, and The Strawbs. Ackles played two short residencies at the Main Point in 1969, in April (supporting Tom Rush) and November (headlining, with David Rea as support).

LYNDA RUTHERFORD I first met David in early April 1969. I was working at a small coffeehouse [the Main Point] and he was opening act for Tom Rush. It was Easter weekend, and that Saturday night, after we closed and we were cleaning up, he came into the kitchen and asked if anyone knew of a church he could go to the next day for Easter services. I told him I was taking my grandmother to her former church in South Philadelphia, and he was welcome to join us. The next morning, he drove to my parents' house to pick me up, then we went to my grandmother's apartment to get her. I remember his voice filling the church during the singing of hymns, and after the service the minister approached him and asked him if he'd like to join their choir! David, with a smile, gracefully declined, saying that he lived in California and the commute would be too much! We then returned to my parents' house for Easter dinner … then off to the Main Point for the last two performances.[2]

In May 1969, between Ackles's two Main Point residencies, he played five nights on home territory, at the Troubadour, West Hollywood, supporting Joni Mitchell. He would play there again a year later, supporting Elton John.

Though Ackles was willing to keep performing in small clubs and theatres, an ambivalence about the very notion of playing live persisted. He never got over this, and it must have contributed to his struggle to make commercial headway later. Part of the problem was finding suitable venues. Ackles wasn't a rock musician, so rock clubs and support slots with rock bands tended to go badly. He tended more toward the folk coffeehouse circuit, but as he wasn't a folk musician, he was always an awkward fit. In an interview feature by Kathy Orloff, widely syndicated in June 1969, his doubts were obvious. Playing live, he said, 'was antithetical to my whole being because I'm extremely private as a person ... the kind of music that I'm writing belongs best, I suppose, either in college concert areas where you have people whose minds are free to accept, or in small back-country bars ... I don't think my kind of music is heard best in a totally commercial environment.'[3]

Rutherford saw Ackles again after his second Main Point appearance, travelling to New York in December to see him perform at the Bitter End on 13 December. Ackles had played the venue before, in March that year, and was not impressed with the house piano. In an age before convincing digital options, this was an issue for all piano performers at the time, unless they were sufficiently supported financially to take their own instrument (and somebody to keep it in tune) on the road. Ackles was never in that category, and he had to work with what he was given. Which was often unsatisfactory.

A writer called Douglas Graham was in the Bitter End audience that night. He didn't know Ackles at the time, but the two later met and became firm friends and colleagues. Graham co-produced Ackles's final album, *Five & Dime*.

DOUGLAS GRAHAM In 1969 I was managing the folk singer Odetta. I happened to be in New York, and I went into a club called the Bitter End on Bleecker Street. And there was David playing, and I'd heard of him because of other people I knew in the business, but I'd never heard him. He was playing a solo set, and he was fantastic. I didn't talk to him or meet him ... but later on that year, my wife at the time and I moved to Hollywood Hills ... Beechwood Canyons, a hilly part near the Hollywood sign. We rented a house and there was a knock on the door, and it was a sweet little English lady who worked in real estate, and she wanted to know if we were interested in selling the house. I said, 'We've just moved into the house, we're renting it, but please come on in.' And she did, and she introduced herself as Queenie Ackles. I said, 'Are you any relation to David Ackles?' She said, 'Oh, that's my son, and we live just down the road on Beechwood Drive, and David's staying at our place at the moment'. And I said, 'Well, tell him I saw him in New York and I'm a big fan of his. And I'm a writer and I'm working for Warner Brothers as a screenwriter, and I'd love to meet him.' A day or so later, I got a call from him, and he said, 'This is David Ackles, I understand you're a neighbour of mine,' and I said, 'Yes, can we meet?' And we did, and we hit it off immediately. And even though we were in different disciplines ... we became very good friends.[4]

In December 1959, Ackles had been in New York, clerking for a rubber wholesaler and dragging himself through a dispiriting round of auditions in the dying days of his failed attempt to break into the theatre world. Ten years later, he was back, thriving and optimistic, seeing out the year and the decade with a flourish. A sense of occasion hung over the December Bitter End residency, which ran from the 13th to the 15th. Bill Haley & The Comets had played six nights earlier in the month. With the temperature hovering around freezing, crowds queued around the block to get a seat in the 230-capacity venue to see Ackles. The shows were widely reviewed, with writers picking up on many of the recurring themes that had cropped up throughout his career so far. There were the usual attempts to describe Ackles's music with Brecht/Weill comparisons and erroneously place him in the folk category. The intense and sometimes murky subject matter was contrasted with Ackles's smiling demeanour, and his tendency to become deeply absorbed in his material as he delivers it. And then there was the somewhat inappropriate billing. This time, Ackles was paired with Morgen, a New York-based prototype heavy rock band whose sole album has since become collectable in psychedelic circles. The general impression given by the accounts that follow—by Mike Jahn of the *New York Times*, and from *Cash Box* and *Billboard*—is of an artist who is growing in confidence and finding his feet on stage.

> At the Bitter End, where he appeared through last night, Mr. Ackles banged heartily on the customarily out-of-tune piano. His voice

> has a grave tone, especially foreboding when he sings songs like his 'Main Line Saloon', which deals with drug use, or 'Inmates Of The Institution', which is either about a mental institution or about the general emptiness of life. ... At other times, Mr. Ackles can be quiet, tender, and tearful. His 'Subway To The Country', about bringing up children in the city, is very good in this way. His habit of singing these songs through the smile of a very intense cherub is quite effective.[5]

> David has been called a 'down' performer. It has been said that his songs are so depressing that he is no fun. Now David makes jokes about the situation, declaring that his amusing song 'Laissez-Faire' is an 'upper-downer'. Entering another song, he warned the audience that at the end of the set he would pass out razor blades to them.
>
> If Ackles is depressing, it is only because he makes everyone see himself clearly for the first time, and that's not supposed to be fun. Lou Christie is supposed to be fun. David does not deal just in entertainment, he deals in revelation through entertainment. If that sounds too strong to you, you haven't heard David yet.[6]

> Ackles was at his communicative best, both in his interpretations of his fine material and in his comments to the packed audience. The Elektra Records artist opened with bitter smiles as he sang 'Main Line Saloon' from his latest album. 'That's No Reason To Cry' and 'Subway To The Country' were other good selections from the LP, while 'What A Happy Day' was a good song from his first Elektra album.[7]

Alongside the live work, Ackles performed on regional television in 1969. In April, he appeared on *The Hy Lit Show* in Philadelphia, and in May on *Upbeat* in Cleveland. The level and rate of this activity throughout the year was not sufficient to expose Ackles to a much wider audience than he'd attracted with the release of his debut album the previous year. It was, though, regular work on a par with labelmates like Tom Rush and Tim Buckley. In 1969, more than any other, Ackles led the working musician's life: preparing a new album while playing live to promote the previous one. There are even indications he worked as a songwriter for hire, though with little success.*

There was a steady drip feed of press coverage, too. Belated assessments of Ackles's 1968 debut continued through much of 1969, alongside live reviews and interviews looking forward to the second album. In her June interview, Orloff indicated that this was still a work in progress. By November, reviews were starting to appear, and it seems that the album—*Subway To The Country*—was on sale in the US in late November, though probably not until January 1970 in the UK. It was preceded in the Elektra schedule by the most un-Elektra album the label ever released, *Wild Thing Partyin'*—a crass collection of covers of contemporary hits.

The main sessions for *Subway To The Country* were conducted over a month from late June until late July 1969, at Elektra's studio in West Hollywood. There was some technical continuity between the new album and its predecessor. Just Russ Miller was credited as producer, but Ackles recalled that David Anderle was present and involved. Engineer Bruce Botnick was on duty again, assisted by Fritz Richmond, a washtub bassist and jug player who also worked as an engineer on many Elektra recordings.

The front cover—another W.S. Harvey production, this time using photos by Frank Bez—contrasted with Ackles's debut. The oblique mystery of the former is replaced with a close-up of a smiling, tousle-haired Ackles in profile. The back cover has Ackles in work clothes and boots, crouching on the tracks at the entrance to a railway tunnel, a hat and knapsack on the ground next to him. A 'lone travelling man' sort of pose, already a

* Writing in *Press & Sun Bulletin* on November 29, 1969, Kathy Orloff reported that Ackles was writing the theme song to the movie *The Way We Live Now*, though nothing seems to have come of this.

familiar trope of singer-songwriter mythology. You can imagine Tom Rush or Fred Neil sitting on those tracks. Ackles's music, though, was moving ever further away from that world.

Subway To The Country was arranged and conducted by Ackles's old USC friend Fred Myrow. In his late teens and through his 20s, Myrow had emerged as a promising modern classical composer, awarded multiple grants and scholarships and winning praise from Dmitri Shostakovich. He explored what is now termed world music and, as he approached thirty, decided to follow his father, the twice Oscar-nominated Josef Myrow, into scoring films. Most of Myrow Jr's film work was done from the 1970s onward. His best-known scores are the Charlton Heston sci-fi vehicle *Soylent Green* and the *Phantasm* series. There's something of the cinematic in his arrangements for *Subway To The Country*. Indeed, twenty-four minutes of unreleased outtakes of the album's 'Candy Man', without vocals, could easily pass as incidental music to some noir thriller, with Myrow referencing his modern classical roots and often drifting toward dissonance. Those outtakes show the arrangement evolving to some extent, though some themes and the general atmosphere of the released version are there from the start. This indicates that Myrow's approach to arranging wasn't simply a matter of getting musicians to read the dots on the charts. Similarly, studio chatter before a take of 'Mainline Saloon' has 'Donny' (presumably Don Gallucci, who is listed on the album credits) discussing with Myrow when and where he should 'lay in' and 'lay off'.

Myrow was two years younger than Ackles. He died of a heart attack in 1999, just six weeks before Ackles himself died. Thirty years earlier, he was drifting into the Elektra orbit.

DAVID ACKLES I was in New York and ran into him [Fred] on the street. He said, 'I understand you're doing rock'n'roll,' and I said, 'Well not really, but it's popular music, with electrical …' He said, 'Well, let me know if you ever need an arranger.' So of course, as soon as the next album was ready to be arranged, I called him, and Fred did the arrangements—

which reflect his background as much as anything, and his understanding of the music.[8]

Around the same time as arranging for Ackles, Myrow was working on the music for Jim Morrison's film *HWY: An American Pastoral* (often referred to as *Highway*). That same year, Myrow also contributed to an album on Jac Holzman's classical imprint, Nonesuch, *Spectrum: New American Music* volume 1. Myrow's score runs through much of *HWY*'s fifty minutes, following Morrison as a hitchhiker—as he makes his way from the desert to the city—with wandering guitar improvisations, keyboard drones, hand percussion, and Japanese-sounding flutes. The film (and music) is very much of its time and was never commercially released, though it can now be watched online. Myrow and Morrison became close and, according to a 1994 interview with Myrow, were planning to write a musical together in France—a scheme curtailed by Morrison's premature death.*

Myrow was the only arranger Ackles tolerated. There were at least three other attempts to work with arrangers, all established figures with impeccable industry credentials, none of which worked out.† The reasons for the success of the partnership between Myrow and Ackles probably went deeper than friendship and shared history. Neither were rock'n'roll men, and—at thirty years of age, give or take a few years—both were stepping into new phases of their respective careers.

AFM session records list ten three-hour sessions, spread over seven days between late June and late July.‡ These logs must be incomplete, as 'Candy Man' doesn't appear in the list of songs recorded, and Lonnie Mack, who is credited on the album sleeve, does not appear among the participants.

---

* Janice Vogel Ackles told Richie Unterberger that she and Ackles briefly sublet a house from Fred Myrow, who in turn let it from Jim Morrison.

† Don Randi on *David Ackles*, Don Ellis, and Al Kooper on *Subway To The Country*, Del Newman on *American Gothic*.

‡ Two three-hour sessions on June 23, 24, and 25, and July 3, and one three-hour session on July 16, 17, and 29.

The other twenty-one musicians credited on the album are listed in these session records, though. Of the five players who backed Ackles on his debut, only Doug Hastings survives on *Subway To The Country*, nestled in the middle of the much longer roll of credits. Hastings, though, has no recollection of the sessions, and he did not even know he was credited.[9] Brass, woodwind, and strings outnumber guitar, bass, and drums. Among the musicians listed in (almost) alphabetical order after Ackles are multiple stalwarts of the Los Angeles session scene, who between them recorded with many of the greats of American popular music, from Glenn Miller to Frank Sinatra to The Beach Boys.* Several Wrecking Crew players appear, including Larry Knechtel, Louie Shelton, Ollie Mitchell, and Tony Terran. And some older jazz musicians, such as Bud Shank, Victor Feldman, and William Ulyate. Ackles's Elektra stablemate Lonnie Mack was one of three guitarists, alongside Hastings and Shelton. The ill-starred Jim Gordon played drums. Don Gallucci, who had served in The Kingsmen and later produced The Stooges' *Fun House*, played keyboards. A mixed bunch, reflecting the varied experiences and tastes of Ackles, Myrow, and Miller, each of whom had a hand in selecting musicians. In addition to the credited musicians, a further six appear in session records: guitarist Thomas Tedesco, and a string section comprising Jeffrey Solow, Audrey King, Mary Ahlborn, Laurence Lesser, and Milton Thomas.

Myrow's arrangements are dense and layered, often creating a blurred effect like a penumbra around Ackles's piano and voice. And while it's unlikely that all twenty-two musicians feature across the whole record, it often sounds like they do. Just reading this list of contributors and knowing a little of their histories, you get the sense—without even hearing it—that the music they contributed to on *Subway To The Country* might not have borne that close a resemblance to the rock music of 1969. And it doesn't, though there are just enough familiar gestures for the people promoting Ackles to present him to the rock market.

* Violinist Gordon Marron appears near the end of the list.

Two of the musicians credited, violinist Gordon Marron and drummer Craig Woodson, were fresh out of The United States Of America, one of the first rock bands to integrate electronic sound into their arrangements. Woodson recalls playing at a single evening session on one song, probably called in by Marron.* There were lots of other musicians present and the lights were low. He was not given a score.

CRAIG WOODSON David came over and said he wanted something mysterious on the drums, so I used mallets, just to try and give a smoky, hazy feel to it, and I was remembering that the last time I used the mallets was in the USA when I was trying to imitate Balinese drumming, because I had been studying that. And I was thinking of that when I did David's thing… and he came up and he thanked me, and said it was great, exactly what he wanted.†[10]

Although *David Ackles* had been borne out of multiple sessions, it ended up sounding like a modest, small ensemble record. By contrast, *Subway To The Country*—with its lush production, complex arrangements and a band of eminent session players—is a consciously big statement. It would not have come cheap. Clearly, Elektra thought Ackles an artist worthy of continuing investment.

Subway To The Country was released on the cusp of a new decade, at a time when—even with hindsight—it is hard to identify much in the way of a musical zeitgeist. The big British bands—The Rolling Stones, The Beatles, The Who, Led Zeppelin—were all active and released international bestsellers in 1969. So did Cream, though they had split up at the end of 1968. Bob Dylan, The Byrds, and The Flying Burrito

* Marron is the only musicians present at all ten sessions listed in the AFM records. He is described as 'leader' for two of these sessions.

† Woodson's description of the song he played on sounds like 'Candy Man', though the session records list him as being present when 'Woman River' was recorded. However, as there are no session records for 'Candy Man', it's possible that Woodson did also play on that song.

Brothers were playing country music to rock audiences. The Temptations, Funkadelic, and Sly Stone were cultivating distinctive brands of elongated psychedelic soul and funk. The careers of many of the artists Ackles was sometimes compared to were gathering commercial momentum. Leonard Cohen's *Songs From A Room* was a number two UK hit. Joni Mitchell's *Clouds* won a Grammy and charted at thirty-one on the *Billboard* 200. Laura Nyro's albums were attracting much critical acclaim, and her songs were hits for other artists. The second wave of male singer-songwriters—who came to embody the term in the 70s—were just getting started. James Taylor's commercial breakthrough came with his second album, *Sweet Baby James*, released a few months after *Subway To The Country*.

What of Elektra's other male singer-songwriters? Fred Neil had left the label some years before and was close to the end of his recording career. Tom Rush decamped to Columbia, as Ackles would eventually, moving into a soft country-rock groove that became a template for the 70s generation of West Coast troubadours. Tom Paxton remained with Elektra until 1971 and in 1969 and 1970 recorded two albums with a broader than usual (for him) instrumental palette. Like Ackles, Tim Buckley was moving ever further away from rock structures—in his case toward a semi-improvised, jazzy folk.

There are eight songs on *Subway To The Country*, four to a side. Ackles indicated that the track list was influenced by Myrow, who chose some songs that Ackles would not have chosen, as he thought they offered more possibilities for his arrangements.[11] In this sense, and allowing for the prominence of Myrow's arrangements, *Subway To The Country* is the Ackles album over which he had least influence. He seemed happy enough about this but never again ceded so much control.

DAVID ACKLES Of all the arrangers I could select out of the whole world, Fred's probably the only one who could come really close to what I wanted without coming so close as to be boring about it—he would bring his own originality to it. And he did, on that second album. I think there's some wonderfully original ideas on there.[12]

In a provocative move, Ackles opens *Subway To The Country* with one of the harshest, most uncompromising songs he ever recorded. 'Mainline Saloon' sees Ackles hammering the piano in a bleak, chaotic, stumbling, barroom threnody for the ravages of drug addiction. To a backdrop of clinking glasses and scattered applause, his barked vocals sometimes anticipating Tom Waits, Ackles dwells on a compulsion unmitigated by euphoria or romance.

'Mainline Saloon' is the first entry in a disquieting and deeply odd trilogy on *Subway To The Country*, along with 'Candy Man' and 'Inmates Of The Institution'. Lurching tempo changes, discords, scurrying piano, declamatory singing, mirthlessly jaunty melodic choruses, abrupt stops. The sound of apparently tenebrous imaginations at work. Myrow like Bernard Herrmann conducting a Las Vegas showband in a nightmare. Ackles the star of a horror musical on some other Broadway, or a wild-eyed preacher. As if recognising that the three songs would be too much to stomach grouped together, Ackles scatters them through the album, buffered by adjacent softer moods.

The softest of those softer moods follows. 'That's No Reason To Cry' is a lovelorn break-up song, with Ackles softly intoning over a gentle swell of brass and woodwind. A pleasant if slight entry—sung in the first person, with the rhythm picking up in the middle, like so many Ackles songs. It's over in two minutes and thirty seconds, but the musicians drift through an extended two-chord instrumental coda, adding nearly another minute of warm, soft-focus meandering. In an unreleased solo version, Ackles accompanies himself with abstract piano chords, coming over like a nightclub cabaret performer. The coda in this version is a bluesy, wordless improvisation.

Then 'Candy Man' creeps up, with its ominous harpsichord arpeggios and bent-out-of-shape muted brass introducing a story of child abuse. Oscar the one-armed Vietnam veteran opens a sweet shop and distributes what we are led to assume is pornography (though it is never explicitly stated) 'in every bag of sweets'. On discovery, his defence is, 'I only did to some of you, what you all did to me.' Oscar's story is told in the third person, but for the last verse Ackles switches to the first person. While declaring that he is not the 'Candy Man', he points a stabbing finger and sneers:

The world that made me what I am
Must owe me something too
And I only want what is my rightful due
From you and you.

The specifics here are not clear and probably weren't meant to be. The message, though, seems to be that the world damages us. And we are all, to some extent, products of our experiences.

After the brooding, claustrophobic menace of 'Candy Man', Ackles assumes his familiar rootless drifter guise for 'Out On The Road'. It's a gospel-style epic in which Ackles bellows out what appears to be a plea for freedom and tolerance over a Myrow arrangement of screaming lead guitar and brass that sounds like it's been relocated from a Percy Sledge record. It's his most impassioned, uninhibited vocal on record.

Side two opens with 'Cabin On The Mountain', not to be confused with the bluegrass standard 'Cabin On A Mountain'. A waltzing first-person murder ballad that nods thematically to 'The Green Green Grass Of Home', it was the first time Ackles worked squarely in the country idiom, something he would do again on his next two albums. Myrow reined in the arrangement, backing Ackles's voice and piano with a traditional country-rock band—bass, drums, and two guitars. Two alternate versions survive: the first, a solo rendition with Ackles accompanying himself on honky-tonk tack piano; the second, the previously described Ellis/Kooper arrangement.

'Woman River', on account of Myrow's arrangement, manages to be simultaneously languorous, romantic, and just a little sinister. All ebbing orchestral textures, jazzy muted trumpet, and elongated phrasing. Rivers were something of a motif for Ackles, in life and song. The boy born next to the Mississippi who pieced together his masterwork in a house on the banks of a tributary of the Thames wrote 'Down River', 'Woman River', and the unreleased 'There Is A River'.

'Woman River' subsides peacefully to a close and a baleful woodwind and brass pattern fades in, sounding like something menacing crawling from the water. Then it's Ackles's stentorian piano and vocals, announcing 'Inmates Of The Institution'. At first, he kids you into thinking you're listening to a song about mental illness and the cruel horrors of institutionalisation. An anti-psychiatry diatribe, maybe—a voguish intellectual topic at the time.* Very soon, though, we realise we're probably being presented with a metaphor for late twentieth-century malaise. Are we the inmates, casting around hopelessly for leaders and solutions in a meaningless existence? The metaphor is obscure in places. Who is the ragman? The spaceman? The flagman? The race man? We never know. Like many of the songs on the album, it's hard to locate a literal meaning here. The impression, though, is clear enough. These inmates, whoever they may be, are trapped and lost and unhappy. With its mental illness conceit delivered in a thespian style, it feels like an unprecedented song.

After so much shifting of mood, and so much darkness, *Subway To The Country* closes with the title track, the album's one fundamentally optimistic song. A sweet tale of a father longing to take his sons away from the grime of the city to a free and clean place, it's another of those Ackles character-driven ballads that ought to have been a hit. In the context of much of the material on the album, it's a heartwarming anomaly, with its big chorus and dynamic shifts. You can imagine Ackles—with his jeans and work boots and tousled hair—baffled to find himself unaccountably crooning the song in an upmarket supper club.

---

* Books by R.D. Laing (*The Divided Self: An Existential Study In Sanity And Madness*, 1960), Erving Goffman (*Asylums: Essays On The Social Situation Of Mental Patients And Other Inmates*, 1961), and Ken Kesey (*One Flew Over The Cuckoo's Nest*, 1962) were popular throughout the decade.

Elektra pushed 'Subway To The Country', rightly recognising it was the most commercial cut on the album. It was released as a single, backed with 'That's No Reason To Cry', and a promo film featured Ackles wandering around New York and Bodie, a ghost town in California. Promotional copies of the album came with a seven-inch single for radio play, featuring the song on one side and Ackles talking about it with an unnamed interviewer on the other.* In this conversation, Ackles explains that the song was inspired in part by an elementary teacher friend who set her children an assignment to paint a winter scene. Some of the children came back with pictures that were completely grey because they associated winter with snow that, in New York, was grey with pollution. The image found its way into the lyrics:

New York City is a town too big for children,
Where there's so much dirt they think that snow is grey.

A few months later, Ackles, talking about his approach to songwriting, had moderated his view of New York, which, on the interview disc, he described as a 'bummer experience':

> When I was at the Bitter End several months ago with Spider John Koerner and Willie Murphy, I was complaining about New York City. My usual bad rap about what it's like to live in the city and how much I longed to get back to the country and all this nonsense. And Willie Murphy had the astuteness to point out that since we are headed for a totally urban society, that we had better evolve some new values based on urban living. Find the things that are good and adjust to them. Make them worthwhile. And I think that's the new positive ethic. And as far as whether country music is a part of that, I don't think so. I mean, it's great to visit the country,

* See Appendix 3 for a full transcript of this interview.

> we all need that. I think we need it at least once a month to get out of the city and get into a place where there is earth and water and a lot of sky. But that isn't really what we are about. We are about streets and concrete, and we had better learn to make a positive value out of that. And I think out of that reassessment of personal values will come a new kind of music that is urban-oriented.[13]

In addition to the aborted Kooper/Ellis sessions, another surviving *Subway To The Country* outtake is a version of 'Such A Woman', a song that later turned up on Ackles's fourth album, *Five & Dime*. With a shifting, dreamily maudlin arrangement that sounds like Myrow's other work on the album, it's a fully realised, finished piece, with Ackles in good voice. It seems an odd omission—especially given that, in its released form, side one of the album was shorter than side two, and there would have been room for another song. Perhaps this was an example of Myrow flexing his producer's muscle and deciding the song didn't fit the album. Perhaps it wasn't included simply because it deployed a gospel-style piano intro very similar to the one we hear in 'Out On The Road'.

Songs and arrangements combine to make *Subway To The Country* an album of varied, even extreme moods. Ackles responds with vocal performances ranging across a spectrum from a husky murmur through an angry snarl to a throaty howl. This is attributable to his growing confidence as a writer and performer, and the depth and range of Myrow's widescreen orchestrations. Such acute mood swings make for an engaging listen but maybe help explain why the songs didn't attract other artists. Who, in 1969, was going to cover 'Inmates Of The Institution'? Whereas half the songs on the first album were covered at least once, only 'Subway To The Country' itself attracted any attention this time.*

The singer, actor, and civil rights activist Harry Belafonte came to prominence performing calypso in the 50s. By the end of the 60s, the hits

---

* 'Down River', 'Be My Friend', 'Road To Cairo', 'His Name Is Andrew', and 'Blue Ribbons'.

had dried up, but Belafonte had evolved into a mature, all-round entertainer, recording, playing live, and acting in film and television. He filmed several TV specials paired with female artists, including a 1970 ABC show with Lena Horne, sponsored by Fabergé. Broadcast on March 22, 1970, it features solo and duet performances. During the show, Belafonte follows an awkward, unlikely interpretation of Creedence Clearwater Revival's 'Willie And The Poor Boys' with 'Subway To The Country', with which he sounded far more comfortable. In a richly orchestrated and elegantly phrased interpretation, Belafonte demonstrates that this particular Ackles song might easily have become a MoR standard, had things turned out just a little differently. But the Belafonte and Horne album was issued initially in a limited, mail-order edition, and was not as widely heard as some of Belafonte's other recordings. 'Subway To The Country' was not covered again until 1988, when New York-based cabaret artist Steve Ross included his piano and vocal version on the album *Most Of Ev'ry Day*.

Though Ackles was not a widely interpreted songwriter, the variety of artists that did cover his songs points to the potential for widespread appeal, and to something unclassifiable in his work. His songs caught the ear of cabaret and stage singers (Ross and, later, Stacy Sullivan), a polished mature entertainer (Belafonte), British rock and pop bands (Spooky Tooth, The Hollies), a sixteen-year-old ingénue (Louisa Jane White), and several English folk performers (including Martin Carthy). But after 'Subway To The Country', there were no more cover versions by established artists. It seems the closer Ackles got to realising his artistic vision, the harder it became for other artists to imagine performing his songs.

Subway To The Country consolidated Ackles's profile rather than developing it. Once again, sales were modest but reviews favourable. There was no promotional visit to Europe this time. Had there been, things might have been different, as much of Ackles's status among his peers was established during that 1968 visit. Around the time the album was released in the UK, there was radio play and a single BBC TV appearance, but no progress. A debut artist who attracts good reviews and admiration from peers and a handful of cover versions might feel like they've made a good start, even if sales are poor. But if it's more of the same on the second album, it can feel like things are stagnating. Ackles's career might have ended with *Subway To The Country*. Afterwards, he withdrew from recording for a while, taking stock and playing live less frequently. But Elektra kept faith and signed him for another album.

'David is now on his second contract with Elektra,' Jac Holzman said at the time. 'I think it's one thing that Elektra does have a history of, and that is sticking with the artists it believes in. David had gone through one four-year contract and two highly unsuccessful and very expensive albums, but we had to re-sign him because we knew if we didn't, we'd regret it.'[14]

BERNIE TAUPIN The fact that he got to make his magnum opus says a lot for the belief people had in him. Certainly Jac Holzman. He has to be given a great deal of credit for believing in David. I think he felt this was his final shot at greatness.[15]

CHAPTER FIVE

THAT'S NO REASON TO CRY

ELTON JOHN • THE TROUBADOUR • ALL SAINTS EPISCOPAL CHURCH • RECORDING WITH LONNIE MACK

"

I make a little list of songs that I'd like to sing. And they don't always correspond to songs you'd like to hear.

DAVID ACKLES

"

Early evening, Tuesday August 25, 1970. David Ackles walks out onto the small stage at the Troubadour in Los Angeles. He sits at the grand piano, to the left of the stage from the audience's viewpoint. In the middle of the stage is a huge drum kit with two bass drums and a set of congas. To the right of the kit is a bass amplifier.

The Troubadour is home territory for Ackles. He played here the year before, supporting Joni Mitchell. There are friends in the audience. Douglas Graham and Jim Friedrich. It's five dollars to get in, but not many people have paid. The club is full of the great and the good of the Los Angeles music world, who get in for nothing. The great and the good aren't there to see Ackles, though. They're there to see the US debut of a British rising star, Elton John, about whom rumours of greatness abound…

On the second day of the new decade, Ackles was braving the New York City winter again, sharing the bill with Al Kooper at the Town Hall. *Subway To The Country* was in the shops and picking up some reviews and airplay. But, compared to the first album, there was less of a concerted promotional push. Even so, like the Bitter End show a few weeks before Christmas, this first performance of 1970 attracted attention, with *Cash Box* reporting:

> The word 'work' is much more fitting than 'song' to describe the music which David Ackles writes. Ackles's 'works' transmit a feeling of lived experience, of honest emotion and, as their creator, his rendition of them is totally effective. As a singer, Ackles is a sort of hybrid. Essentially he has the vocal character of a cabaret singer; one perfectly suited for intimate clubs where he can deal with the audience on a note-to-note basis. But there is also a great deal of the minstrel, the open road singer, in him as well.[1]

Finally realising that describing Ackles as a folk artist was plain wrong, critics instead began trying to place him by casting around for comparisons with an unconnected litany of artists and composers—almost all of whom had nothing whatsoever to do with rock music. The *Village Voice*:

> I heard everything from Jelly Roll Morton to Kurt Weill and Charles Ives in his piano—polytonalities, freaky counterpoint, multi-rhythms and all sorts of other 'technical' things that make music fascinating. Ackles's songs are a perfect reflection of his performing style. He writes the kind of stuff that probably turns off more light-headed listeners ... stuff that owes more to the poetry of Brecht than to the usual pop influences.[2]

The *Chicago Tribune* likened the album to 'Burl Ives doing Brecht/Weill songs. Or Edgar Lee Masters poems set to music not by Aaron Copland, but by Charles Ives.'[3] While there is something in these attempts to locate Ackles, reviewers were pointing to names that probably meant nothing to the greater proportion of the rock audience to which he was being promoted—at that time dominated by teenagers and young adults up to about thirty years.

In a discursive opinion piece in *Zig Zag*, Jeff Cloves picked up on something similar. Declaring Ackles the most important songwriter since Dylan, Cloves saw a set of European influences not often obvious in American artists, though he offered Judy Collins's *In My Life* as a reference point. 'This very distinctive European flavour I've been talking about, and the underlying piano (rather than guitar) sound of his songs tends to steer them toward Brecht, Jacques Prévert, Brel, and even, perhaps, Leonard Cohen.'[4]

An *International Times* review said Ackles sounded like French singer Gilbert Bécaud.[5] A syndicated US review compared Ackles favourably with James Taylor, Randy Newman, and Van Morrison; called *Subway To The Country* magnificent, like its predecessor; and then declared, 'There's no use trying to describe the songs.'[6]

The *Village Voice* review of Ackles's New York Town Hall show was quoted in adverts for his third residency at Canterbury House, from February 13 to 15. The tickets were now $2, and Ackles was paid $750 for the residency, on a boilerplate AFM contract. Mike Gershman (1939–2000) signed the contract on Ackles's behalf. Gershman, later a renowned author of books about baseball, worked at the time as a music publicist. His other clients included The Doors and Elton John.

A perceptive and laudatory review of this third stint noted Ackles's ability to generate energy without relying on volume and pointed out the warm audience reception on a night when he was called back for two encores. 'Ackles's voice was powerful, his music intriguing, his poetry moving,' wrote Gary Baldwin of the *Michigan Daily*. 'Combined with his strong, friendly presence, it is no wonder the crowd was so reluctant to leave.'[7] Baldwin also commented that Ackles seemed nervous, though less so than when he'd performed at the same venue the previous year.

JANICE VOGEL ACKLES He enjoyed singing, but I don't think he enjoyed performing live. Some of that came through in his performances. It was very difficult for him. He was just a bundle of anxiety. He would always get sick, literally, right before he would perform. It was sort of amazing to me because of the amount of stage experience that he'd had in his life. I just don't think he was comfortable being up there as David Ackles… any theatre piece would have been fine, but to be out there just kind of exposing your soul, I think, was extremely difficult.[8]

That so experienced a performer as Ackles should be nervous playing live as a singer-songwriter is explained in part by the nature of that previous experience. Though he had been performing since early childhood, almost all of his work up to the age of thirty-one was as part of a cast or as half of a duo—in theatre, television, or film. In front of quiet, seated audiences expected to pay attention, or no audience at all, apart from camera technicians. Performing alone, the sole focus of attention, to a live audience that might not necessarily conform to theatrical conventions about sitting quietly and still, apart from during interludes, was an alien experience for Ackles, and one he was never quite at ease with.

A highlight on the first night of this third residency at Canterbury House was the introduction of a new song, 'Family Band', which Ackles later recorded for *American Gothic*. The title track of that album was also in the set. Though it was more than two years until he presented it to the world, Ackles was already preparing his masterwork.

In December 1970, an article reviewing Canterbury House's activities through the year recorded an intriguing vignette. During a spring 1970 residency, Ackles attended Sunday morning worship, as he always did when performing at the venue. On this occasion—for unspecified reasons—things didn't go well. The meeting was halted and a discussion commenced, trying to identify what the problem was. Ackles, the weekend's guest performer, stood up and said he had been to three worship sessions at Canterbury House: the first was exciting, the second less so, and the third (the session abandoned that day) unpleasant. He went on to say that working through problems was a feature of most communities and could lead to the most exciting time of all. David Ackles, the Elektra singer-songwriter, was nervous performing his songs, but confident enough to stand up in a church service where he was a guest and offer comment and advice.[9]

When *David Ackles* was released in 1968, Elektra promoted Ackles heavily in Europe and particularly the UK. With some success. Ackles's visit that year attracted widespread press, concert, television, and radio exposure. Though there was no commercial breakthrough, in the UK at least 1968 ended with the sense that Ackles was a coming thing. There was no promotional visit for *Subway To The Country*, though, and consequently less coverage. Despite this, the response was still favourable. In those days, before the digital archiving of almost everything, cultural memories were shorter than they are now. Most reviewers felt obliged to remind readers that Ackles had found favour just over a year earlier with his debut. The *New Musical Express* said, 'This LP is extremely good and will enhance Ackles.'[10]

Ackles did feature on an episode of *Disco 2*—which replaced *Colour Me Pop* as BBC2's 'serious' music show—in an episode broadcast on January 10, 1970, presented by Tommy Vance. The footage of the programme does not survive, but records show that Ackles's contribution was a repeat of his performance of 'Road To Cairo' on *Colour Me Pop* in 1968.

Ackles spent the rest of 1970 playing intermittent shows—fewer than 1969—and plotting his next move, which did not involve going straight back into the studio to record a third album. It's as if he was adopting a holding position. Meanwhile, his friendship with Douglas Graham continued.

DOUGLAS GRAHAM On my twenty-fifth birthday, which was in 1970—in July—I had a dinner party at my house, and my parents were there from Texas, and Kris Kristofferson was there, and his bass player Billy Swann was there, and David was there, and we had this wonderful dinner. And David, of course, could charm anybody. He just had a natural charm, and my parents who'd never met him, and Kris who'd never met him—they were all charmed by him.[11]

That same month, *Hit Parader* magazine published a short article credited to Ackles in which he shared his thoughts on the art of songwriting. It's not the most articulate or informative piece and was probably transcribed from a conversation rather than written. Even so, one sentence is revealing, summing up Ackles's own motivation: 'I think either you really desperately want to write and will eventually do it, or you don't.'[12]

Ackles spent at least some of this year living back in the family home near the Hollywood sign.

LYNDA RUTHERFORD In the summer of 1970, [a friend] and I began our cross-country drive. I remember we ended up in LA at, like, 10pm, not knowing where to go or where we were going to stay. We had an address for David and somehow got to that house in the Hollywood Hills.

Lights are on at the house, and we walk up to the door and knock. A woman about our age or a bit older came to the door. We asked for David, and she said he wasn't there. 'Okay, well, just tell him Lynda and Alison stopped by.' We walk back to the car and are about to get in when we hear yelling: 'ALISON! LYNDA! Get back here!' It was David! Seems this was his parents' house, and he was staying there (can't remember the reason), but there was a woman 'stalking' him, and he told his sister if any females come to the door, just say he's not there. Anyway, David's lovely parents offered us the den floor. We grabbed our sleeping bags and slept the night. In the morning, David's dad, wearing tennis whites and carrying a racket, wakes us telling us to go out back and pick the fruit we wanted with our breakfast. I remember orange and grapefruit trees. David made us the best scrambled eggs with chives! We left after a bit, but later in the week David took us to the beach in Malibu.[13]

Toward the end of the summer in what was an otherwise quiet year for Ackles, he played a supporting part in an event that is now written into rock lore. On the surface, perhaps not a part he would have chosen to play. Yet without his participation in this event, Ackles's third album might have been a very different prospect.

Doug Weston opened the Troubadour on La Cienega Boulevard in 1957. In 1961 he moved it to Santa Monica Boulevard, West Hollywood, where it remains to this day. Weston modelled the venue on the Troubadour in London, which had opened in 1954, and which he had visited on a trip to England. In the early years, the LA Troubadour thrived on the more commercial end of the folk boom. But as younger musicians moved from folk to rock, the Troubadour followed suit, rather like Elektra Records. From the mid-60s it attracted young bohemian folkies, up-and-coming rock musicians, and writers. The Byrds first aired 'Mr Tambourine Man' in the club, and Buffalo Springfield debuted there in 1966. In 1962, Lenny Bruce was arrested on obscenity charges after an appearance at the Troubadour. In the 70s, the writer Charles Bukowski read from the stage seated at a reading desk, a refrigerator packed with beer next to him. The six-foot-six, long-haired Weston presided over it all, a proprietor with an ego to match those of the performers who hung around the place, on stage, and in the audience. He was not universally popular, on account of booking upcoming artists with the proviso that they do return gigs at the same rate. Even if, by the time the return date came around, they'd become multi-million-selling, stadium-filling megastars. Weston died at seventy-two in February 1999, just a few weeks before Ackles.

From the late 60s, the club became linked with the singer-songwriter movement and country-rock, and for a while it seemed like almost everyone from those worlds played significant Troubadour gigs. Jackson Browne, Tim Buckley, Neil Diamond, Billy Joel, Carole King, Kris Kristofferson, Gordon Lightfoot, Don McLean, Joni Mitchell, Van Morrison, Randy Newman, Phil Ochs, Bonnie Raitt, Linda Ronstadt, J.D. Souther, James Taylor, Tom Waits, Neil Young. Tim Hardin played one of his last gigs there. Fledgling Eagles Glenn Frey and Don Henley met at the bar.

By 1970, Los Angeles was the centre of the American music industry, following a transfer of power from New York that had begun in the middle of the previous decade. You could place a lot of the music coming out of Los Angeles at the time in the country-rock and singer-songwriter camps, and the Troubadour was a locus for those overlapping scenes. On paper, Ackles—a singer-songwriter who sometimes drew on country influences—ought to have fitted in. But he didn't.

BERNIE TAUPIN When I think of that time period I think of the people who used to hand out in the bar at the Troubadour, like the fledgling Eagles, Jackson Browne, J.D. Souther, and then there were the other people like James Taylor, Carole King, but he just didn't seem a part of that clique whatsoever, and I don't think he cared to be a part of it. He was just a different human being, and he came from a different background, and his whole worldview was different.[14]

Barney Hoskyns's 2006 book *Hotel California* ranges through the emergence, achievements, and subsequent decline of the music coming out of Los Angeles in this period, recounting interweaving tales about its big stars and behind-the-scenes influencers. As much as it was a music venue, the Troubadour was a social club for Hoskyns's cast of characters, many of whom lived a life of cocaine and bed-hopping in Laurel Canyon, or further out in Topanga Canyon. Selling the world a dream of sunshine and easy living. The book's epigraph is a few lines from Ackles's song 'Oh California!', which he recorded in 1972 for *American Gothic*. It's an interesting choice. Ackles was nearby, geographically, but he didn't live in Laurel Canyon. This geographical proximity to but separation from the heart of the action was mirrored in his social and musical life. He was on the fringes of everything that was happening (almost) on his doorstep. Musically, it was still possible to connect him with some contemporaries also on the fringes—Judee Sill and Randy Newman, for example—but he wasn't an insider. He was never a member of the club.

So, in May 1969, when Ackles played the Troubadour supporting Joni Mitchell, who had made her LA debut there a year earlier, his status was ambiguous. He was on home territory where he didn't really belong. In August 1970, Ackles was back, this time sharing a bill with one of his biggest admirers.

Born Reginald Kenneth Dwight in 1947, Elton John was ten years Ackles's junior and yet, by 1970, a far more experienced music-industry hand. He had been playing pub piano gigs from the age of fifteen, and by the mid-60s his band, Bluesology, was backing American soul musicians touring the UK, including The Isley Brothers and Patti LaBelle & The Bluebelles. In 1967, Elton teamed up with Bernie Taupin to form their enduring songwriting partnership, initially providing middle-of-the-road pop material for other performers. Alongside this, he was very much the jobbing musician, playing sessions whenever he could and plotting a solo career. This he launched in 1968, with a single on Philips: 'I've Been Loving You' b/w 'Here's To The Next Time', both songs written with

Taupin. Another single and a debut album, *Empty Sky*, followed. None of these records sold particularly well, and it wasn't until the release of a second, eponymous album in April 1970 that the weather changed. The album got good reviews in the UK, and John Peel played it.

By the time he arrived in the US in August to promote the album, Elton John hadn't yet had a hit, but there was the feeling it was coming. *Elton John* was released on Uni, which also included Neil Diamond in its roster. When Elton and his entourage flew into Los Angeles on Friday, August 21, Uni arranged for them to be picked up from the airport in an open-top double-decker bus with a sign declaring 'Elton John has arrived'. Elton told *Rolling Stone* a year later that he found this deeply embarrassing. Four days later, at 11pm on Tuesday, August 25, after Ackles had opened the evening's proceedings at 9pm, Neil Diamond introduced the first of Elton's eight gigs over six nights.

Elton had been ambivalent about the Troubadour booking, wondering if it would have been better if he'd stayed in the UK and built on the growing interest there. He saw The Dillards play at the club the day he arrived. He loved the show but was struck by how small the club was, and he wondered if there would be room for his piano and his rhythm section. Feelings became more mixed when Elton and lyricist Bernie Taupin discovered that Ackles would be their support act. They were, at this point, fully conversant with and great admirers of Ackles's two albums.

'You know, it's funny,' Elton told *Cash Box*. 'David doesn't seem to be as well known here as he should. In Britain he's a huge star and could sell out any theater he chose to play in. We think he's incredible.[15]

BERNIE TAUPIN To our amazement, David was Elton's opening act, a fact that equally thrilled and embarrassed us. However, David's charm and complete disregard for anything approaching professional jealousy soon defused any discomfort.[16]

We couldn't believe he was actually opening for us. Because to us he was so established. But I suppose in the big picture he wasn't, as his records didn't sell. People didn't really know who he was. They didn't really know who we were, but we had the hype and he didn't. And we became great friends. We were thrilled to meet him and know him.[17]

Both Janice Ackles and Douglas Graham state that Ackles was initially scheduled to headline but swapped billing with Elton.

DOUGLAS GRAHAM David said, 'I can't follow Elton John—he'll just blow this place away, he's so good.' So, he made an arrangement with the owner of the Troubadour that they would swap billing. So, David went on first, then Elton went on and really rocked the place—he was fantastic. Both were.[18]

Janice was in England at the time and recalls Ackles writing to her shortly before the opening night, saying that he'd be supporting Elton John, who he'd never heard of, and saying, 'I hope he's good.'[19] There's nothing to suggest Ackles might have initiated this switch himself, conscious of his limitations as a live performer. Elektra's Jac Holzman wrote much later that Ackles *was* the headline act. He wasn't, but perhaps Holzman was remembering that he had been, initially.[20]

Years later, Doug Weston implied a different sequence of events when he talked about hearing Elton John's second album and booking him to headline at the Troubadour straight away, despite knowing little of him.[21]

The British writer Johnny Black quoted Travis Michael Holder, the Troubadour's 'talent coordinator', telling yet another variant of the story. Holder said he initially booked Elton to support Jerry Jeff Walker. This was a ruse on Holder's part, as he wanted to book Elton, but Weston wasn't keen, and he bargained that Walker—who was finishing off an album—would drop out and that Elton could then be promoted to headliner.[22]

There are some inconsistencies, too, in accounts of what happened next, which may be due to people remembering different shows. It was a six-night residency, not a single event. But there is no doubt that the Los

Angeles music business grandees turned out in force to see Elton, and that his shows caused a sensation—the opening night especially. The set started quietly, with 'Your Song', and gradually built up from there. During 'Take Me To The Pilot', Odetta got up and danced. Along with Odetta and Neil Diamond, confirmed sightings through the week included T-Bone Burnett, David Crosby, Micky Dolenz, David Gates, Don Henley, Danny Hutton, Quincy Jones, Carole King, Gordon Lightfoot, Mike Love, Henry Mancini, Graham Nash, Randy Newman, Van Dyke Parks, Diana Ross, Leon Russell, Stephen Stills, Brian Wilson, and Neil Young. The *Los Angeles Times* music critic Robert Hilburn was there on the opening night and filed an ecstatic review that was published on August 27. There was, he noted, a large gathering of rock writers in attendance. Numbers dipped after the first night, but once Hilburn's review was out, the crowds flocked to the club and queued down the street. The review barely mentioned Ackles, though it did include a description of Elton's music that said he was creating his own field, like Randy Newman and Laura Nyro. An irony, as many other writers made similar observations about Ackles throughout his recording career.

It's a given that Elton John's Troubadour residency accelerated his rise. But if he hadn't played those shows he would have become a star anyway, sooner or later. The wave was building up, and it was going to break. It would be a mistake, though, to frame Elton's triumph as being at the expense of Ackles. Whether or not Ackles was going to headline initially, it's not as if the crowds and journalists and rock stars would have turned out for him in their droves. Elton didn't steal the attention that Ackles would otherwise have got. The event does, though, underline a feature of Ackles's story. He wasn't a rock showman in the way Elton John was. In an article in the *Guardian* prompted by the death of Zoot Money, Elton wrote about the challenges of being a performer if you're a keyboard player. You tend to be at the side of the stage, and you can't move around much, compared to a guitar player.[23] But it is possible to put on a flamboyant show, as he demonstrated at the Troubadour, and as Jerry Lee Lewis and

Little Richard had before. Ackles, by contrast, could not attract attention in that way. He could play and sing beautifully on stage, but he would never kick away the piano stool and do handstands. That approach would never have worked for his songs anyway, but it wasn't in his nature.

In a BBC documentary many years later, Elton reflected that the residency and Hilburn's review saved him a year's work. Yet the shows became a cherished part of Elton's creation myth, a story repeatedly told, hardening in the retelling into a simplistic, stylised sequence of events: the moment when everything changed. The apotheosis of this mythmaking can be seen in the Elton John biopic *Rocketman* (2019), with the Troubadour gigs bathed in an almost mystical light. There's no mention of Ackles in *Rocketman*, and indeed if he is mentioned at all in accounts of the shows, it tends to be as a hapless bit player, ignored by the audience as he played. Elton, always gracious about Ackles and unstinting in his praise, concurred to an extent:

> David Ackles was brilliant. I made a point of watching him every night. He told me how much he enjoyed working with me... which is utterly incredible, because I had been a number-one fan of his. To see the audience just chatting away while he was singing those lovely songs just tore me apart. People were there because the buzz had got around that I was the guy to see, and they didn't give a toss about a great person like him.[24]

Others remember differently. Jim Friedrich, once of Canterbury House, moved back to Los Angeles, his hometown, in May 1970, and was ordained to the priesthood in September.

JIM FRIEDRICH In August I saw that David was playing at the Troubadour. And I wondered if he'd agree to play at my ordination... I didn't really know who Elton John was, but I was really excited about seeing David. I found my way to the dressing room before the show to see David and ask him if he'd play at my ordination. He said yes. He was just the most gracious person you'd ever meet… then the next month we had the ordination.[25]

Friedrich recalls sitting at a table with Odetta at the Troubadour, and the excitement of the night. He did not detect in Ackles any discomfort at not being the star of the night, the centre of attention.

JIM FRIEDRICH Then Elton John walked in… it seemed like that was their first meeting. As I recall… it seemed like Elton was saying, 'I just wanted to tell you how much I respect your music and I'm honoured to sing with you'—that kind of stuff.[26]

If Friedrich's backstage encounter with Ackles and Elton was the first time the two singers had met, it was probably the first show of the residency.

JIM FRIEDRICH David was wonderful, and people were just absorbed. And then Elton comes on, and once he starts doing his playing with his feet stuff… the Jerry Lee Lewis stuff… the energy level went up. But I had no sense that people were bored or inattentive [of Ackles] at all… but then of course I was totally into it, and I can't speak for what was in other people's hearts, but if I'm at a concert and people are being inattentive and it's interfering with my absorption of it, I do notice that.[27]

Though Elton's performances got the most attention from reviewers, Ackles picked up some favourable coverage too. 'David Ackles is an intellectual troubadour,' *Phonograph Record* reported. 'He is a man who can say so much but still leave the coloration to one's imagination.… His story songs are of common human experience, but his viewpoint is original and often startling… Ackles's voice is clear and manly and his phrasing, as with all good folk storytellers, is all his own. He leaves an audience thinking and not just sitting there.'[28]

The Troubadour residency closed with the final shows on Sunday,

August 30. When the music was over, Elton sat with Ackles at the bar, sharing a bottle of Scotch that Ackles had bought Elton as a congratulatory gift. Elton's third album *Tumbleweed Connection*, which had been recorded in March, was released in October. It carried the dedication 'To David, with love'. Elton and Bernie Taupin say that the piano-and-vocal only 'Talking Old Soldiers' from the album was their homage to Ackles's conversational, narrative style of songwriting—as heard in 'Down River' and 'Road To Cairo'. After a day's rest, the pair performed a similar six-night residency at Doug Weston's short-lived San Francisco outpost, Troubadour North. The venue had only just opened, and within a few months it closed. Once again, Elton played a rocking set to a packed crowd of media people, but the gigs attracted little attention, reviews were ambivalent, and this second residency is now all but forgotten. Michael Kelton, reviewing the opening night in the *San Francisco Examiner*, considered there was an artifice in Elton's performance. He offered a prescient tautological closing remark that managed to summarise Ackles's recording career as if by hindsight, though it still had years to run, describing him as 'a singer, pianist, songwriter whose appeal is limited but profoundly appealing to those who like him'.[29]

It wasn't long after the Troubadour gigs that Ackles was playing a very different sort of show. On September 17, Jim Friedrich got ordained at All Saints Episcopal Church, Beverly Hills. He planned his ordination service to run something like the happenings he'd helped organise at Canterbury House, starting with a twenty-minute audiovisual collage, including fragments of the moon landing broadcasts, T.S. Eliot reading from the *Four Quartets* and snatches of rock'n'roll. The opening hymn would be The Beatles' 'Let It Be'. The prayers would be interspersed with quotes from The Rolling Stones' song 'Salt Of The Earth'. The organist from the LA Philharmonic would play the church organ, and Ackles would sing two songs.

When Friedrich presented this scheme to the church authorities a few days before, there were reservations, but he was allowed to proceed on the condition that Ackles's song 'Be My Friend' was moved from its intended slot before the gospel reading and replaced with a hymn. In the event, Ackles sang 'Be My Friend' as the congregation filed up to take communion and played the as-yet unrecorded 'Family Band' to close the service.

There were no commercial releases of new Ackles material in 1970, though he recorded a single toward the end of the year.* Produced by fellow Elektra artist Lonnie Mack, who had appeared on *Subway To The Country*, it paired a new song, 'One Night Stand', with an old one, 'Be My Friend', both in different versions from their respective album releases. 'One Night Stand' later turned up on *American Gothic*. Mack gave it a more conventional soft-rock singer-songwriter treatment, with Ackles's piano and vocal taken at a relaxed pace, backed with bass, drums, and a delicate string arrangement. 'Be My Friend', familiar as the closing song on *David Ackles*, is taken at a slightly faster pace than its first outing, with acoustic guitars, bass, and drums, plus strings in place of Michael Fonfara's organ, which dominated the original. It's a pleasing record that was circulated as a promotional item, but it attracted little attention.

Of all his Elektra contemporaries, Ackles was probably closest to Lonnie Mack. He played shows with Tim Buckley and Tom Rush, but he didn't know them well. Later, when Harry Chapin—who admired Ackles—signed to the label, he too became a friend. But Mack was more of a confidante, and another example of Ackles gravitating toward friends as producers and arrangers.

Ackles kept quiet through the first months of 1971, just as he had for most of the previous year. Eighteen months later, he said in a radio interview that he had thoughts of giving up music during this time. There were occasional live shows and even a few stray reviews of *Subway To The Country*, a year too late. 'David Ackles is a singer-songwriter who has

* The liner notes to *There Is A River* state that this was recorded October/November 1970 and released as Elektra (US) EKM-45712. It appears it was only released as a promotional item, not commercially, and circulated in early 1971.

somehow been passed over, and it's a shame,' said one.[30] But most of the time he was lying low, making plans. March saw the last recorded evidence of Ackles's continuing involvement in his mother's church-based theatre group, The Geneva Players. A column in the *Los Angeles Times* announced the first performance of *The Second Disciples* on March 29, written by Ackles, 'a pianist and singer who has made two record albums.'[31] The play imagines the impact of the life of Christ on people who witnessed the crucifixion.

Ackles was, by now, ready to record again, but he had no producer. Lonnie Mack had been considered, and the promo single was probably a try-out. It might have been a good pairing, but Mack's Elektra contract expired in 1971, and he retreated from the mainstream for a decade. Mack and Ackles were similar in some respects—fellow Elektra artists, both brilliant musicians, but temperamentally not best suited to the music industry. In the end, events converged to suggest another solution.

CHAPTER SIX

WOMAN RIVER

BERNIE TAUPIN • MOVING TO WARGRAVE • *THE OLD GREY WHISTLE TEST* • THE SALVATION ARMY CHOIR • RECORDING *AMERICAN GOTHIC*

"

Mellowed in the drowsy sunlight of a summer's afternoon, Wargrave, nestling where the river bends, makes a sweet old picture as you pass it, and one that lingers upon the retina of memory.

JEROME K. JEROME, *THREE MEN IN A BOAT*

"

A day in March, 1972. A Salvation Army choir more used to street parades and revival halls assembles in the live room of IBC studios, in London, standing where The Kinks and The Who have stood before them. David Ackles is teaching them his song 'Family Band'. He hasn't bargained on the English accents. The vowel pronunciation isn't what he was imagining. In his head he hears an American Salvation Army choir, and the sound is quite different. But Ackles coaches the choir from behind the piano, sometimes running up the stairs to the control room to talk to producer Bernie Taupin and his soon-to-be wife, Janice. Pronunciation issues aside, the mood is good, and before long they're ready for a take…

Ackles had kept in touch with Elton John and Bernie Taupin since the Troubadour residency in August 1970. His relationship with Taupin in particular blossomed, and the two became great friends. By 1971 Taupin was an Elektra recording artist himself, with the label taking on the American release of his debut spoken-word album, *Taupin*. By this time the John/Taupin partnership had written two US Top 10 albums (Elton John's *Elton John* and *Tumbleweed Connection*). As a lyricist, Taupin was eminently bankable, but he had no obvious production experience. Somehow, though, the idea came up that he might be the man to occupy the producer's seat for Ackles's now overdue third album. Taupin sensed that Ackles was on the verge of making his magnum opus and, inexperienced or not, wasn't about to miss the opportunity to take part:

DAVID ACKLES Then Taupin expressed to Jac Holzman at one point that he was interested—Jac was talking about casting around for another producer, Lonnie [Mack] was going to produce me, and then he left…and Bernie said he'd like to produce me in England. So Jac called me, and we talked about it, and I said I thought it was a very good idea.[1]

BERNIE TAUPIN As luck would have it, the great Jac Holzman, founder and architect of Elektra Records, a man I also respected tremendously, saw the possibilities in the merging of this mutual admiration society and offered me the production position on David's forthcoming album.[2]

I had a sort of relationship with Jac. And I guess he just . . . thought it would be a good idea. One, the fact that I was a good friend of David's. Two, that I was a tremendous fan of his music.[3]

JAC HOLZMAN I don't know who came up with the idea of recording the third one in England with Bernie Taupin. . . . There was such a good relationship between the three of them—Elton, Taupin, and Ackles—my guess is it was Anderle's idea. Why not?[4]

However it came about, at some point in the middle of 1971, Elektra commissioned Taupin to produce Ackles's next album. The decision was made to record in England, where studio facilities were a little cheaper.

For each of his four albums, Ackles ended up working with a collaborator who was also a friend. David Anderle on *David Ackles* and Fred Myrow on *Subway To The Country*, both fellow USC alumni. Taupin on *American Gothic*. Later, on *Five & Dime*, Douglas Graham, already a friend and neighbour of several years, who went on to work on writing projects with Ackles into the 1980s. Then there were other people Ackles attempted to collaborate with, without success. Don Randi leading a group of Wrecking Crew stalwarts (*David Ackles*). Al Kooper and Don Ellis (*Subway To The Country*). Del Newman—more of whom later—on *American Gothic*. As best as I can judge, none of these people were personal friends but rather experienced music industry insiders who were probably recommended to Ackles by Elektra as suitable partners.

What does this say about Ackles? Most likely his first ever experience in a recording studio was with those Wrecking Crew players, who between them had played on hundreds of hit records. Ackles (and Anderle) decided it wasn't working. Newman was at the top of his game as an arranger and conductor when Ackles decided he wasn't working at all for *American Gothic*. There's a seam of diamond-hard confidence and purity of artistic vision that endured and enabled those strong leadership decisions. Conversely, perhaps there was a vulnerability, too. Maybe Ackles needed a friendly sounding board—a trusted wingman who could challenge him at times but wouldn't take control.

And so it was that in September 1971, Ackles moved to England to start work. It was a dry and sunny month. Compared to California, life was led on a smaller, more parochial scale. The newspapers were full of the Baker Street burglary, where a criminal gang inspired by a Sherlock Holmes story tunnelled into a bank vault close to the fictitious home of the fictitious detective. The Prime Minister, Edward Heath, raced yachts and conducted the London Symphony Orchestra. BBC television shut down for a few hours in the afternoon before resuming at 4:20pm with children's programmes. It banned *Sesame Street* for its 'authoritarian aims', so the Independent Television Network took up the series. *Who's Next* topped the album charts. Rod Stewart finally had a hit with 'Maggie May / Reason To Believe'.

Just before leaving for England, Ackles signed with Renaissance Entertainment Corp, a newly formed management company led by Abe Hoch and Dallas Smith.[5] It was a relationship that ended badly for Ackles. Smith, who was mainly active from the mid-60s to the mid-70s, had form as a producer, working with artists including Canned Heat, Del Shannon, and Bobby Vee (the latter also signed to the new company). Hoch was married to Lynne Randell, a big Australian pop star in the mid-60s. He later managed Led Zeppelin's label, Swan Song.

A few days after Ackles arrived in England, his friend Douglas Graham joined him. In 1971, Graham was contracted as a writer for Warners and could work remotely. And he was looking to escape an unhappy domestic situation. Like Steve Spellman, he was a very different character to Ackles in many ways, yet the two formed an enduring friendship.

DOUGLAS GRAHAM We were like opposites. David was the dignified one. David was the intellectual. David was the classiest guy I ever met. David was the personification of class and humour, and we'd hang out all the time. I was like the street kid from Detroit and David was the sophisticated guy from Los Angeles who'd studied in Edinburgh.

We stayed in an apartment in Chelsea for a couple of weeks and he found a house in the country, in a little town called Wargrave, in Berkshire. I joked and said, 'It's the only house in England that looks like a Californian house.'[6]

Wargrave stands on the banks of the River Thames and along the confluence of the River Loddon, about thirty-five miles west of London. The house Ackles found might have looked American, but leafy Wargrave, with its manor house and half-timbered cottages and old pubs and winding streets and boating clubs, is like a Hollywood set builder's dream of a sleepy English village. The church, St Mary's, dates from the twelfth century, but little of the original building survives on account of the most dramatic event in Wargrave's history. This occurred in 1914, when the church was gutted by a fire in the early hours after Whitsunday. At 3:15am the clock struck the quarter hour, and then the hands abruptly dropped to a vertical position as the clock workings fell to the floor in the inside of the tower. Oddly worded postcards referring to 'women torturers' found inside the building, and the sightings of unknown women in the area the night before, led to a rumour that suffragette arsonists were responsible.[7] Nobody was ever convicted for the crime, if indeed there was one, but the drama of that night has provided local history content ever since. It might have been the most dramatic event in the village's history. For the most part, though, Wargrave has always been the sort of place where big events do not happen.

The proximity to waterways has done much to shape Wargrave's development. During Victorian times—when boating became a leisure pursuit—the area was a popular destination, and by the 1920s, river tourists were buying up plots along the bank of the Loddon and establishing summer dwellings. Often these were simply houseboats pulled up out of the water. Even in 1971, when Ackles lived in Wargrave, this continued. One of his next-door neighbours lived in such a grounded houseboat. When the settlements were first established, there were no services. Water was drawn from the river, and cooking was done on paraffin stoves. In time, more substantial structures sprung up, and people began to live in the houses all year round. The Californian-looking house that Ackles found was one of these. Graham thinks Ackles located it through an estate agent. Taupin thinks maybe his office helped. Both might be right.

The author Jeremy Harding artfully evokes the character of this patch of Wargrave in his memoir, *Mother Country*. His family had several properties in what he called floodlands. Shacks, boats, bungalows. Brian Jones of The Rolling Stones rented one from Harding's adoptive parents for a short time.[8] They were eccentric people leading somewhat louche, rackety lives—escaping from Notting Hill to Wargrave at weekends and drinking from late morning onward in one of the houseboats, called *Nirvana*, which had been pulled up onto the bank and propped up on brick pillars, or in a similarly elevated bungalow. This was in the 50s and 60s. It was damp and misty. The whole area often flooded, and when it did, Harding's parents got their car as near as possible to their dwelling and covered the remaining distance in a rowing boat. A trick Ackles deployed during his tenure in the district.

Something of that idiosyncratic, bohemian atmosphere survived when Ackles arrived. This, and the proximity to London, made the Loddon houses and the rest of Wargrave popular with artists and entertainers. During Ackles's months in the village, the singer Mary Hopkins and her then-husband, Tony Visconti, lived nearby, as did the character actor Robert Morley. Wargrave also attracted the wealthy commuter wanting to escape the cut and thrust of London life for evenings and weekends.

The house Ackles rented was called Farthings. It was built in the early 1920s by John Hector Seale and his wife, Fanny, on an approximately two-acre plot just a few feet from the river. Seale came from a family of sculptors, stonemasons, modellers, and plasterers. He worked for the family firm, Gilbert Seale & Son (Gilbert being his father), and evidence of his skill survived in Farthings into Ackles's time, in the form of moulded cornicing. Initially, Seale built a studio at ground level, which tended to flood. He then extended the property into a bungalow built on brick stilts, like Harding's parents' house. Even the stilts didn't save the house from flooding in 1947, when the Seales were evacuated. A pet cat survived in the loft for three weeks, until the family returned. When John Hector died, in 1949, Farthings was bought by Colonel and Mrs Blaber. For sixteen years, Colonel Blaber bred prize-winning Aylesbury ducks there, selling day-old ducklings around the country and abroad.[9]

DOUGLAS GRAHAM David was an anomaly in that he was very much an Anglophile, and also very much into Americana. I always thought David was more of an Anglophile than an American. For instance, he loved *Beyond The Fringe*, and he could do the voices and the accents, funnier than hell. So, when he went to England to record *American Gothic*, he was really at home there, at Farthings.[10]

By the time Ackles arrived, in 1971, David and Tibs Partridge owned Farthings and used it as a holiday home. David Partridge was a Canadian painter and sculptor of some repute who lived in England with Tibs and their two children from 1962 to 1974. He was renowned for his relief sculptures made from nails and plywood.

As the dwellings along the Loddon became established, so did Loddon Drive, a private road that, in Ackles's time, was an unmetalled gravel track. This emerges onto Station Road, right by Wargrave Railway Station. Opened in 1900, initially double-tracked with a station building and a pedestrian bridge linking the platforms, it is now a single-track halt. You can see it (as Auchengillan station) in *The Magic Christian* (1969) and in the opening scene of *Porridge* (1979), when the station looked as it did during Ackles's tenure at Farthings, with the station building still standing.* By changing at Twyford you can get from Wargrave to London Paddington Station in under an hour. This places Wargrave in prime commuter belt territory, and Ackles himself commuted into London during his months in the village. A tousle-haired American, probably wearing jeans, boots, and a work shirt, sitting among the men (and it would have been men, then) with briefcases reading the *Times* and *Telegraph*.

Once established in Farthings, Ackles rented a baby grand piano from Harrods and acquired a handful of orchestral instruments to help him write the scores he felt his new songs demanded. He could not play the instruments but became familiar enough with them to know their range. Ackles and Graham were early risers. While Graham wrote, Ackles sat at the piano with his manuscript paper, surrounded by his collection of instruments, laboriously writing the arrangements, note by note.

After the 1970 Troubadour residency, Bernie Taupin spent most of his time in California, where he saw Ackles from time to time. But when Ackles ensconced himself in Farthings, Taupin became a regular visitor.

BERNIE TAUPIN We became much more acquainted on a day-to-day level when he came to England ... I made a point of being there when he was there.[11]

The house got cold, especially when the nights drew in. Graham had a girlfriend in Sevenoaks and often visited her, leaving Ackles alone at the piano. Graham and Ackles sometimes went into London for meetings, driving the second-hand car Ackles had bought.

When the river burst its banks around Farthings—a not uncommon occurrence because the property's garden was almost at the same level as the river—the house stood marooned on its brick stilts. To get to his car,

* *The Magic Christian* starred Peter Sellers and Ringo Starr. *Porridge* was a film spin-off from the popular TV comedy series of the same name, starring Ronnie Barker.

Ackles had to row across the flooded garden in a small boat to the garage by the road. A few months later, *Rolling Stone* characterised this period as Ackles's version of 'getting his head together in the country', while acknowledging that he wouldn't apply the term himself.[12]

Most—if not all—of the songs for *American Gothic* were already written by the time Ackles moved into Farthings. Ackles had performed the title track and 'Family Band' live since 1970. 'One Night Stand' had featured on the promo single recorded the previous year with Lonnie Mack. 'Montana Song' goes back even further and is listed (and crossed out) on the box of a quarter-inch tape reel kept by David Anderle, dated December 20, 1968. It was the arranging that took the time. With the ten-minute 'Montana Song' in particular, the distinction between composing and arranging blurs into near irrelevance. Musically, the song is the arrangement.

Recording was preceded by the now familiar unsuccessful encounter with an arranger. This time it was Del Newman who fell short of Ackles's high expectations. Newman (1930–2020) was a British conductor, arranger, and producer. Active from the 60s to the 90s, he worked with great success for many name artists, including Donovan, Peter Frampton, George Harrison, Elton John, Harry Nilsson, Carly Simon, Paul Simon, Scott Walker, and 10cc. The predictably fruitless encounter with Newman gave Ackles the opening to do what he wanted to do all along.

DAVID ACKLES What we did was, we went over first and got Del Newman to arrange a couple of songs on a trial basis. I think he did four songs, and we went in . . . and recorded them, and I just hated them—they bore no relationship with the material whatsoever. They were beautiful arrangements, he's a fine arranger, but not for my material.* I guess that was in November, so in December I hastily arranged myself. You know, typical musician, I sat home and listened to it and thought, *I can do better*

* Whereas recorded evidence of Ackles's unsuccessful trials with arrangers for *David Ackles* and *Subway To The Country* survive, it isn't clear if the Newman trial recordings still exist. If they do, I haven't been able to find them.

than that! and did some arrangements and begged Elektra and Bernie and everyone to let us at least go in and try a couple of songs, so we did. We went in and did 'Billy Whitecloud' and 'American Gothic'.[13]

Ackles then took the tapes of these two songs back to New York and then Los Angeles, playing them to Jac Holzman and Russ Miller, convincing them that he was up to the job of arranging the album. Which he was, but it wasn't easy for him. Without the necessary formal training, it was a matter of diligent trial and error.

DAVID ACKLES Then there was this long hiatus while I actually did the arrangements, which, because they were the first things I had ever arranged, it took me forever... it was just a monumental task, only because of my ignorance.[14]

Graham remembers a slightly different timescale, saying that by the time he and Ackles arrived at Farthings, in very late September or early October, Ackles was already committed to writing the arrangements himself:

DOUGLAS GRAHAM He was working on the arrangements, meticulously by hand . . . he was writing all these charts. In the beginning he was worried about who was going to do the arrangements—this is very, very complicated work—and I suggested Paul Buckmaster, who neither of us knew, but who had done a lot of arranging for Elton. He was a great string arranger, but he was so booked up he was not available. David said, 'I'm going to do it myself. I'm going to write these charts myself.' So, that's what he did. I just hung out there and I went into London periodically for meetings, and David worked slavishly on his charts for months. And I left in November... I think he was still working on the charts when I left.[15]

Ackles spent some time alone at Farthings in the run-up to Christmas, working on arrangements. December was warm by English standards that year, but the days were short and the nights long. He flew back to the US to spend Christmas at home, but he was back in England by the first days of 1972.

On January 4 of the new year, Ackles travelled to Television Centre at White City for his final appearance on BBC television. *The Old Grey Whistle Test* had launched on BBC2 in September 1971, replacing *Disco 2*, which itself replaced *Colour Me Pop*. Ackles appeared on all three shows, which focussed on album material, in contrast to the BBC's flagship music show, *Top Of The Pops*, which featured chart hits. *The Old Grey Whistle Test* and its two predecessors were devised by Rowan Ayers, a former naval officer who served in the Battle Of The Atlantic in World War II and was the father of Soft Machine founder Kevin Ayers. Mike Appleton, who had also worked on *Colour Me Pop* and *Disco 2*, was the *Whistle Test*'s producer. The journalist Richard Williams presented the first series, in which Ackles featured, in episode 16. From the start, the *Whistle Test* matched established names with lesser-known performers. Ackles shared the bill with The Kinks and Muddy Waters. Some footage of the show survives in the archives of the British Film Institute: excerpts of The Kinks' performance and an interview with Muddy Waters. But nothing of Ackles. All the shows on that first series went out live, though sometimes cut to prerecorded footage. Ackles played solo, probably two songs, though what the songs were is not known. Williams does not recall if the footage was prerecorded or live in the studio.[16]

In late January or early February, Ackles's future wife, Janice, joined him at Farthings, remaining there until June. They sometimes socialised with the house's owners, David and Tibs Partridge. Later, they both looked back at this period as an idyll, even if the English winter was a shock to people used to a Californian climate.

DAVID ACKLES I was fortunate enough to do a couple of live concerts, and I did a club date. I did several television shows, including *The Old Grey Whistle Test*, and had a lot of fun doing them: I got to meet some terrific people. As a matter of fact, my wife and I wished that I had been able to secure jobs in England so that we could have stayed there.[17]

JANICE VOGEL ACKLES There wasn't much heating. You had to huddle around the stove, but the village was perfect. The people were perfect.[18]

By March 1972, Ackles had completed his arrangements and was ready to record. Elektra booked him into one of London's leading studios. International Broadcasting Company studios (IBC) hid in plain sight behind the façade of a grand central London townhouse at 35 Portland Place, just up the road from the BBC's Broadcasting House. The studio had opened before World War II to record radio programmes but in the post-war years moved toward recording music. By the 1960s it was a favoured place of work for many of the era's biggest names, including The Who, The Bee Gees, Cream, The Yardbirds, and Jimi Hendrix. The Rolling Stones cut early demos at IBC with Glyn Johns. Not long after, The Kinks recorded 'You Really Got Me' there with Shel Talmy.*

There were two studios at IBC. Studio A, the larger one, was where most recording happened and where Ackles made *American Gothic*. The live room comprised two rooms knocked together, creating a space roughly sixty feet by thirty-two feet, with a ceiling height of twenty feet—a large space heated by an open fire. Stairs led up to the mezzanine control room, with a vocal booth beneath it. When Ackles recorded *American Gothic*, the studio was still equipped with a custom-designed mixing console dating from the 1960s, paired with a sixteen-track Ampex tape machine. Studio B, usually used for vocal overdubs, was smaller. In the basement there was an echo chamber, and another room housing EMT plate reverbs. At the back, beyond a covered courtyard, a separate building housed a cutting

* Chas Chandler, the Animals bassist who later managed Hendrix and Slade, bought the studios in 1978 and renamed them Portland Recording Studios. He then sold the facility to Don Arden, who used it for his Jet Records. In 1985 the studio shut down and the site was converted to office space. It is now a Columbian Consulate building.

facility. From 1974 to 1984 it was occupied by George 'Porky' Peckham, whose signature—'A Porky Prime Cut'—was scratched into the runout grooves of dozens of punk and new wave records.[19]

Taupin was a novice producer, but he was aided through the sessions by Damon Lyon-Shaw, an IBC house engineer. Lyon-Shaw had considerable previous form, including engineering The Who's *Tommy*. He was assisted at the session by a young apprentice, Hugh Jones, who later worked at Rockfield Studios in Wales. Elektra also hired Robert Kirby, who had written string arrangements for Nick Drake, to conduct Ackles's arrangements. Ackles could have conducted himself, and he might have preferred to, but the approach to recording precluded this. After the lengthy creative process, after so much thought and planning, Ackles was confident, ready, and in command.

DAVID ACKLES It was one of those things where most of the preparation was done as a result of being able to work on the arrangements and orchestrations in our little house out in the country for quite a while, well actually for a matter of months before we ever went into the studio. There were no decisions to be made on the occasion of being in the studio—we went in pretty thoroughly prepared.[20]

BERNIE TAUPIN David knew exactly what he wanted. He was fully in charge. Nobody was in charge more than him. All I was doing was being there as a support system for him ... he knew what he wanted out of the arrangements, he knew the way he wanted his voice to sound, he knew how we wanted the instruments to sound. Between the rest of us, we just made sure that could happen.[21]

Apart from Ackles, no musicians are credited on *American Gothic*, but even a casual listen reveals that many took part. Certainly, more than the twenty-two credited on *Subway To The Country*. Strings, brass, woodwind, acoustic, electric and pedal steel guitars, bass, drums, and multiple backing singers. According to Janice, who was present at all the sessions, most of the orchestral musicians were from the London Symphony Orchestra. There was also a Salvation Army choir. It wasn't a rock'n'roll session.

For two weeks or so in March, David and Janice commuted daily to IBC from their riparian paradise, usually by train, walking from Farthings to Wargrave train station, then catching the train from Wargrave into Paddington (via Twyford). From Paddington they got onto the tube, the Bakerloo Line down to Oxford Circus, where they walked the few minutes up Great Portland Street, past Broadcasting House, to IBC. You can do it in ninety minutes if you're lucky with the connections.

After such a long and sometimes fraught gestation, including the failed Del Newman arrangements, the recording of *American Gothic* went smoothly. Comments made over the years by people who were there—Janice, Taupin, Lyon-Shaw—combine to create the impression of a focused, efficient, good-natured working environment.

BERNIE TAUPIN I definitely admired David's spirit in the studio. He was not intimidated at all by the musicians. The atmosphere was always wonderful.[22]

Ackles was a perfectionist in the studio and knew his songs inside out. But he was a convivial presence too, cracking jokes in an exaggerated English accent and making people feel at ease. Taupin recalls him being greatly concerned with fettling his voice into the best working order. Lyon-Shaw thought him musically brilliant and masterful at the sessions. Taupin thought Ackles could have produced the album himself but benefitted from having somebody he trusted on hand to act as an advocate, a sounding board and support system.

BERNIE TAUPIN To my way of thinking at the time, I'm sure I felt that what I couldn't provide in technical know-how I might be able to contribute in simple human support. I knew full well that David had a vision and the wherewithal to execute it, but you must understand that, at the time, Elton's star and mine was on the rise, which gave us a certain influence in the industry. In a nutshell, if I had the muscle, then I was more than happy to use it in helping David get the necessary funding for this project.[23]

Lyon-Shaw and Taupin complemented each other. Lyon-Shaw had the technical skill to record complex orchestral arrangements and knew his way around the IBC studio. Taupin had the personal touch with Ackles.

DAMON LYON-SHAW I worked very well with him [Taupin]—he appreciated my technical input and very much let me get on with it. However, the way he oversaw the recordings in a quiet assertive manner and very much supported David, was a huge asset to the success of the project.[24]

Ackles came to the sessions ready, presenting the musicians with the charts he had prepared meticulously over the previous months. Then, with Ackles seated at the piano with the rest of the musicians and Robert Kirby conducting, Taupin and Lyon-Shaw standing up to look over the mixing desk and down from the upraised control room, the recordings were captured with the minimum of fuss.

DAMON LYON-SHAW As far as I remember, all sessions were live, as in, all musicians played together, including David, no overdubs of musicians to rhythm tracks were undertaken. All parts would have been scored for both the rhythm section and the orchestra. There would have been one or two run-throughs before recording and no more than a couple of takes at most… as far as I remember, all vocals would have been overdubbed at a later stage.[25]

Janice had witnessed Ackles working on the charts and knew the songs but was stunned when she heard the arrangements played for the first time. So was Ackles, as he wasn't familiar enough with each instrument he was writing for to understand exactly what it would all sound like until he heard it played. According to Mike Jahn, writing a few months later, the London Symphony Orchestra musicians present stood and applauded Ackles at the end of the sessions.[26]

American Gothic was recorded, mixed, and mastered by the end of March. Within weeks Ackles's manager Abe Hoch began circulating advance cassettes of the album to American journalists. Ackles stayed on in Farthings through the spring and early summer of 1972, while Elektra geared up for the album's release. He was still in England when word came from his homeland of euphoric early reviews.

CHAPTER SEVEN

THERE IS A RIVER

THE *SGT. PEPPER* OF FOLK • RETURN TO LOS ANGELES • A CHANGE IN THE CRITICAL WEATHER • DISAPPOINTING SALES • MARRIAGE TO JANICE

“

Mr Ackles is thirty-five, born (forgive my xenophobia) of British parents and currently living in Britain.

DEREK JEWELL, *SUNDAY TIMES*

”

A day in April, 1972. Chris Van Ness, a Los Angeles-based journalist, slots the cassette tape into his cassette machine and presses play. It's an advance copy of a new album by David Ackles. Van Ness and Ackles have history. Van Ness thinks of their relationship as a 'reserved friendship'. The most scathing review he ever wrote was of an Ackles album. For that reason, he isn't expecting much from the cassette. But he is drawn in listening to the opening song, 'American Gothic'. To his ears, this is a completely different David Ackles. In the following two weeks, he listens to the album at least twenty times…

With recording wrapped up, Elektra set to work packaging *American Gothic*. Robert L. Heimall was assigned as art director, and photographer Mike Ross, who had worked with Elton John, was dispatched to Wargrave to take the cover shots. His images captured the peculiar, ambiguous circumstances in which Ackles found himself. An American songwriter, half-English by parentage, holed up in the most American-looking house in the heart of England. Minutes from the Thames, meandering its way into London. Casting a perceptive eye over the Atlantic to the homeland he had—temporarily at least—left behind. The American musician and producer and Ackles admirer Jim O'Rourke picks up on this contradictory dynamic—the combination of belonging and not belonging.

JIM O'ROURKE He sounds to me like an ex-pat who never got around to becoming an ex-pat. An ex-pat who never left the country. There is a critical eye in a lot of his songs, but there's also an embracing of the characters that keeps them [the songs] from being completely critically distant.[1]

The front cover of *American Gothic* shows Ackles sitting in a rowing boat, floating on the Loddon at the back of Farthings. Janice sits on the covered balcony. You can see right underneath the building through the gaps between the supporting brick pillars that were of sufficient height to keep the house from flooding, most of the time. The back cover references

Grant Wood's 1930 painting which gave *American Gothic* its title. In the painting, a man and woman dominate the image, their heads framing an arched window in an otherwise folksy-looking white weatherboarded house. The man stares balefully at the camera holding a three-prong fork. The woman looks slightly to her left. The flat, severe figures evoke the rigidity of posture and expression in early long-exposure photographic portraits. In the Ross photo, David and Janice are placed in the bottom left of the image. Farthings presents a similar white-boarded gable end but with a square leaded window and a round porthole next to it. David manages his own baleful stare, holding a four-prong fork; Janice looks to her left. The photo, by alluding to without directly replicating such a mythic rural American image, seems to deliberately position the album as a tangential comment on culture, tradition, and a nation's own self-image. It tells us this is a view of America, seen from an oblique perspective. A sentiment Ackles underlines with an explanatory note superimposed on Farthing's white boards:

> It is now two years since the last album.* I suppose that's almost too long between songs, but it was needed as a kind of sorting-out period. I've been living in England for part of that time in a house in the country with apple trees and swans and a river running past the back porch. It seems like you get a sharper perspective on your own country when you're away from it, so the time has been a big help in a lot of ways. This album is the result of distance and peace and a lot of patience and kindness from a lot of friends. Many, many thanks.[2]

By the standards of the vinyl age, *American Gothic* is quite a long album, at around forty-three minutes. Its eleven songs break down into three broad categories. First, four conventionally structured ballads ('Love's Enough',

* It was actually more than two and a half years since the last album.

'One Night Stand', 'Another Friday Night', and 'Waiting For The Moving Van'). With different arrangements, these songs would have fitted neatly enough onto either of Ackles's first two albums. Poignant, faintly country-influenced story songs, with 'Another Friday Night', 'One Night Stand', and 'Waiting For The Moving Van' told from the perspective of Ackles's now familiar world-weary, beaten-down-by-life character.

Then there are two songs that explicitly reference older American forms. 'Family Band' sounds like an evangelical hymn, and 'Blues For Billie Whitecloud' nods to finger-clicking 1930s swing.

Third, there is the inimitable theatrical art song, which Ackles hinted at on the first two albums and here realises fully. There are five numbers in this category—'American Gothic', 'Ballad Of The Ship Of State', 'Oh, California', 'Midnight Carousel', and 'Montana Song'—which, on account of the length of 'Montana Song', take up more than half the album's running time. As good as the other songs are, it's these five—eccentrically-shaped mini-operas, with their time changes and intricate orchestrations and thespian delivery—that give *American Gothic* its unique character. They are also the reason why rock audiences found it hard to relate to the album. No guitar solos, often no rhythm section, no easily graspable verse/chorus structures. There just wasn't enough of the familiar. And yet this is the sound of Ackles finally making the record he wanted to make.

The most obvious explanation for why *American Gothic* doesn't sound like rock music is that rock wasn't Ackles's primary influence. He was familiar with artists recording for Elektra at the same time he was, such as Tom Rush and Tim Buckley, not all of whom operated strictly within rock conventions. Much later in his life, when asked what songwriters he liked, he replied with a list of long-established big names, which might indicate that he didn't dig too deeply into the rock world.* In an interview just

* In an email to me dated October 18, 1998, Ackles said, 'The individual songwriters I admire are from the old school, i.e., Leonard Cohen, Randy Newman, Paul Simon, David Bowie, Elton John, and Bernie Taupin.'

before the album was released, Ackles mentioned the song 'Sally Go Round The Roses' as instructive in his emerging understanding that rock and folk music could combine into something new. Credited to The Jaynetts, 'Sally Go Round The Roses' was a big hit in 1963 and was subsequently much covered. Tim Buckley quoted liberally from it in his 1973 song of the same title, on *Sefronia*. The Jaynetts were a made-to-order studio creation in the style of girl vocal groups of the day. The song has an intriguing ambiguity about it, a hint of ominous mystery which perhaps appealed to Ackles. But he tended to look beyond rock music for inspiration. West Coast jazz. Musical theatre. Brecht & Weill especially, with Weill's preference for woodwind and brass over strings and a singing style ranging through conversational, declamatory, and oratorical. Classical music, particularly Aaron Copland and Mahler. (Ackles presented engineer Damon Lyon-Shaw with a bust of Mahler as a thank-you at the end of sessions for *American Gothic*). And a strand of Protestant hymns that in turn seeped into country music. The album fuses this array of influences into a distinctive whole. They can all be detected in the first two albums, but here they come to the foreground. *David Ackles* and *Subway To The Country* are the sound of Ackles and his producers and arrangers presenting his songs in a more-or-less rock idiom. On *American Gothic*, the rock gestures are relegated so far in the background as to be barely noticeable.

Lyrically, *American Gothic* combines sweeping big-picture commentary with acute personal scrutiny. The loss of youthful dreams, racism, divorce, a changing relationship with the land, a war on foreign soil, faith and family, usually viewed through the lens of individual experience. It's a short story collection as much as it's a song cycle.

American Gothic opens with its title track, and there's no sense of breaking in the listener gradually to the album's extremities. A claustrophobic domestic nightmare in which Ackles exposes the gap between tawdry experience and aspiration, 'American Gothic' stars a married couple, Molly and Horace Jenkins, living as strangers under the same roof. She wants material luxury; he aspires to piety. Neither gets what they want,

RIGHT The Ackles Twins, Sally and David, pictured circa 1944. *Kim Nixon* **BELOW** Promotional poster for *The Return Of Rusty* (1946), the first *Rusty* film that Ackles (second right, top) appeared in.

DAVID ACKLES

ABOVE An Elektra Records promotional photo issued in support of *David Ackles*.

ABOVE & BELOW Ackles performs on Norwegian television, August 29, 1968.
LEFT Poster advertising an Ackles appearance at Canterbury House, 1970.
Jim Friedrich

RIGHT A press ad for Ackles's appearance at the Troubadour in August 1970. **BELOW** Ackles performing at Jim Friedrich's ordination service, All Saints Episcopal Church, Beverly Hills, September 17, 1970. *Marilyn Robertson*

THIS PAGE Contact sheets showing David Ackles in IBC studios during the recording of *American Gothic. Mike Ross*

ABOVE Farthings, Wargrave, where Ackles lived while preparing and recording *American Gothic*. *Douglas Graham* **RIGHT** A press ad announcing 'the album of the year'. **BELOW** Douglas Graham in the home studio where Ackles recorded *Five & Dime*. *Douglas Graham*

THIS PAGE The front covers for Ackles's albums *David Ackles* (1968), *The Road To Cairo* (1969 reissue of *David Ackles*), *Subway To The Country* (1970), *American Gothic* (1972), and *Five & Dime* (1973).

ABOVE A UK press advert for the withdrawn *There Is A River* collection (2007). **LEFT** Ackles in the early 1990s. *Janice Vogel Ackles* **BELOW** *Sister Aimee* demo cassette (1994). *Stacy Sullivan*

and both look for escape in slummy distractions—she, prostitution to raise money for new shoes; he, pornography and alcohol. Ackles presides over the sorry situation with a clear eye and something like compassion: 'They suffer least who suffers what they choose.' Never mind how pitiful, how shabby his characters, Ackles is never judgemental.

The arrangement is built on an anxious, bustling piano pattern and layered brass and woodwind. No guitar, bass, and drums. Structurally, the song comprises three sections, repeated twice—the first run-through telling Molly's side of the story, the second Horace's. The first section then repeats a third time, with the couple sitting down to breakfast, before the song ends on final judgement. It isn't a rock song. More like a sermon or a morality tale.

'Love's Enough', a simple, poised ballad about falling in love, shifts the mood. With a conventional verse/chorus/bridge structure, the piano and voice are supported by picked acoustic guitar, soft woodwind and organ, and the gentlest percussion. Ackles's singing is measured, almost formal.

In 1972, the long, bloody story of American involvement in the Vietnam War was reaching its conclusion. 'Ballad Of The Ship Of State', while not referencing the conflict directly, sounds like a barbed comment on what was increasingly viewed as a futile foreign policy disaster. Ackles voices an exchange between a group of soldiers abandoned on some foreign shore and an officious voice booming from a passing ship. The soldiers forlornly plead for rescue to a backing of melancholic woodwind and brass. The voice from the ship (pointedly not the captain, who is 'locked in his quarters') refuses—in a manner gratingly hearty and evasively legalistic, offset with a comic opera backing. The first time we hear a rock drum kit played with intent is a minute into this, the album's third song.

An Ackles staple character, the down-at-heel drifter with commitment issues, makes his first showing in 'One Night Stand', the second of the album's four ballads. Here he's a travelling musician, though he could be the same person we meet at different stages of life in 'Down River', 'Road

To Cairo', 'Out On The Road', and more. This album cut contrasts with the version of the same song Ackles recorded in 1970 with Lonnie Mack, though it's taken at a similar pace and intensity. Here, the easy-going piano, percussion, acoustic guitar, and woodwind arrangement supplant the slow rock backbeat and strings of the Mack take, which aligned that earlier version with Jimmy Webb and Glen Campbell.

'Oh, California!' is a comedic jazz-hands show-tune satire, with Ackles rhyming 'warn ya' with 'California'. California seems to be a symbol of a certain type of encroaching, all-consuming materialism, bringing with it dire consequences 'when the oil meets the Red Woods, then the sun grows dim'. A coda of lush strings running through the chorus at a slower pace builds to a crescendo ending, a device borrowed from film musicals.

'Another Friday Night' closes side one, a ballad that—lyrically and musically—explores similar territory to 'Out On The Road', from *Subway To The Country*. The Ackles transient appears again, this time labouring on the roads and musing on the quotidian ennui of working life. Within a simple verse/chorus structure, he moves between regret at lost time in the verses, before youthful dreams reassert themselves in the rousing choruses. With a backing of country-soul piano, harmonica, guitar, bass, pedal steel, and organ, it's the most conventional arrangement on the album—and the closest to the zeitgeist, if there was one in 1972. Gospel-style female backing vocals sing in the choruses, the first time we hear backing vocals of any sort on an Ackles record.*

Though in common with most writers Ackles sometimes drew on personal experience for subject matter, he was rarely an autobiographical or confessional songwriter in the manner of somebody like Tim Hardin. The brief 'Family Band', which opens side two of *American Gothic*, is an exception. To a sparse piano-and-organ arrangement, Ackles remembers

* These singers are probably not the Salvation Army choir we hear later in the album. Bernie Taupin, speaking to Richie Unterberger in 2002, thought they might be a combination of Lesley Duncan, Madeleine Bell, and Doris Troy, all of whom were session regulars in England at the time.

the hymns he played in church with his father (on bass) and his mother (on drums), while 'Jesus sang the song'—pitching his strident voice against a choral counter melody he arranged for the Salvation Army singers hired for the sessions. Ackles had to work hard to get them approximating the feel he was after, as he discovered that British Salvation Army choirs sounded quite different to American ones, on account of diction and pronunciation. It's a song that talks of enduring, if fluctuating, faith, and that manages to give the general impression of an evangelical hymn without—to my knowledge—directly quoting from one.

The mood shades into something darker with 'Midnight Carousel', a poetically opaque tale of temptation and lust that, musically, conjures a similar atmosphere to 'American Gothic'. It's structurally complex, comprising three distinct voices—a narrator, a young woman tempted to throw in her lot with a 'man in red', and a carnival barker who serves as both Shakespearian-style chorus and the warning voice of conscience. Each voice has a corresponding musical passage, with the hoedown fiddle underneath the barker's passage at odds with the more involved orchestral scoring of the rest of the song. Ackles's arrangements, hovering on the margins of discord, at times recall Fred Myrow's for 'Candy Man' on *Subway To The Country*.

'Waiting For The Moving Van', the fourth and last of *American Gothic's* simple ballads, is next—four verses, each anchored with a lyrical refrain. Against piano, acoustic guitar, melancholy woodwind, and brass, Ackles sings a first-person lament to lost love. In the last verse, he pulls off a trick deployed in 'Down River', adopting a positive stance—'I like it on my own'—that isn't fooling anyone. Including him. In his sole interview just before the album's release, Ackles alluded to this song 'indirectly' referencing his brief first marriage.[3]

The album's penultimate track takes aim at American racism. As with most of his social-comment songs, Ackles explores the subject through a personal story. In 'Blues For Billy Whitecloud', the titular character is a Native American who gets a good education but is excluded from getting a correspondingly good job. Turning to drink, he eventually bombs his old school. Ackles deliberately exacerbates the grimness of the vignette by placing it in a perky swing setting. It's an uncomfortable listen, which was the desired effect.

American Gothic closes with the ten-minute statement piece 'Montana Song', an elegiac widescreen orchestral tone poem that nods conspicuously to the atmosphere of Copland's *Appalachian Spring Suite* while falling just short of quoting it. The first-person narrative reads like a blank verse précis of a John Steinbeck novel, with the central character looking for his forbears on a 'long abandoned farm' in a 'long forgotten town'. (Was Ackles visualising Bodie, the ghost town where he shot the 'Subway To The Country' promo film, as he wrote those words?) The lyrics explore generational change, with sons leaving their parents' farm and way of life in the early twentieth century. A ragtime piano section represents the new world the sons have gone looking for. As usual, Ackles anchors the big themes to a small, human drama. If he needed distance to see his homeland clearly—as he says in the album's sleeve notes—he also required close attention to detail, to the minutiae of his character's lives, to help him understand. Taupin later commented that you'd have to be dead inside not to be moved.

BERNIE TAUPIN I remember listening back to that and thinking, *Wow, this is really something else. This is really something very, very special.*[4]

'Montana Song' is complex and self-assured, a fitting end to an album that is the sound of an artist at his creative peak. Ackles's songwriting expanded and refined the themes and styles present on his first two releases, wrapping up his influences into an individual package. An untried and untrained novice, he stepped into the arranger's role with some nerve. As a singer and performer, he matured. We hear his voice ranging across the same emotions and variations in intensity as on *David Ackles* and *Subway To The Country*, but with greater control.

BERNIE TAUPIN The main thing I remember about the sessions was David was very, very concerned about keeping his voice in perfect condition. He used to take medications and different kinds of herbal teas and stuff, honey and all this stuff. Very concerned about, quote-unquote, the *timbre* of his voice. I remember that was a big thing, the timbre of his voice. And being able to record that correctly.[5]

Even now, *American Gothic* defies easy categorisation. Although traces of soul, rock, folk, gospel, blues, and country are present, most of the songs go well beyond the normal parameters of pop music. All the greats of twentieth-century American music the reviewers mentioned—such as Dylan, Copland, Al Jolson, Burl Ives, Ira Gershwin, Leonard Bernstein—Ackles throws into the mix. Taupin detects a noirish sensibility, comparing the album to the Orson Welles film *Touch Of Evil*. Alongside the American forms, there's a European sensibility too, attributable in part to the shadow of Kurt Weill's Weimar cabaret. Yet despite the wild eclecticism, Ackles achieves an artistic unity and a strong sense of identity on *American Gothic*. This is exactly the point that the reviewers hailed. Most considered *American Gothic* his masterpiece, and yet it is also the most inaccessible of his records.

American Gothic requires close attention and rewards it if it is given. Though the more challenging tracks are spaced around a handful of more readily understandable ones, it isn't an easy listen in the sense of being catchy. There are no obvious singles. Most of the critics who praised it effusively talked of spending time with it over weeks. For a long time, I admired its virtuosity more than I enjoyed it. Only when I sat down to concentrate on it time and again did its charms reveal themselves. It's not a record for the streaming age. It is, though, an extraordinary bravura performance by Ackles the singer, songwriter, and autodidactic arranger.

Two complete studio out-takes survive, one a more conventional country-influenced ballad, the other perhaps the strangest song Ackles ever recorded.

'I'm Only Passing Through' is yet another of the Ackles drifter songs, with his tough yet fragile 'man's man' character this time cast as a peripatetic card player. Featuring a fully realised country-soul band arrangement (bass, drums, guitar, piano, organ, horns), it shares an atmosphere with the ornate country music Mickey Newbury was recording for Elektra at the same time. A pared-back mix with piano, bass, drums, and vocals indicates that other arrangement details might have been added to this basic track. It's as good a song as the four country-influenced ballads included on *American Gothic*.

In 2007 Rhino prepared (and then aborted at the last minute) a box set of Ackles's Elektra recordings called *There Is A River*. The title came from another *American Gothic* outtake. British writer Penny Valentine spent time in the studio in late March and witnessed the recording of the song.[6] Tape boxes from the sessions list it as divided into two parts, one starting the album, the other ending it, indicating the song was withdrawn late in proceedings. Had it not been, *American Gothic* would have been an even more unusual album.

'There Is A River' comes across like a location recording. To a backdrop of traffic noise and piano chords, Ackles delivers a sonorous vocal like a street corner preacher. The Salvation Army choir and a brass band then join in behind him, as if Ackles is leading them on a parade. The choir sound less rehearsed, more as if they're just singing along, compared to their appearance on 'Family Band'. The song then reverts to Ackles's voice and piano, and a traffic-noise fade. Fragments comprising elements of the finished production on their own (the traffic noise, Ackles's voice and piano) indicate that the field recording effect was most likely studio sleight of hand.

The lyrics to this oddity manage to appear hymnal without mentioning God. It's as if Ackles is leading his congregation with a rallying cry, the precise meaning of which remains elusive. It's a yearning song of alienation and the possibility of reunion. Ackles stands at a distance, looking back with nostalgia and regret ('If I care about you, then can I come home').

The river—so often a symbol of life—here is more a symbol of division that must be traversed ('In my dreams I see a river, running through the land. With all of you on the other side, and here I stand').

—

When *David Ackles* was released in 1968, Ackles was sometimes bracketed with other singer-songwriters by virtue of being on the same label as them, or because critics noticed a shared tendency to draw on influences outside of rock's conventions, or both. By the time *American Gothic* came out, these peers had all gone off in their own directions. Fred Neil and Laura Nyro had withdrawn from recording (though Nyro would later re-emerge). Leonard Cohen was a third of the way through a three-year pause in studio albums. The artistically restless Tim Buckley had already moved through his folk-rock and experimental jazz-influenced periods, left Elektra, and was about to release a soul/R&B album. Tom Rush had also left Elektra and found an easy-going country-rock sound that was a template for the 70s generation of West Coast male singer-songwriters. When Ackles first visited London on a promotional tour, in September 1968, Harry Nilsson was also in town. An article by Ray Connolly in the London *Evening Standard* compared them. By coincidence, Nilsson recorded his *Son Of Schmilsson* album in London at the same time as Ackles recorded *American Gothic*. Listening to the albums now, it's hard to detect any of the similarities that Connolly had noticed just four years earlier. The same can be said for all the other artists Ackles had once been compared to. He didn't sound like them anymore, if he ever did.

This disconnect from his contemporaries extended beyond musical differences. Most of them were making a lot more money than Ackles was. Even Fred Neil, who didn't sell many of his own records, was flush off the back of Nilsson's cover of 'Everybody's Talkin'', as used in *Midnight Cowboy*. Financially, Ackles was still in the 'shows potential' category, with some commercial interest in his early songs, yet heavily in debt to Elektra on account of his albums' production costs. This made him vulnerable. In contrast to his friends Bernie Taupin and Elton John. Elton's fifth album, *Honky Château*, was released two months before *American Gothic* and went on to become one of the biggest releases of 1972. Commercially, *American Gothic* came nowhere near.

Ackles stayed in England until shortly before *American Gothic*'s release. Elektra held a small album launch party at Farthings. The guests, mainly Elektra staffers and some music journalists, meandered down the dirt and gravel track to find Ackles standing on the balcony to greet them. The group assembled in the living room, still featuring the plaster cornicing made by John Hector Seale when he built the house in the 1920s. Ackles sat at the Harrods piano and sang some songs. It was a damp, drizzly day. British music journalist John Tobler was there with his dog, called Elektra. The dog jumped up at the film producer Jonathan Clyde (the brother of Jeremy Clyde, of Chad & Jeremy).[7]

Ackles's younger sister Kim joined Ackles for his last weeks in England and was present when Elektra organised a farewell press lunch in London. Ackles had grown a beard and shaved it off. 'I didn't look Christ-like, and if you can't look Christ-like, why, there seems to be no reason to have one.'[8]

In the weeks before leaving England, and later in life, Ackles said he would have liked to stay. Farthings fitted him well. It's an indication of his affection for the place that he, Janice, their son George, and his parents all visited in the 1980s, welcomed by the Bond family, who had bought the house in 1978. Had he stayed in England, he might have had a longer career. Looking back with the benefit of decades of hindsight, it's clear he was better understood in his mother's homeland than his father's. But he couldn't find a way to make it work.

By early July, after a holiday in Ireland, Ackles was back in Los Angeles, gearing up for a projected six months of concerts and promotional events, right up to Christmas. On his return, Elektra put on another launch event for *American Gothic* at the University Of Southern California, Ackles's alma mater.* The writer Mark Leviton attended. He was already primed to expect something special. Chris Van Ness had written an enraptured pre-release review that Elektra was circulating with press kits for the album and running in adverts.

MARK LEVITON I was invited to the USC performance by Pat Faralla, Elektra's publicity head, who was always so nice to me. In the 60s, I used to get written invites in the mail to Elektra events, often telegrams if things happened quickly. I have a vague memory of getting a written invitation to the Ackles performance, like a card that invites you to a wedding.

If I had to estimate, I'd say there were no more than fifty people there, a cosy library-like room with a grand piano and chairs set up. I was sitting very close to the piano, maybe even the front row, with Ackles to my left, so I couldn't see his hands on the keyboard. I think Jac did an introduction, and then Ackles played the album all the way through.[9]

This modest affair was out of proportion to the considerable media noise that had already built up around *American Gothic*. Ackles's manager, Abe Hoch, held a listening party at his house and began circulating advance cassettes of the album in April 1972. One of these went to Chris Van Ness, who was then writing for the *Los Angeles Free Press*, a big-circulation underground newspaper. Van Ness, like Ackles, was a USC theatre and communications alumnus. With its extensive music coverage, the *Freep*, as it was known, was a cultural tastemaker. At the time, Van Ness, who rose to editor in 1974, was reviewing music.

In a detailed feature in the May edition, he declared *American Gothic* the album of the year, starting by explaining why he thought *Sgt. Pepper* the best album ever made (it channelled the psychedelic era's experimentation into concise songs, and introduced listeners to forms rarely heard in rock

* Most likely this was on July 6, as invites to an Ackles concert at USC on that date put on in association with Elektra survive. If it was the July 6 event, the concert doubled as a benefit for the 'Art Scholarship Programme For Talented Minority Youth'.

music). 'I never really imagined that anyone could ever come along and make another album that would be as important—and for the same reasons as *Sgt. Pepper* was... but someone has,' he continued. 'His name is David Ackles, and the album (his third) is called *American Gothic*.'[10]

Van Ness went on to explain that he had written a bad review of an earlier Ackles album for *Entertainment Now*, which had led to the two men meeting and becoming friends. In April, Hoch had given Van Ness one of the advance cassettes of *American Gothic* at Ackles's suggestion. The album had been mixed just weeks before, and Ackles was still in England.

> It was as if somehow in the last two years David had managed to cleanse himself and purify his art to a point where he finally had total control over his genius ... *American Gothic* is either the best pop album ever made—or maybe the second best.[11]

Van Ness then went on to analyse the album track by track, expressing mild reservations about just one song, 'Family Band', finding himself unable to judge whether it was intended as a parody or not. After hundreds of words of effusive hyperbole, he then wondered if he had overdone it and raised expectations too much. Those words would ring gratingly true in Ackles's ears before the year was out.

The Elektra publicity machine jumped on the review and played it for all it was worth. Copies were included in their press and radio promotional mail out for the album so that most of Ackles's potential media supporters heard the album for the first time with the words 'album of the year' in front of their eyes. Portentous newspaper ads declared that 'on the 4th of July Elektra Records will release *American Gothic*, the album of the year'. It was a deliberate attempt to position the release of *American Gothic* as a big cultural event. As an attention-grabbing strategy, it worked to the extent that most other critics seemed to agree with Van Ness. For a while, at least.

A month after Van Ness, John Weisman in the *Detroit Free Press* recycled the *Sgt. Pepper* comparison and declared *American Gothic* the finest

American album since the days of George Gershwin. After a review almost as detailed as Van Ness's, he rose to a similarly acclamatory conclusion:

> With *American Gothic* David Ackles has pulled together the best elements of American pop music—jazz, 'serious composers', the musical theatre and film music, and combined them with exquisite taste ... The best album of the year? Undoubtedly. The best of the decade? Probably.[12]

Weisman's enthusiasm endured until the end of 1972, when he published his annual 'best of' list, in which he held to his earlier assertion that *American Gothic* was album of the year, beating The Rolling Stones' *Exile On Main St.* into second place.

Across the country, dozens of similarly panegyrical responses appeared. Album of the week, or month, or year, or decade. Adjectives like brilliant, inventive, extraordinary, and magnificent piling up. Comparisons to the royalty of twentieth-century American popular music. A milestone, a towering achievement, an ambitious work, a lofty peak. Meticulously fashioned and rich in detail. It became almost boringly predictable.

Mark Starr's review in the *Democrat & Chronicle* was typical. He started by explaining that he bought *American Gothic* on reading the Van Ness review, which Elektra had printed as an ad in *Rolling Stone*:

> Van Ness's problem is he can't decide whether *American Gothic* or *Sgt. Pepper* is the best pop album ever made. I can't go that far, but Ackles's third album is one of the best, most exciting, most innovative albums of this year ... the album is so good that deciding the best cuts is too difficult.[13]

By the time *Rolling Stone* got around to publishing a thoughtful review of the album by Stephen Holden, in September, its relative restraint seemed anticlimactic. Even though the review was entirely positive and full of praise. 'Ackles is an important artist whose work eludes categorization,' he wrote. '*American Gothic* is an impressive and original record that deserves a wide audience.'[14]

In the UK, where Ackles was more established, it was much the same.

The idea that rock music, in the broadest sense, might be a form worthy of serious critical attention took root in the US earlier than it did in the UK. In the late 60s, when Ackles emerged, much writing in the British music press still adopted a forced 'teenage' vernacular that seems risible now. By the time *American Gothic* was released, that had changed, and the dominant style had more of an earnest polytechnic undergraduate feel to it. Broadsheets were starting to take notice too.

The journalist, author, and broadcaster Derek Jewell was one of the first British critics to pay close attention and became an unlikely champion of progressive, experimental rock music in the *Sunday Times*, a bastion of establishment, conservative journalism. Whereas John Peel, who was writing and broadcasting at the same time, was part of the culture he was promoting, Jewell came from a very different world. Born in 1927 and educated at Oxford, he was a good twenty years older than most of the rock critics on *the New Musical Express*, *Sounds*, and *Melody Maker*. Alongside his *Sunday Times* writing, Jewell presented *Sounds Interesting* on BBC Radio 3, a station primarily given over to classical music. Jewell championed Ackles on air and in print, and as late as 1976—three years after Ackles stopped recording—he was playing 'Montana Song' on the radio.* His *Sunday Times* review of *American Gothic* was a match for Van Ness in enthusiasm, though shorter, and could not have been more laudatory. Under the title 'Record Masterpiece', Jewell, in just over three hundred words, bracketed Ackles with the greats of American popular music, from George Gershwin through Duke Ellington, Count Basie, Frank Sinatra, Leonard Bernstein, and Elvis Presley to Bob Dylan. He then threw in The Beatles as another comparator.

---

* Jewell featured Ackles four times on *Sounds Interesting* between 1973 and 1976.

> Now, another event to contend with such achievements is here—an album called *American Gothic* (Elektra £2.09), by the American singer and musician David Ackles. It's a masterpiece. Its achievement is comparable with *Sgt. Pepper.*[15]

That was just Jewell's introduction, but the rhapsodical tone continued. There were further comparisons to Burl Ives, Aaron Copland, Al Jolson, Benjamin Britten. Ackles is special, brilliant, full of verbal wit. 'Never has popular music sounded more dramatic ... The beauty, surprise and sheer perfection of his songs will confound you.'

Mark Plummer of *Melody Maker*, who had attended the Farthings launch party, indirectly referenced the Jewell and Van Ness reviews when finding his angle. '*American Gothic* has been likened to *Sgt. Pepper* in a number of reviews, but that cannot be, for *American Gothic* is an album that is stunningly important in its own right ... a classic.'[16]

Elektra must have been delighted at the critical attention. Ackles himself was ambivalent. Speaking a year later, he reflected on his feelings.

> All it is is an album, one record album of a handful of songs. They can only be so good, right? They can't be any better than that ... to have people fall down and say 'this is a whole new direction to music' is embarrassing, because I can't support that, my music can't support it, nothing can support it. ... I was, thrilled that many people were that enthusiastic, and I appreciate their enthusiasm and their faith and all of that, but at the same time, it caused me no end of grief. I knew what the album was worth, and I still know—it's a good album. I'm not putting it down, but it's only an album, only a group of songs.[17]

After a few months of unremitting critical lionisation, occasional dissenting voices made themselves heard. Bill Mann, writing in the *Montreal Gazette*, saw some worth in Ackles's songs and arrangements but complained that he couldn't sing. 'There is really no way to describe Ackles's moaning except to say that he sings like Richard Harris in *MacArthur Park*, only worse,' he concluded.[18]

A month later, Nick Tosches, writing in *Creem*, could barely contain himself. 'I mean, is this guy serious or what? I've heard of living in the past and all, but this Ackles fellow really takes the cake … with his pretentious two-years-since-the-last-album piece of atavistic Sunday School dooty … Send the sap back to his farm.'[19]

The thread that runs through these and other negative reviews—there were a few, though not many—was that the writers were opposing the gushing excesses of Van Ness and Jewell as much as criticising the music. 'People are reacting to the reviews and not the album, which is not fair,' Ackles lamented to *Phonograph Record*. 'It's just music, it's just a way of communicating, and if it doesn't reach you, it doesn't, and that's valid.'[20]

Critical acclaim doesn't always sell records, and there's often a negative reaction to hype. Sometimes it seems like critics end up speaking to each other, and nobody else listens. One review described Ackles as a darling of the rock press, unknown to the public.[21] In the end, Elektra's use of the Van Ness and Jewell reviews in the promotion of *American Gothic* backfired. Yes, the column inches of praise added up spectacularly, but after a few months there was a discernible shift in attitudes. It was a hard album to promote, in that it had to be consumed whole. In those days, as now, singles or maybe short TV and radio sessions were entry points. You hear one or two representative songs and that's enough to persuade you to buy the album. The problem with *American Gothic* is that there aren't really any representative songs. The shorter, more conventional ballads—'One Night Stand', for example—don't prepare you for 'Ballad Of The Ship Of State'. 'Blues For Billie Whitecloud' sounds nothing like 'Montana Song'. There were no obvious singles. Elektra released 'Oh! California', backed with 'One Night Stand'. Judging by the current collectors' market, there were more promo copies than commercially released copies. On top of that, it didn't really fit with what was happening elsewhere. While Ackles's first two albums could be—and were—connected with other artists then working, *American Gothic* was in a category of its own.

BERNIE TAUPIN It was definitely a difficult sell. It didn't really meld in with what was happening at the time. The kind of music that was selling. It was a completely different animal.[22]

By September 1972, even when discounting the more extreme negative reactions, you could detect an almost audible change of mood. *Well, it's a good album, but not that good. What was all that fuss about?* Which is much what Ackles himself thought.

DAVID ACKLES I appreciate the fact that Chris [Van Ness] was trying to convey his sense of excitement over the album, and he chose as his means the comparison to *Sgt. Pepper* and the overpraising of it on certain levels. I appreciate that, but I can't agree with it, because I just wrote it as an album. I'm not trying to shake the world. I'm not trying to change the course of music. I'm just trying to express what I know about music; what I feel about it with the utmost honesty possible, that's all.[23]

That statement appeared in a piece by Jeff Walker in *Phonograph Record* magazine, which was as much a critique of the media response to *American Gothic* as it was to the album itself. An album that Walker judged equal parts pleasant, depressing, intriguing and boring. He quite liked Ackles and *American Gothic*, but he thought the claims of Van Ness and Jewell, which Elektra magnified, were inflated and misleading and in the end did Ackles a disservice.

> If you buy *American Gothic*, do so without expecting it to knock you on your ass. Just listen, carefully and objectively, and see if something comes to you. If you do buy it to hear the 'album of the decade' and your first reaction doesn't quite see it that way, don't blame Ackles.

> Just think twice the next time about succumbing to far-reaching statements by crusading critics. We should all know better.[24]

From May 1972, Ackles was getting reviews to die for. In July, he returned to his homeland, to embark on what should have been a triumphal victory parade of dates around the country. Yet after just a few months there were unmistakable signs of the energy leaking away.

After the Elektra-sponsored USC launch event, Ackles launched into a round of live appearances—not something he particularly relished. Many were uncomfortable, for all sorts of reasons. There was a particularly awkward experience supporting Mountain. The bills often seemed incongruous, as if still nobody knew where Ackles fitted in. In July, he supported the Dillards in Chicago. He also played at San Francisco's Boarding House, supporting the folk and bluegrass artist John Hartford. He returned to the Main Point, in Bryn Mawr, Pennsylvania, for a short weekend residency. There was a week in August headlining at the Troubadour, which seemed to go well. That same month, he was back at the Bitter End in New York, sharing the bill with Merry Clayton and complaining about the piano. According to Mike Jahn's report in the *Baltimore Sun*, 'He's paying a piano tuner out of his own pocket to come into the Bitter End and reason with the piano, but it hasn't helped. Ackles feels it sitting next door waiting for him like a sniper in the trees.'[25]

Piano problems aside, the Bitter End shows were well-received, with reports again of queues stretching down the street.

There were several shows in October and November, supporting the Canadian comedian David Steinberg. This unlikely double bill appeared at the Academy Of Music in Philadelphia, where Ackles was well-received, but the venue was only a quarter full.[26] Also in October was a support slot with Jackie De Shannon at Utah State University. Once again, the audience was sparse. Closer to home in the same month, Ackles played two nights at the Salt Company coffeehouse in Hollywood, a Christian venue born out of the 60s 'Jesus People' movement.

The Salt Company started in the First Presbyterian Church Of Hollywood (Hollywood Presbyterian), where as a child Ackles had taken part in one of his mother's first church productions. The original venue opened in 1968, and there was a house band of the same name. By 1972, another larger coffeehouse opened on Highland Avenue in Hollywood, one block below Hollywood Boulevard and just across from Hollywood High School. It was at this larger venue that Ackles performed. In common with many coffeehouses of the time, the Salt Company cultivated a folksy vibe, with bare floorboards, wood panelling on the walls, and bentwood chairs around forty-eight-inch cable drums laid on their sides, which served as tables.

Ackles was an atypical Salt Company performer, but he got the booking through Don Williams, a pastor at Hollywood Presbyterian who he knew. The venue usually hosted overtly Christian rock and folk acts, including Larry Norman, Randy Stonehill, and Keith Green. A post-conversion Barry McGuire, of 'Eve Of Destruction' fame, also performed there.

By the Salt Company's standards, Ackles was an unusually high-profile artist, and they made the most of it. Tim McAlmont, who ran the venue, covered Hollywood with promotional posters for Ackles's appearance and was ticketed by the LA County sheriff for stapling posters on power poles on the Sunset Strip. A judge threw out the case on the basis that the Salt Company was a church-affiliated venture that worked with street kids.

Speaking to *Melody Maker* in September, Jac Holzman said of Ackles, 'His moment was going to come. Artistically the moment is on the *American Gothic* album.'[27] Artistically, yes, but commercially, no. And if an artist doesn't sell to expectations, doesn't cover his costs (as Ackles didn't), there will be a reckoning sooner or later.

Just when Ackles's continuing tenure at Elektra began to look uncertain, there were changes at the label, too. In 1970, Holzman sold Elektra to the Kinney Corporation, which had already acquired Warner Bros, Reprise, and Atlantic. A condition was that Elektra be allowed to continue to operate with total autonomy under Holzman's leadership. He was obliged to stay for three years, with an option for another two. By the time the three-year deadline (mid-1973) was visible on the horizon, Holzman was ready to move on. David Anderle had jumped ship for A&M in 1970. Bread and Carly Simon were earning big money for Elektra. The label was taking on a new character. More mainstream, less maverick.

Commercially, *American Gothic* wasn't an outright failure. It didn't sink without a trace. It performed better than Ackles's two previous albums. It even managed a lowly chart placing, making number 167 on the *Billboard* listings. But it didn't sell in a way commensurate with the red-hot expectations stoked by all the critical cheerleading. It just didn't catch the record-buying public's imagination. In those days, before streaming and social media and twenty-four-hour media, modest-selling records tended to disappear quite quickly. For a while, they became just another record in the racks, then they were gone. For an album to live on you needed radio play, hit singles, media attention, cover versions, touring, and informal word-of-mouth promotion—one listener saying 'you'd really like this' to another. *American Gothic* didn't get much radio play, and the media attention had tailed off by December, though the album did make a few 'best of the year' lists. There were no cover versions. Though there were a decent number of covers of songs from *David Ackles*, and Harry Belafonte's version of *Subway To The Country*'s title track, nobody was inclined to take on anything from *American Gothic*. The album's great strength, its particularity, the idea that 'only Ackles could do that', frightened other artists off. Ackles was playing live regularly, but to small audiences. As for word-of-mouth promotion, Ackles always had enthusiastic fans, then as now, but there weren't that many of them.

This must have been a disorientating time for Ackles. The early part of 1972 was spent happily living in an idyllic riverside setting, in the countryside in England, preparing and then recording an album. It went well. He was pleased. Then, for a few months—roughly May to August—he found himself hailed as a genius. After that, things started to slow down. Relations with Elektra faltered. By the end of the year, Ackles was trailing around inappropriate small venues, playing out-of-tune pianos to dwindling audiences, wondering if he'd ever make another record.

But while the year drew to an uncertain, unsatisfactory close professionally, personally it ended in the best of ways. In October, Ackles proposed to Janice at an airport before flying off to a gig. They married on December 9, 1972.

CHAPTER EIGHT

EVERYBODY HAS A STORY

LEAVING ELEKTRA • CLIVE DAVIS AND COLUMBIA • HOME RECORDING WITH DOUGLAS GRAHAM • DEAN TORRENCE AND A JAMES BOND VILLAIN • *FIVE & DIME* • US TV PROFILE • CAST ADRIFT

“

Rather fail with honour than succeed by fraud.

SOPHOCLES

”

June 20, 1973. It's 10am in the morning and David Ackles is sitting in the live room at Paramount Recording Studios, a sixteen-track facility on Santa Monica Boulevard, Los Angeles. His friend Douglas Graham is in the control room with Brian Bruderlin, who owns the studio. Gathered in the live room with Ackles is an unusual mix of musicians, including one-time Bob Dylan sideman Bruce Langhorne and the acclaimed jazz drummer Colin Bailey. And Dean Torrence from Jan & Dean, and the bassist and James Bond villain Putter Smith. There's a three-hour session booked. One of the songs requires a bass voice, but nobody can sing low enough…

What do you do when the critics say you've released the album of the decade and defined a whole new direction in popular music and still hardly anybody listens? This was the quandary Ackles found himself in in late 1972. He agonised over it to the extent that it precipitated writer's block for a while.

DAVID ACKLES I figured there was no way I could surpass what I had done in terms of the reviewers, because they had already committed themselves to it being better than peanut butter. I was literally stymied. Within the first few months after *American Gothic* came out, I couldn't write a song.[1]

Jac Holzman at Elektra Records also ruminated on the same point. The label had invested heavily in Ackles. *David Ackles*, *Subway To The Country*, and *American Gothic* were expensive productions, with their false starts and long lists of session players. And they put some promotional heft into *David Ackles* and *American Gothic* (less so *Subway To The Country*). Contractually, Ackles could have held out for a fourth album on Elektra, and indeed he began discussing it. But it didn't happen. He thought that Elektra should have done more to promote *American Gothic* after the initial rapturous press response, while at the same time realising that the reason they didn't was because he was so in debt to the company after three expensive but poor-selling albums. Though Elektra was the sort of label that would let artists develop over several albums, there was a limit. The outcome wasn't a surprise:

DAVID ACKLES I'd had three strikes at bat with Elektra and got nowhere. The records had all been well reviewed and hadn't done much else, so Jac Holzman and I sat down and decided between us that it might be time to try somewhere new. It was thoroughly mutual. Jac was as frustrated at the lack of sales as I was, and we decided it was an opportune moment to move on.[2]

JAC HOLZMAN We did everything we could for *American Gothic*, but it didn't do anywhere near as well as a record of that quality should have done... If we couldn't get anything going after that, I had no idea what we could do with him. That's why we parted company, but very amicably. There were artists on the label, Ackles being one of them, that I had real regrets about that we were never able to connect him to an audience. Part of it was the personality of the man—very introspective—just very content to do what he was doing.[3]

DAVID ACKLES I remain enormously grateful to Jac Holzman for everything he did personally on my behalf. I don't believe anything more could have been done to make me a commercial success. It just wasn't on the cards.[4]

The conversation between Ackles and Holzman happened in late 1972 or early 1973. Elektra formally terminated Ackles's contract on February 5, 1973. Holzman himself was gone by July, and the label lost its distinct identity thereafter, even though there were many more great releases. Ackles was disappointed, even though the relationship ended cordially. But almost immediately a saviour appeared on the horizon. Clive Davis, president of Columbia Records since 1967, was a longtime admirer of Ackles. On hearing he was a free agent, Davis stepped in with an offer.

Ackles signed, saying a few months later that he did so on the condition that he could record at home, removed from the usual pressures that come with decisions about producers and arrangers. He wanted to make a more personal record, and he wanted control. He wanted to not only write, arrange, and perform, as he did on *American Gothic*. He also wanted to produce. There wasn't much money in the deal, but Ackles was optimistic. Although *American Gothic* had not been the commercial success that he and Elektra hoped it would be, it elevated his status, particularly in the USA. Starting again on another label, there was good reason to believe that Ackles's next album would cement his position as an important songwriting voice.

DOUGLAS GRAHAM Clive gave him a deal . . . but there was very little money, because of the non-commercial perception of David's work . . . you know how record labels are. If they can't pigeonhole it, package it, market it as a particular genre, they're not interested. But I think the deal was, Clive gave David $50,000 or something, out of which he had to deliver a finished album.[5]

The newlyweds David and Janice had moved to a house in Pacific Palisades, near the ocean, where they stayed for about five years. It was a beautiful spot. Avocadoes and limes grew around the pool in the back garden, and raccoons gathered at a window at night—on the other side of which sat Ackles's piano—as if they were fans of his music. Recording at home is commonplace now, but not so much in 1973, so his decision to record most of his new album in the Pacific Palisades house—helped by Douglas Graham, credited as production supervisor—was unconventional.

JANICE VOGEL ACKLES He thought at the time he would like to have . . . a less *studio* sort of sound, for lack of a better term, and he thought it might be interesting to record at our house, and also for economic reasons, as he was functioning as producer, he thought he might see a little more money upfront. But mainly it was for the sound, and he thought it might have a sound he was really looking for by doing it that way ... we set up in the living room, and got a bunch of baffles, and we were in a somewhat rural place anyway, so it seemed to work out pretty well, but there was some studio work, obviously, but the vast majority of it was done in our living room.[6]

DOUGLAS GRAHAM Well, you can't make much of an album for $50,000 ... so he had this dilemma, and he said, 'Do you have any idea what we can do?' I said, 'I don't know how you're going to do this,' and he said, 'Can you help me?' and I said, 'I can try.' I had a new four-track TEAC machine. It was quarter-inch tape. I said, 'If we record this at home and get a really great piano in there ... if we get some decent microphones, I think we can record the basic tracks at your house and go in the studio and finish it up. That way we can record on the cheap, but you can still make a living from this album until the next one comes along.' So, we did that, and I was tasked to find musicians.[7]

Once the decision to record at home was made, things moved fast. It's likely that work was underway by March 1973.* Through calling in favours and word of mouth, Graham and Ackles drafted an incongruously expert cast of supporting musicians for a low-budget, home-recorded venture. Some were brilliant young orchestral players at the start of their careers. Others were storied veterans who had been working for decades.

DOUGLAS GRAHAM I got a friend of mine, Loren Pickford ... a wonderful musician, primarily a jazz sax player, but he could play multiple instruments. So, I recruited him, and he got for me Colin Bailey, who was in my opinion one of the best jazz drummers of the twentieth century ... and he got a

---

* Janice Ackles told me in 2002 that she'd discovered a file of notes about *Five & Dime* and realised that it was recorded four months after she and David married, which was in December 1972.

bass player called Putter Smith, who was brilliant. And I got Bruce Langhorne.[8]

The rhythm section alone boasted an impressive pedigree. By the time he played for Ackles, the British-born Bailey had drummed for Winifred Atwell, Benny Goodman, Dizzy Gillespie, Frank Sinatra, Chet Baker, and dozens of others. Smith's credits included Thelonious Monk, Art Blakey, Duke Ellington, Burt Bacharach, Ray Charles, Sonny & Cher, The Beach Boys, and The Righteous Brothers. In a curious adjunct to his musical career, two years earlier Smith had played the assassin Mr. Kidd in the James Bond film *Diamonds Are Forever*.

Ackles called in the Trojan String Quartet from USC, who had played at his and Janice's wedding a few months previously. Red Rhodes played pedal steel. Another familiar, if surprising, name in the credits is Dean Torrence, of Jan & Dean. Ackles didn't know Torrence but cold-called him as he needed a classic surf voice on the album.[9] Lou Anne Neill, who later worked with Frank Zappa and became the principal harpist of the Los Angeles Philharmonic, was at the beginning of her career. Fiddler Bobby Bruce was born in 1925 and had been playing professionally since just after World War II. Like Ackles, he had been half of a childhood vaudeville duo with his sister.

More than twenty musicians appeared on *Five & Dime*. Though they were never all playing in the house at the same time, it was quite a squeeze, and Ackles and Graham had to improvise. There were compromises, but what they got in return was time, and freedom from the tyranny of the studio clock. The sessions were relaxed and elongated, sometimes running on into the early hours. A few months later, being interviewed in the same house where he recorded the album, Ackles called this a luxury.

DAVID ACKLES Oh yes, right here, this is the room. There was a string quartet right there in front of the fireplace, and instead of that lamp, we had an umbrella hanging up with some foam inside it, so the drummer had his own little booth set up under that. We had a concert grand piano, guitar here, bass in the hall, then we closed the door to the bathroom hall and used it as a sort of echo chamber. And the control room is in the office around that corner.[10]

DOUGLAS GRAHAM We rented a nine-foot Steinway piano, from Studio Instrument Rentals. It was the same piano that Rubenstein used to use whenever he played in Los Angeles… it was quite an undertaking. I set up my machine, we got some really good mics—we got a Neumann U47 for the voice and piano—anyway, everybody set up in different rooms, so we could hear each other but we couldn't see each other.[11]

JANICE VOGEL ACKLES They [the musicians] weren't all recorded at once, as I recall, but at any given time there were usually six or seven working.[12]

Apart from the more complex 'Aberfan', all the basic tracks and some overdubs were recorded in the Pacific Palisades house. This involved sub-mixing some instruments into a single track and bouncing between tracks. Though by 1973 most professional recording studios were at least sixteen-track, recording onto four-track had been normal practice through much of the 1960s. So, in a sense, Ackles and Graham were reviving an approach that had only gone out of common usage a few years previously. But their makeshift recording environment lacked almost all the features of a professional studio, like a separate recording booth, outboard equipment, and monitor speakers. The improvised control room was a rudimentary setup. Graham sat at a small desk in the corner of Ackles's study, on which the TEAC four-track was placed. To the left of the desk, a shelf in a bookcase was cleared to hold some bits and pieces, including a pre-amp. They did not use compressors.

Graham's friend Bruce Langhorne provided some inspiration. He had recorded the soundtrack to Peter Fonda's Western *The Hired Hand* on a two-track Revox tape machine two years earlier, playing along to a black and white copy of the film, layering up tracks of organ, piano, banjo, fiddle, harmonica, recorder, and Appalachian dulcimer.

DOUGLAS GRAHAM He played all the instruments. And he just bounced tracks back and forth, and it's a stunning score. The music is superb. So, I knew it could be done. If you could do it on a two-track, you could do it on a four-track.[13]

Langhorne's primitive technical approach allowed him to create a soundtrack that conjured a dusty, hazy ambience that matched the film. Ackles and Graham's home-recorded effort achieved a close-up intimacy. What it loses in technical sophistication it gains in that sense of being right in the room, with the musicians in front of you. Ackles wanted to do something more personal, and he succeeded—as if he has invited the listener to his house to hear his new songs.

DOUGLAS GRAHAM So, the piano's going into one channel; David's voice going into another channel; the drums are going into another channel; and the bass—stand-up bass—into another channel. Somehow, I recorded some acoustic guitars and Bruce Langhorne on electric guitar at David's house. How I did that I don't know. There's one flute part that Loren Pickford played. We did that at David's house. I might have bounced some [tracks]. I must have.[14]

With the bulk of the recording done at home, Ackles and Graham took the tapes to Paramount Recording Studios on Santa Monica Boulevard. Here, they transferred the four-tracks to sixteen-track to create space for overdubs, and recorded the album's most ambitious arrangement, 'Aberfan'.

Also recorded in Paramount were the backing vocals for the surf spoof 'Surf's Down', featuring Dean Torrence. Bruce Johnston of The Beach Boys—with whom Ackles was friendly—was due to sing, but he couldn't make it on the day because he had a cold, hence the call to Torrence.

When recording was finished, Ackles and Graham mixed the album in two straight days, at Paramount. They then teamed up with Doug Sax to master the album in a single overnight session.

Though the Columbia deal was modest commercially, Ackles felt some security in the knowledge that Clive Davis, Columbia's president, was a supporter. Davis had been at Columbia since the mid-60s and was a heavyweight music business powerbroker. By the time he offered Ackles a deal, he'd already signed Janis Joplin, Laura Nyro, Aerosmith, Santana, and Earth, Wind & Fire—among many others. In 1973, Davis was one of the most powerful people in American music, but on a day in May he walked into his office at Columbia to be told he was fired. The reason was an entanglement of allegations about payola, fraudulent invoicing, and using company funds to pay for his son's bar mitzvah. In time, Davis was exonerated, and he returned to thrive at Arista, RCA, and elsewhere. But that was in the future. By June 1973, Davis, who had signed Ackles, was out of the picture. This news filtered through to Ackles while he was still recording *Five & Dime*. American Federation Of Musicians records show that three three-hour studio sessions at Paramount took place between June 14 and 20. In those nine hours, Ackles recorded 'Aberfan' and the overdubs on all the other songs. He would have heard about Davis's departure just before those sessions.

Unusually for such a senior executive in a company as big as Columbia, Davis took a personal interest in the artists he signed. This was generally to the artists' benefit, but in Ackles's case, the relationship with Davis did not have time to mature to the extent that Ackles got integrated into the company. When the album was finished, he delivered the masters to Columbia without knowing a single person there. He was stranded at a label that didn't appreciate him, with a new album almost ready for release. 'I was a strange, alien presence to them,' he later noted, 'and I equally didn't understand what made Columbia tick.'[15]

Ackles's former Elektra labelmate Tom Rush had moved to Columbia in 1970. Though he recorded four albums for the label, like Ackles he never felt at home. 'Elektra was a small shop where everybody knew everybody. Columbia operated on layers and layers of bureaucracy. It was hard to figure out who did what.'[16]

Around the same time as Davis's departure, Ackles was hit with another stroke of bad luck, entirely unrelated, when his management dropped him without warning or explanation. Ackles was a great musician, but he lacked the temperament and experience to navigate the labyrinthine intricacies, competing commercial concerns, and vaunting egos of the music business. Just when he needed a manager to help him find a way to engage with the new regime at Columbia, and to help organise album promotion, he was on his own. The timing couldn't have been worse.

DOUGLAS GRAHAM When a new regime comes in, they kill all the projects of the old regime. If you're not a superstar, nobody wants to take the blame for any failure. Consequently, there was no promotion on the record. Nothing happened... they could have created a niche for him, they could have promoted a tour, they could have done a lot of things, but they didn't. *Five & Dime* went nowhere. There was no promotion whatsoever.[17]

JANICE VOGEL ACKLES It was kind of a double whammy, if you will, both in Clive Davis leaving, as he was the major force behind signing David, and therefore the impetus for pushing the album went awry, as well as the fact that David's manager disappeared about the same time. Both of those things were quite devastating, particularly the loss of the manager, because it left David just hanging there, and I think—like a lot of artists—it was hard for him to push himself, in terms of the promotion, and the marketing. He had left that to the 'professionals'.[18]

Speaking just a week after *Five & Dime* was released, Ackles was adopting a wait-and-see posture toward Columbia. At that point there had been no promotional activity. He didn't yet know that there would be hardly any, and that the album would fail commercially. He was reserving judgment about the label while trying to remain optimistic. But even then he recognised the tension, understanding that Columbia wouldn't invest in promotional support unless they saw signs that the album was attracting attention. Yet few albums attract attention without promotional support.[19]

In late August and early September, Ackles was back at the Troubadour, relegated again to a supporting role after the previous year's bill-topping residency. This time he was second on the bill to Dave Mason, formerly of Traffic. There were sporadic gigs for the rest of the year, but Ackles's live work rate was nowhere near the level it reached in 1969, or the second half of 1972 when he toured in support of *American Gothic*. For anyone paying attention, it was obvious that his profile was slipping. As if to underline this, in September the *Kansas City Star* published a long feature wondering what had happened to *American Gothic*—an album then not much more than a year old. The tone and content are illuminating. The writer, Robert W Butler, felt it necessary to explain who Ackles was ('a former protest/folk singer') and that *American Gothic* was buried with praise. He then hinted at distribution problems, saying it was hard to find the album on release and now—a year later—it was even harder. He liked the album a lot, but the whole thrust of the piece was that Ackles was an obscure figure who once made an album that got a lot of praise but had already all but vanished.

A month or so after this feature was published, Columbia released *Five & Dime*. Or rather, let it loose in the wild, where it was ill-equipped to survive on its own. This time, there were no full-page adverts, no launch events, no tours, no radio sessions, no convivial lunches for selected journalists at the record company's expense, no promotional seven-inch singles for radio play. The campaign for *Five & Dime* amounted to a cursory mail-out of review copies. Hardly surprising, then, that the press response compared to that for *American Gothic* was muted. From May to December 1972, *American Gothic* had dozens, maybe hundreds of reviews, most of them pitched somewhere between positive and adulatory. *Five & Dime* got a handful. True, they were generally positive, but there was no sense of occasion.

Chris Van Ness, whose extravagant accolade in the *Los Angeles Free*

Press had ignited the media hysteria about *American Gothic*, restricted himself to a paragraph of more reserved praise for *Five & Dime*. *Rolling Stone* thought the album 'quietly satisfying'. *Variety* and *Billboard* each afforded the album two sentences. *Walrus*, a 'progressive music newsletter' out of Philadelphia, put the album in its 'merit' category—the second to top ranking. In the UK, where the album was never released anyway, there was a *Melody Maker* feature. And the ever-loyal Derek Jewell gave over part of his January 20, 1974, edition of *Sounds Interesting* on BBC Radio 3 to playing extracts 'from a new American album by David Ackles'.[20]

With no support at the label and no management, Ackles became desperate. He and Graham contacted TEAC to demonstrate what they had accomplished by using the company's four-track to record basic tracks at home. The idea was to get TEAC to sponsor a promotional tour for *Five & Dime*, thus emphasising the quality of the tape machine and the possibilities for saving money by recording in this way. But nothing came of it.

The one beacon of hope in this disappointing response was the longest television appearance of Ackles's career. *One Of A Kind* was a series of thirty-minute artist performances broadcast on KCET public television in California and widely syndicated. Jim Croce was another subject. The Ackles edition was first broadcast in November 1973, just after the release of *Five & Dime*. Ackles, sitting at the piano in a brown jacket and light-coloured open-necked shirt, performs six songs from the album: 'Everybody Has A Story', 'I've Been Loved', 'Berry Tree', 'Jenna Saves', 'Aberfan', and 'One Good Woman's Man'. The set is completed with four older songs: 'Subway To The Country', 'Laissez-Faire', 'Oh, California!', and the traditional set closer, 'Be My Friend'. Ackles performs on a bare stage in a small auditorium, with three rows of seats containing an audience of not much more than fifty people. This might have been a facility in USC.* He looks confident and at ease, smiling a lot and joking self-deprecatingly

* Several people remember the show as being recorded in a theatre in USC, though, judging from memories of the set list, this was more likely the Elektra launch of *American Gothic* in 1972. Having said that, there's a good chance that *One Of A Kind* was recorded at the same venue.

between songs, as in this moment between 'Laissez-Faire' and 'Aberfan':

> Enough of this levity. I once did a show in Pennsylvania, which is, heaven knows, a serious place. Out in Bryn Mawr, which is as serious as you can get. And that's almost terminal seriousness. And I was playing... a few songs I had written since the last time I was there. And in the end of one of these... lively numbers [someone in the audience said] we came here to be depressed. So, lest you get too lively, let me depress you.*

One Of A Kind was repeated frequently throughout 1974 and 1975 and must have been seen by a lot of people, though it didn't do much to lift the profile of *Five & Dime*. The show was still being shown after Ackles's recording career had finished.

To reinforce the idea that *Five & Dime* is an outlier in Ackles's body of recorded work, the album's artwork departs from type in not having a photo of the artist anywhere. Instead, we see what appear to be two photo-realist paintings of a shop front on the front and back covers, faintly reminiscent of Edward Hopper. (In fact, the two images are parts of a single painting). The title of *Five & Dime* and the idea to have a painting of a shop on the cover came from Janice. The painting was by Mike Henderson, using the name Michael Wasp. The part used for the front cover shows an empty, shabby-looking, double-fronted store, with a red, white, and green canopy. There is no text—no album title or artist name.

DAVID ACKLES I thought it would be interesting to have an absolutely blank cover—not blank, but that did not contain any other information than the picture itself, which I think is arresting. But we had lots of trouble. That's why that awful sticker is there: 'New from David Ackles.'[21]

---

* A copy of *One Of A Kind* is archived in the Paley Centre, New York. I am indebted to Richie Unterberger, who viewed this copy and sent me a full account of it.

The back cover shows a similar but not quite the same shop front. There is no canopy, the windows above are different, and the tiles around the shop are pale blue, as opposed to the maroon of the front cover image. The painting was based on a photo of adjacent shops.

In the back cover image, the shop is open, and we see Ackles illustrated as the proprietor, standing in the doorway wearing sunglasses and a vivid Hawaiian shirt. The sign above the shop front reads 'DT Ackles, Five & Dime'. Taped in the window to Ackles's right are two posters—one titled '5¢', listing side one's song, the other titled '10¢', with side two's songs. The cover gives no sense whatsoever about what sort of music might be hidden on the album within. Douglas Graham didn't like it, but Ackles did. Subsequent CD reissues have mistakenly but understandably reversed the images, so that the original back cover with the track listing becomes the front cover.

As with *American Gothic* and *Subway To The Country*, Ackles chose to open *Five & Dime* with one of the album's more challenging listens. 'Everybody Has A Story' deploys the strict rhythm used on 'Laissez-Faire', from *David Ackles*, to propel what sounds like a disturbed cabaret band through two minutes of fraught anxiety. The lyrics are a withering put down of a barroom bore. 'No one wants to listen, nor do we.'

The switch in mood on song two is another familiar Ackles device, one he utilised across all his albums. This time, after unsettling us with 'Everybody Has A Story', he charms us with the gently sad chamber-pop ballad 'I've Been Loved'. With its delicate piano figure, string quartet, and classical guitar flourishes, it's a poignant reflection on the loneliness of old age. Regretful but not lachrymose.

JIM O'ROURKE It's probably the saddest song I've heard in my life, but so precise, so profound, and every bit of fat's been cut away from the sentiment.[22]

'Jenna Saves', more than any other song on *Five & Dime*, evokes *American*

Gothic. The bustling, chasing-itself piano is redolent of the earlier record's title track, and the saturnine parable, leavened with sarcastic humour, fits its mood. This time, Ackles takes aim at Jenna, a miser who renounces all else—including a suitor and love—for money. Ackles is supported by urgent electric guitar, bass, and drums, with brass overdubs.

DAVID ACKLES I like parables, little morality plays, and I thought it was moderately amusing in its own way, though it wasn't about anyone specific.[23]

On the most atypical of Ackles's albums, 'Surf's Down' is the most atypical song. A credible pastiche of early Beach Boys and Jan & Dean records, with a middle-eight Brian Wilson would have been proud of in 1965, 'Surf's Down' is a gentle poke at 60s surfers who had grown up but not moved on. Perhaps surprisingly, Ackles himself had been a surfer, and even in 1973 he sometimes still took his board out. To a backing of electric piano, bass, drums, and electric guitar, Ackles transforms his normally austere, throaty voice into a suitably adenoidal whine to deliver lines about Dick Dale records, leaking wetsuits, and disappearing knots. Torrence's falsetto and Johnston's help with arranging lend the whole thing a veneer of authenticity. Taken on its own merits, it's a pitch-perfect surf skit. Mike Jahn, writing in *Cue* magazine, thought it 'hysterically funny'. *Rolling Stone* judged it an 'outright failure'.

DAVID ACKLES Bruce and I sat at the piano working out different vocal lines for every song on the album, how he would have done it, à la the Beach Boys—and we fell down. It's got to be one of the funniest sessions we've ever done. The sad part was that he called me the day we were scheduled to record—we had to do that one in the studio, because of the multiple voices—and he had this cold [and] he could barely speak.[24]

DOUGLAS GRAHAM There's one little bit in the song where it goes 'surf's down' in a baritone voice. Who's going to sing that? Nobody had a voice that low except me, and my voice wasn't that low, so we went in the studio at nine o'clock in the morning to do that overdub, and I said, 'I can't get my voice down that low,' so I got a little bottle of cognac and I took a couple of shots of cognac to drop my voice half an octave so I could actually hit that note twice.[25]

For 'Berry Tree', Ackles assumes an old-time vernacular and delves into his church music roots again, as he had on 'Family Band' from *American Gothic*. Red Rhodes (pedal steel) and Bobby Bruce (fiddle) mesh complementary counter melodies over a country rhythm. Brass overdubs flesh out the arrangement as the song moves through its three verses. It's a song of the rhythm of life, faith, and family, with the berry tree a symbol of constancy and flourishing. A short, simply constructed song of three verses, three choruses, and a short linking instrumental that serves also as an intro and an outro. Across his recording career, Ackles delivered several songs that might have found favour in Nashville. This is the last of them.

Side one closes with 'One Good Woman's Man', another nostalgic piano-and-strings ballad, with Ackles singing in the first person of a brief one-night stand. This is the closest he gets to adopting the drifter persona that recurs through earlier albums. He's not quite in character, though. This time the regret isn't pitched against dreams not yet dead or macho posturing. It's just regret.

Side two opens with the first of the album's two issue songs. 'Run Pony Run' sets off with *Five & Dime*'s most zeitgeist-capturing arrangement, a country-rock canter of bass, drums, piano, electric guitar, and pedal steel. Ackles sings another of his oblique protest lyrics, this time quietly lambasting the rise in the industrial slaughtering of horses for food prompted by the rise in beef prices.

DAVID ACKLES They're hunted with helicopters and what have you—it's quite mechanised. They just round them up and slaughter them and make dog food out of them.[26]

'Aberfan' is *Five & Dime*'s centrepiece. It recounts the Welsh mining disaster of 1966, when a coal slag heap collapsed on a school, killing 144 people, including 116 children. The Welsh writer Tom Davies was a rookie reporter when he was dispatched to Aberfan on the day of the disaster. Decades later, he wrote of the desolation. Policeman crying. Miners digging to uncover the buried school full of children and their teachers. Pausing every thirty seconds and standing in silence to listen for survivors.[27] Ackles read about the tragedy in a feature in *Life* magazine a few months after the event. He was deeply shocked, but he filed away his feelings until 1972, when he sat down to write his song. It's a risky subject for anyone to take on. A black horror looms over the tragedy to this day, and in 1972 it was still a raw, recent memory. Writing about it ran the risk of slipping into mawkish sentimentality on the one hand or of exploiting unspeakable loss for art's sake on the other.

Ackles's comment on the calamity was understated. Lyrically, his quiet excoriation of corporate greed and neglect fingers the banal incompetence and corner-cutting that precipitated the landslip as much as the rain that washed the slag down the hill. Phone calls to Swansea and cups of tea. Musically, Ackles harks back to the mood of *American Gothic*, with a bleak, sinister, suspenseful arrangement. The menacing, stabbing woodwind; the sombre, pounding bass piano notes like a tolling bell. 'Aberfan' had started out as a longer song, which Ackles called a ten-minute polemic, with another section about the My Lai atrocities in Vietnam. By containing his anger and sadness in more modest proportions, by avoiding the big statement, Ackles increases the impact.

Technically, 'Aberfan' is an anomaly on *Five & Dime*. The only song wholly recorded in a professional recording studio, it has a fuller sound and is the album's most complex and challenging composition. It bears hardly any relation to anything else in rock music and, the geographical specificity of the subject matter aside, sounds oddly stateless. If it were possible to listen to 'Aberfan' without contextual knowledge, you would have no idea where the music came from.

'Aberfan' was recorded in a single three-hour session on June 15. Ackles played, sang, and conducted a fifteen-piece chamber ensemble comprising the rhythm section of Bailey and Smith, harpist Lou Anne Neill, a wind octet, and a string quartet. It took two takes.* They also made time to record overdubs for 'House Above The Strand' and 'I've Been Loved'.

After the compressed drama of 'Abervan', Ackles moves into a run of four first-person ballads that close out his recording career. 'House Above The Strand' was a recently written autobiographical love song. Ackles said it was inspired by the very house in which he recorded the album, the 'Strand' being the beach. A short ballad that builds up to two crescendos of lush strings, with Ackles at his most impassioned, it is the one song on *Five & Dime* that sounds like it is struggling with the limitations of the improvised recording environment. It deserves a full orchestra, and the voice sounds like it needs a wider band of frequencies.

'A Photograph Of You' is a little longer and tends toward maudlin, where 'House Above The Strand' is heartfelt. Bailey adds vibraphone to the piano and woodwind. It's an example of Ackles using his life experience to inform the song while falling short of writing strictly autobiographically.

DAVID ACKLES I was going through some effects after I moved here … and I came across an old photograph of someone that I had once thought I was desperately in love with, and couldn't live without, and had managed to live an extra fifteen years since! But it did bring back a sort of keen feeling, so I wrote a song about that feeling, from that standpoint.[28]

'Such A Woman' is probably the one older song on *Five & Dime*, recorded

* AFM records indicate the session took place between 10am and 1pm on June 20, with the following musicians: Patrick Smith, double bass; Colin Bailey, percussion; Georgia Mohammar, flute; James Kanter, clarinet; Robert Henderson, French horn; Todd Miller, French horn; Earle Dumler, oboe, English horn; Dawn Weiss, piccolo flute; John Daley, trombone; Russell Kidd, trumpet; Lou Anne Neill, harp; Barbara Thomason, viola; Cynthia Cole Daley, first violin; Donald Ambroson, second violin; Robert L. Adcock, cello.

during the *Subway To The Country* sessions in 1969 but not included on that album. That earlier version grew to epic proportions with Fred Myrow's swelling arrangement. The second time around, with the more modest recording facilities at his disposal, Ackles and his four-track tape machine couldn't match Myrow's grandiose sweep, but he sings with passion to a piano-and-brass arrangement, with Bruce Langhorne contributing economical lead guitar flourishes in the manner of Steve Cropper.

Ackles exits with 'Postcards', inspired by his stay in England when recording *American Gothic*. He wrote the first verse and chorus on the flight home to Los Angeles after leaving Farthings. It's a small-hours, man-alone-at-the-piano type of song. Langhorne joins in with subtle guitar textures that evoke Doug Hastings's playing on 'Be My Friend'. An understated sign-off to a modest record.

Ackles left the recording business not clamouring for attention but unostentatiously presenting his lovingly crafted work. It sounds like the work of an artist comfortable in his own skin. He knows he's good, and he doesn't feel the need to shout about it.

Artistically, *Five & Dime* was a qualified success. The songs were impeccably written, as usual, and Ackles—emboldened by his experience with *American Gothic*—arranged with confidence. For the most part, he and Graham turned the production constraints into assets.

JANICE VOGEL ACKLES I think there were some production issues, and I think maybe that's because they were trying to bring it in for very little money. Some of it turned out the way he wanted it to, some of it didn't. I think maybe he would have liked to do a little bit more with it, but I think, overall, he was pretty satisfied.[29]

With *Five & Dime*, Ackles wanted to make a more personal, intimate record—a step back from the big statement of *American Gothic*. In this, he succeeded. The technical conditions in which the record was made, without compression and studio reverb, contribute to a natural, unmediated sound. Of his albums, *Five & Dime* conforms least to type. Though there are songs and arrangement flourishes that could only have come from Ackles, it's a smaller, warmer, even happier record, at least in places, compared to its three predecessors. The Ackles drifter—the down-on-his-luck, disappointed, phlegmatic, tough but vulnerable man of the world, a recurring character in multiple guises across *David Ackles*, *Subway To The Country*, and *American Gothic*—does not appear. The theatrical eccentricities—though present—are more contained. And though the album isn't short of Ackles's seriousness, there's the mordant humour of 'Jenna Saves' and 'Surf's Down'. This was all intentional.

DAVID ACKLES The songs are intended to be much more easy to get into, and I felt that it was time I lightened up a bit and made the album a little more accessible. Columbia didn't suggest that I made things more commercial, for which I'm most grateful.[30]

JANICE VOGEL ACKLES Well, I think part of that was that David had more control, and that made him more relaxed. Obviously, he'd done some other albums, so he felt more secure, and quite honestly, we'd just gotten married, and most of that music was written just prior to us getting married and shortly thereafter ... I think he felt good about the fact that we were finally married, and things were looking very optimistic for him, and I just think he felt really good about his life, so that's probably reflected in the music.[31]

Graham was pleased with the album he and Ackles delivered to Columbia, though not with the final sound of the record and subsequent reissues. The original pressing was on flimsy vinyl and sounded weak compared to the master tape they provided.* This might have contributed to its commercial

* A digital transfer of the original quarter-inch master tape Ackles and Graham sent to Columbia has a warmer sound, with more bass.

failure. Nobody covered any of the songs on *Five & Dime*, just as nobody had covered any from *American Gothic*. With little promotion, few reviews, and no release in the UK (where Ackles had his biggest audience), *Five & Dime* slipped almost immediately into obscurity.

DOUGLAS GRAHAM They could have launched in the UK and done much better if they'd had any creative chops... obviously they had the means to do it, if they had the inclination to do it. His music was not popular, and unless they can pigeonhole you ... they didn't know where to put him. Airplay was out of the question, which was very disappointing, but the important thing to him was to do the music he wanted to do and do it well, and he did.[32]

The fissure between talent and sales that was a feature of Ackles's recording career from the start became a chasm. By this time, the first wave of singer-songwriters with whom Ackles was sometimes associated were losing steam. For every Jackson Browne or James Taylor, who came a little later and sold millions of records, there was a Tim Hardin or a Tim Rose or a David Blue, laying down their weary tunes to ever-diminishing artistic and commercial returns. It wasn't like that for Ackles. There was a commercial decline—*Five & Dime* performed poorly compared to the previous three albums, which had only performed modestly anyway. But there was no discernible artistic decline. He left the stage maybe just a step down from the very peak of his powers, with every indication that he was capable of more great albums. And he was expecting to continue. He didn't think at the time it was released that *Five & Dime* would be his swan song. But by early 1974, Ackles had been dropped by Columbia and was without a record deal. He was never offered another one.

CHAPTER NINE

DOWN RIVER

SONGWRITING VS SCRIPTWRITING • MUSICAL THEATRE • CAR ACCIDENT • *SISTER AIMEE* • LUNG CANCER

"

One must live well to know what living is.

BERTOLT BRECHT, *THE THREEPENNY OPERA*

"

Early on a Sunday afternoon in June 1991, David Ackles is in a rehearsal space in the Dorothy Chandler Pavillion, Los Angeles. He's a little nervous. In a few minutes, the first reading of his musical, Sister Aimee, will commence. Ackles has already been working on it for years. He will continue to work on it for several more years after this day. It's quite an occasion. There are twenty-two new songs. A cast of twenty-six. In the programme, Ackles has included an invitation for audience members to send written feedback to his home address…

To almost all of Ackles's small following, it appeared as if his career as a singer-songwriter shuddered to an abrupt stop after the release of *Five & Dime* at the end of 1973. It wasn't quite like that, though he never made another record. Ackles still had a publishing contract with Warners, and he reverted to how he had started in late 1967, pitching songs for other artists to record.

JANICE VOGEL ACKLES David was not one to sit around and moan, but he was very devastated actually and had hoped to do another album, but what he did instead was he just rolled with it, and probably, with hindsight, maybe he should have been more aggressive, and gone schmoozing with the right people, but he didn't do that. He was under contract for, I think, another ten years, with Warner Bros as a writer, so what he would do is go to their weekly writing meetings and he'd turn in tons of songs hoping to get covers, and he did some really great material that, as far as I can tell, they never did anything with. That's how he mollified himself with the creative part of it—he just kept turning out material. He really pushed himself, because he loved songwriting.[1]

Ackles's career as a recording artist had started almost by happenstance when he signed to Elektra in 1967. He hadn't been looking for a deal. It's likely he didn't look for one in 1974, either. Later, he spoke of a sort of resignation, as if giving in to the heavy hand of fate. Like many artists, the business side of self-promotion did not come easily to him. And he didn't have any management.

JANICE VOGEL ACKLES It's not that he was shy or didn't have confidence in his work. He just wasn't somebody to work the room. I don't remember him talking to anyone else.[2]

DOUGLAS GRAHAM I think he gave up ... if you didn't get label support, if you didn't get tour support, if you didn't get publicity—the machinery working for you—you were out of luck. For David, I think the writing was on the wall. There was no market for him. No one knew how to market him. I think an audience could have been developed for him, but it would have been a niche market.

If he was despondent about it, he didn't indicate that to me. He wasn't in it for stardom, he was in it for music. He wanted to do the music he wanted to do and was maybe a little bullheaded about that. He probably could have compromised and gone a more popular route. But maybe not, because his music was authentic and anything else would have been inauthentic.[3]

In 1974, after Ackles had been dropped by Columbia, there were a few stray late reviews for *Five & Dime*. In February of that year, *Melody Maker* ran a long interview feature, anticipating a UK release for the album that never happened. It was the last substantial UK press coverage for Ackles until the Elektra albums were reissued on CD in 1993. In March, *High Fidelity* judged the album's lyrics 'wry and clever'.* The 1973 TV special was shown several times a year across the US in 1974 and 1975. Appearances in listings were sometimes accompanied by quotes from the Chris Van Ness and Derek Jewell reviews of *American Gothic*. An indication of the near invisibility of *Five & Dime* was a 1976 feature titled 'Blasts From The

* The Ackles review appeared alongside a put down of Jobriath's hyped debut on Elektra, less than two years after Ackles was the object of the label's promotional attentions.

Past That Never Took Off', which included an assessment of *American Gothic*, describing it as Ackles's most recent album.[4]

For a few more years, you could catch Ackles playing occasional low-key college and coffeehouse shows in the Los Angeles area. On April 1, 1977, he shared a bill with blues guitarist Paul Geremia at Golden West College, Huntington Beach. But it was the sound of a career winding down, a once nearly famous musician drifting into obscurity. By 1979, only *Five & Dime* remained on catalogue. Nobody recorded the songs he pitched to Warners, and they remain unheard. Ackles, reflecting toward the end of his life, seemed philosophical.

DAVID ACKLES They [Columbia] just didn't know what to do with me, and after nothing happened with *Five & Dime*, they released me. And I just found it was hard to get a deal. A part of it, I would have to say, was my own doing. I didn't come away from Columbia thinking, *Well, by God, I'm going to go elsewhere!* There was so little support that I thought to myself, *Maybe this isn't what you're intended to do*. Of course, I should have been more aggressive, but in retrospect I took it as more of a sign than I should have. It was kind of hard to get motivated, but I kept at it. Finally, I decided I had to make a living and started to look at other things.[5]

I got really discouraged and decided that I wouldn't do any more performing. Instead, I concentrated on writing songs for other people. After my contract ran out, I quit the music business entirely.[6]

JIM FRIEDRICH For a while he just stopped doing music. One time I visited his house, and he was working at USC, and he had a loom and was weaving rugs. He said he was happy, and he'd put music aside, but a part of me wondered.[7]

Those 'other things' Ackles did to make a living included scriptwriting, teaching, and fundraising. But although his career as a recording singer-songwriter was now behind him, writing songs and trying to find an audience for them was not. The Columbia press release for *Five & Dime* said Ackles's one remaining ambition was to write a stage musical. At the time, it wasn't the *only* one, but it was an ambition, nonetheless. Ackles reverted to this first love, and for the rest of his life he expended much of his considerable creative energy writing and developing stage musicals.

In 1976 or 1977, Ackles recorded some demos at Bruce Langhorne's studio, with Douglas Graham helping with production. This was separate from his Warners staff songwriter work.

DOUGLAS GRAHAM He was working on a medieval concept thing called *Allendor*. David played, and I got a couple of friends of mine to play guitar parts and lute parts—stuff like that. I don't know what ever happened to those tapes. The studio ended up closing years later because the co-owner—or the guy who bought it from Bruce—died, and all the tapes were in the vault in the studio. Those tapes are gone.[8]

Ackles was still pushing a retitled version of this project in the mid-1980s. But, in the meantime, life was changing. Ackles turned forty in 1977. He and Janice had a son. Middle-aged and with new parental responsibilities and no regular income, Ackles had to start afresh. Douglas Graham, though younger, found himself in a similar position. They started to write scripts together.

DOUGLAS GRAHAM In 1977, both of us were new fathers. We had to make a living, and the business was not hospitable to either one of us anymore ... and David couldn't get a deal. We did some really embarrassing little television work, freelance, for a kid's show that was syndicated. It was dreadful, but we had to make a few dollars. That lasted for a few months, but it wasn't much.[9]

Ackles and Graham collaborated well if they agreed on their subject matter. Another opportunity that presented itself was a contemporary musical adaptation of Puccini's *La Bohème*. Ackles was well versed in opera and classical music, though Graham wasn't, and started writing some songs adapting the Puccini themes. Graham was tasked with writing the libretto, but he clashed with the producer, who he describes as 'disagreeable'. Ackles struggled with this producer as well, and in the end, nothing came of the project.

In terms of public profile and income, the high-water mark of the Ackles/Graham writing partnership was a TV movie, *Word Of Honor*. First broadcast on January 6, 1981, it was a decent effort with a strong cast, including Karl Malden, Ron Silver, and a young John Malkovich in his first substantial film role. The plot explores a journalist's moral dilemma about protecting his sources in the case of a child murder. Graham had pitched the idea to CBS and brought in Ackles as co-writer. *Word Of Honor* was produced by Alex Karras, a former professional footballer, and his wife Susan Clark, an actress, whose production company Ackles subsequently did further work for. Bruce Langhorne provided the music. As is often the way in movies, the creators lost control of their creation. Graham especially was unhappy with the way director Mel Damski dealt with the subject matter.

Word Of Honor was Ackles's sole substantial credit in his brief career as a screenwriter. A few months after it was first shown, he nearly lost his life. During Holy Week, April 1981, Ackles picked up his four-year-old son George from preschool and set off for home, a route he'd driven many times. Janice had gone on before them. Shortly after getting back to their house, she answered a knock at the door. A policeman told her that her husband and son had been involved in a serious road traffic accident on a narrow public highway near the house. Ackles had been hit by another car that was driving erratically on the wrong side of the road. It turned out this car was driven by an uninsured woman with a history of drug abuse. George was unhurt. The left-handed Ackles's left arm was almost severed at the elbow, and his left hip was pushed into his pelvis. Recovery was slow, and at first he had to use a wheelchair. It was a long time before he was back to playing the piano. His shattered hip was replaced. There were multiple operations. Later, Ackles related how Janice stood outside the operating theatre, imploring the surgeons not to amputate his arm because he was a pianist. They saved the arm, but Ackles had residual pain and numbness for the rest of his life.

JIM FRIEDRICH After the Easter liturgy I took him some lilies from the altar. Even after the accident, he was in good spirits.[10]

DAVID ACKLES I spent six months in a wheelchair, but after getting asked to choreograph a new production of a show I did twenty years beforehand, I got out of the wheelchair to do it.[11]

A lot of Ackles's friends and colleagues from the music business mention losing track of him in the early 80s. This was on account of the accident and a necessary withdrawal from activity while recuperating. By the time Ackles completed his recovery and re-emerged into working life, he was in his mid-forties. It was a decade since his recording career had quietly drawn to a close, but he kept writing when time allowed. He persisted with *Allendor*. In October 1984, the forty-seven-year-old Ackles, with nearly three decades of on/off theatrical experience behind him, was firing off demos like anyone else trying to break into the business. He sent three cassettes and an accompanying letter to Joe Papp.

> I hope you hear in these songs what I had hoped to put there—joy, anger, laughter, sorrow, the works.[12]

Joseph Papp (1921–1991), a New York impresario, launched what is now the Public Theater (or just the Public) in 1954. The nonprofit venue in Lower Manhattan is famous for hosting the premiere runs of *Hair* (1967) and *Hamilton* (2015). Papp's belief that theatre should not be the preserve of a privileged cultural elite endures in the Public's mission, long making it a locus for emerging playwrights and performers.

Ackles's approach to Papp had been set up by an introduction from the actress Linda Miller, a friend of Janice's, who knew Papp:*

> So! Why am I writing? I have a dear friend here named David Ackles. He is a multi-talented writer and composer. He is here in the land of the catchy jingle sitting on a Broadway musical talent. The dilemma as always is the forum and the contact. I believe he is someone you could collaborate and produce some very successful and valuable work with.[13]

After that introduction, Ackles's letter goes on to describe the contents of his three enclosed cassettes. Cassette one is titled *Allendor* and includes four sketches of songs for a proposed musical adaption of *The Little Lame Prince*, a children's book by the prolific and bestselling British novelist and poet Dinah Craik (1826–1887).

> You may recall this is the story of a handicapped orphan prince who is denied his rightful place until, with the help of his fairy godmother, he is able to fly and, finally to achieve justice.[14]

Ackles explains that he proposes to set the musical as a reading for potential backers in a rehearsal hall, thus creating a play within a play. He was familiar with readings like this as a usually necessary phase in the life of an emerging work for the stage. Among the potential backers is an angry old man who is himself disabled and who rejects the story because it offers what he considers false hopes. Though Ackles's inception of this project predates his car crash, the prospect of life-changing long-term disability must have informed him as he continued to work on it after the accident.

---

* Linda Miller was the daughter of Jackie Gleason. From 1963 to 1973, she was married to the actor and playwright Jason Miller, who played Father Damien Karras in *The Exorcist*.

> After... he returns to the empty hall and confronts his bitterness in the form of the boy he was and the man he could have been and discovers that even he can learn to fly.[15]

This *Allendor* cassette is not a copy of the recording Ackles made with Douglas Graham's help at Bruce Langhorne's studio. It sounds more like a home demo but seems to be one stage up from Ackles playing and singing into a cassette recorder. One song has an acoustic guitar part complementing the piano, and there's light reverb on the vocals.*

Tape two contains four songs from the proposed adaptation of *La Bohème*, transposed to 1960s New York and a cast of down-at-heel flower children. Like the *Allendor* demo, this cassette sounds like a home demo with some rudimentary production flourishes. In some places Ackles double tracks his voice, panning parts hard left and right, with the piano in the centre.

Tape three has a selection of songs from Ackles's recording career.

> Here are eight songs that I thought might give you an idea of the range of my abilities, including my ability as an arranger and orchestrator. The songs are taken from several different albums, which is why there is such a difference in volume and clarity among them.[16]

Assuming Ackles intended the choice to be representative of his best work (or at least, most relevant for persuading a theatre producer of his ability to write for the stage) the choice of songs is telling: nothing from the first album, just the title track of the second, five from *American Gothic* (the title track, 'Love's Enough', 'Ballad Of The Ship Of State', 'Midnight Carousel', 'Oh, California!') and two from *Five & Dime* ('Everybody Has A Story', 'One Good Woman's Man').

---

* See Appendix 2

Judging by subsequent correspondence, Joe Papp passed Ackles's letter and cassettes to Gail Merrifield Papp, his partner in life and work and Director Of New Works Development at the Public Theater. Her handwritten notes on Ackles's first letter and subsequent correspondence indicate that she was impressed. *Allendor* is a 'good concept', the *La Bohème* adaptation a 'very intelligent and appealing restyling of the music + story'. Of cassette three, she notes:

> Excellent song—story lyrics—strong character + narrative [unclear word] also present in the music which is emotionally intense + powerful. Orchestrations show variety of style—most often tending to tonal complexity + Kurt Weill derivation.[17]

Merrifield Papp called Ackles on October 17, and the two arranged to meet in November, when Ackles visited New York. At that meeting, Ackles agreed to complete *Allendor* in three months. The following April, he wrote again:

> It is now five months and there is still a great deal to do. But progress is being made, I assure you. The show is now called *Prince Jack*, and it is a marvel of musical invention. (Well, I like it, and so does my wife.)[18]

Whether to remind herself or as a note to her husband (or someone else), Merrifield Papp annotated this second letter from Ackles with the words 'one-time hot songwriter'.

One further letter from Ackles survives, dated July 30, 1985, which indicates that by then he had sent Merrifield Papp an entire draft of *Prince Jack*. It is presumably this draft that survives in the Papp archive in the New York Public Library, a 144-page typewritten script with dialogue and the lyrics to twenty-one songs. Ackles does not mention any accompanying demo in his final letter.

The trail goes cold after this, and there was no production of *Prince*

Jack. By the time Ackles put it aside, he might already have been thinking about his last big creative project. It was another musical, *Sister Aimee*. This one occupied him for the last decade or more of his life. It was a return to the themes of faith and doubt that Ackles had been exploring since 'His Name Is Andrew' and the unreleased 'The Grave Of God', from the first album sessions. Ackles mentioned the idea to Douglas Graham early on in its gestation, though Graham did not get involved beyond providing sound effects for an early reading.

In the end, *Sister Aimee* went further than *Prince Jack*, and there were workshop performances and readings and a studio demo recording, though it did not get a full production. Apart from small funding awards to stage readings, Ackles did not earn money from *Sister Aimee*—and, in fact, invested considerably in making the demo. It was the same with *Prince Jack* before. Consequently, he worked to earn a living throughout the 80s and 90s, when life wasn't interrupted by illness or injury. He was involved in fundraising from the 80s. He must have put considerable time and effort into this, and he did well—by the mid-90s, he was serving as executive director of the National Society Of Fundraising Executives' Los Angeles chapter. Even so, this probably did not rank high among his passions. It was more a day job, the sort of thing to which artists often resort to fund the real work. Much more congenial was teaching at the School Of Theatre at USC, where he ended his working life.

The subject of *Sister Aimee* was Aimee Semple McPherson. She requires some introduction now. Though once famous—in North America, at least—she was never widely known internationally beyond Pentecostal church circles.

Popularly known as Sister Aimee, the Canadian-born McPherson (1890–1944) was an unlikely evangelist. Three times married, twice divorced, she died of an overdose in a hotel room after a preaching engagement. The coroner concluded it was an accident after newspapers had reported it as suicide. She was entrepreneurial, energetic, strong-willed, and a natural self-promoter. For a while, she was the best-known preacher in North America, first touring the continent with her tent-revival crusades and preaching with a megaphone from an open-top car, latterly speaking to thousands every week from the church she built—Angelus Temple, Echo Park, Los Angeles. When it opened in 1923, it was the biggest church building in the US, with space for a congregation of more than five thousand. She published magazines. She spoke in tongues and practised healing with the laying on of hands. Many miracles were attributed to her ministry. She appealed to the poor and disenfranchised—black and white—and deliberately crossed the race divide, inviting a black minister to baptise her daughter. She founded the Foursquare Church, now an international denomination claiming more than eight million members spread across 150 countries. In the early days of flight, she once promoted a meeting by leaflet bombing from a biplane. She opened a show about her life on Broadway, which closed after a week. During the Great Depression, she was said to live in some luxury, yet in 1928 she opened the Angelus Temple commissary, which fed and clothed over 1.5 million people at no charge. She was preaching on radio almost as soon as public radio broadcasts started, and in 1924 she launched KFSG Radio, the second woman in the US to be granted a broadcast license. Shortly before her death, she applied for a TV broadcasting licence. Critics scorned her for her 'entertainment religion', but millions hung on her every word. Yet for all that, McPherson is best remembered now for a mysterious, ambiguous incident that took place when she was at the height of her fame.

On May 18, 1926, McPherson vanished from Ocean Park Beach in Santa Monica, California. She was last seen swimming and was presumed drowned. For days, hundreds of followers stood vigil on the sands. McPherson was at the very peak of her fame, and the crank calls and ransom demands and sightings that often accompany the disappearance of a famous personality followed.*

---

* McPherson's disappearance, never properly explained, shares some features with the disappearance of the crime writer Agatha Christie later the same year.

Then, on June 23, McPherson turned up in a hospital in Douglas, Arizona, saying she had been kidnapped. Her story was that a couple had approached her at the beach and asked her to pray for their sick child. She accompanied them to their car, where she was chloroformed and driven away, bound and unconscious. She ended up, she said, a prisoner in a shack in the Mexican desert, eventually escaping through a window and walking about twenty miles across the desert, to Agua Prieta, Sonora, from where she was taken to Douglas. The media and public interest, already high, intensified. There were photos of a washed-out-looking McPherson in her hospital bed, surrounded by family. When she returned to Los Angeles, a crowd of at least thirty thousand turned out to welcome her.

But almost as soon as she reappeared, conflicting theories about the disappearance began to circulate. Some said the whole thing was a publicity stunt and McPherson's mother was in on it. Others that McPherson had run off with one Kenneth Ormiston, her one-time radio engineer. Others still that she'd had some kind of breakdown due to the pressure of work. McPherson stuck to her story, broadcasting it from her radio station and pulpit. Journalists passed counter-assertions and information to the police. The Los Angeles prosecution fed the press with new developments. Then, after some months of feverish speculation, she and several co-defendants, including her mother, were charged with criminal conspiracy, perjury, and obstruction of justice. But on January 10, 1927, charges were dropped due to lack of evidence. McPherson continued to be a big draw for the rest of her life, but she never quite shook off the questions about her integrity. Whether the whole kidnapping story was a publicity stunt or not, it certainly got McPherson publicity. But it wasn't always good publicity. Like many celebrities before and since, she learned that the media is an unreliable friend. By the 1980s, the scandal-ridden mega-church TV evangelist had become a trope of American religious life. McPherson was the mother of them all.

This mass of contradictions appealed to Ackles. He understood the challenge of maintaining an authentic religious sensibility in a world of temptation and conflicting demands. He understood human frailty, and in song he was ever reluctant to reduce people to one-dimensional cyphers. The tough guy, man-of-the-world drifters turn out to be lonely and fragile too. The protagonist of 'Candy Man' is undoubtedly a sinner, but he's also sinned against. The marriage of Horace and Molly Jenkins, in 'American Gothic', isn't what it seems. She's promiscuously unfaithful, and he comforts himself with drink and pornography. But the song's punchline suggests they might not be as unhappy as their sordid shenanigans suggest. And then there's the religion. Ackles the lifelong churchgoing believer could celebrate simple faith ('Family Band' and 'Berry Tree') and question it ('His Name Is Andrew' and 'The Grave Of God').

DAVID ACKLES I felt an affinity for her conflict between being a committed Christian and someone in love with fleshly things, as it were. She was frustrated by the established church ... she was trying to interest people in subjects that weren't particularly part of everyday conversation.[19]

McPherson's story reads now like an American archetype. Her personal style, the scale of her ambition, the impact of her work, her fame, the manner of her partial but not complete fall from grace—none of this could have happened anywhere else in quite the way it did. And, by the time Ackles began to plan his telling of her life, she was once again a timely subject. In the 80s and 90s, TV evangelists and big-name preachers were living out McPherson's equivocal story all over again. Like Jim and Tammy Bakker, with their TV shows and Christian theme parks and gold-plated bathroom taps and prescription drug addictions and sexual misconduct and apparently enduring faith. And—in Tammy's case—AIDS activism and support for the gay community. It was against this backdrop that Ackles embarked on *Sister Aimee*, a musical about McPherson's disappearance, which became the creative project that dominated his later years. He wasn't the first to realise that McPherson's life was a ripe subject for artistic interpretation, nor the last. There was at least one silent movie about the disappearance. And in 1976, a starry TV movie, *The Disappearance Of Aimee*, with Bette Davis and Faye Dunaway.*

In 1988, twenty years after the release of his debut album, Ackles enrolled in the Lehman Engel Musical Theatre Workshop (LEMTW) in Los Angeles, one of a cohort of twenty-four hopefuls on the roster that year. The director and animator Kevin Lima was a fellow student. At fifty-one, Ackles was older than almost everyone else, including the workshop leaders. Even so, he made lasting friendships. Workshop member Jan Powell collaborated with Ackles on some of his later creative projects.

JAN POWELL My background was always musical theatre, and David and I clicked on that level almost immediately. At that point I was a professional musical director and pianist—had been a singer for ten years—and David recognised that he wanted to be associated with someone who could help him with his work as far as being able to sit down, read it, play it, teach it to singers—so we hooked up on that level in the workshop.[20]

Students enrolled for a curriculum year in which they learned the foundations of musical theatre, including how songwriting works in that medium, and storytelling. There was an emphasis on practical work, collaboration, and tutor and peer feedback. Sessions were clustered together, two or three evenings at a time, once a month.

The LEMTW's founder and director, John Sparks, knew nothing of Ackles and his recording career when he applied. Most people who knew Ackles at this time say he rarely spoke of that period of his life. Indeed, many friends and colleagues from the 1980s and 1990s didn't know about his albums until reading of them in Ackles's obituaries.

JOHN SPARKS He applied for the workshop, and it was very clear from

* A 2006 biopic (*Sister Aimee: The Aimee Semple McPherson Story*) was followed by another in 2019 (*Sister Aimee*). The stage show *Scandalous: The Life And Trials Of Aimee Semple McPherson* was first produced in 2005.

the beginning that he was a very accomplished songwriter, but he had an interest in musical theatre, and he had a project that he was very serious about developing into a full-blown musical about Aimee Semple McPherson.[21]

The workshop curriculum started with assignments that had nothing to do with participants' own projects. For example, students were tasked with writing songs to order within a set of parameters. Collaboration was encouraged, and mutual criticism too. You played your songs to the group, and everyone commented. Ackles quickly demonstrated not only his ability as a songwriter and storyteller but also a capacity to offer pertinent, articulate, helpful criticism, as another fellow member of the LEMTW recalls:

KEN STONE At first, we knew him strictly as a musical theatre guy. He was a large presence in the room, I remember, but kind, knowledgeable ... there was a bias toward kindness in what he had to say. At that point I didn't know of his background in music and recording. I became aware of that over the years.[22]

After the first year, particularly promising students were invited to continue at LEMTW, developing their own projects. Ackles was selected, and he developed *Sister Aimee* at the workshop for most of the rest of his life—only stopping when his final illness made it impossible to continue.

JAN POWELL Anyone who was interested in American history and Los Angeles of that period was completely fascinated by Aimee Semple McPherson and her mother and her boyfriends and the fact that she vanished magically and then came back again. It's just an incredible story.

KEN STONE It is a story of somebody who's maybe a fake, maybe a con. But you never know if such a person believed her own stories. Or comes to believe her own stories. The space between those two ideas is dramatically fascinating—you can go wherever you want with that.[23]

The workshop's role was to offer feedback but also practical support, including hiring actors, directors, and venues for theatre readings and productions. There were at least three LEMTW-supported reading performances of *Sister Aimee*, between 1991 and 1995.* It was during preparations for the first of these that Sparks discovered Ackles's previous life as a recording artist.

JOHN SPARKS They were very successful events. At the first reading it was very clear that the score worked. The lyrics were very sophisticated, and the score was very accomplished. The only reason to do another reading was that David continued to work on the project, based on what he learned from the first reading.[24]

The programmes for two of the readings invited audience members to write to Ackles giving their feedback. Stone, well-versed in the culture of providing a constructive peer critique, sent Ackles a nine-page letter.

KEN STONE I've never written so much after a reading—which is a good sign. The show is a marvel and worth all the effort you've obviously put into it. It is brimming with theatrical know-how and musical treasures.[25]

How Ackles responded to this particular, very detailed appraisal, or any other, isn't known. But he would have been expecting comment, and he would have reflected on it. He was known in the workshop for his

* The first reading took place on Sunday, June 9, at 1:30pm and Monday, June 10, 1991, at 7:30pm, at the Dorothy Chandler Pavilion, Los Angeles Music Center. There was another reading almost exactly four years later, on Thursday, June 15, 1995 location and time unclear. Probably that year there was another reading, without scripts, at the Los Angeles Theater Center. This was a more produced event, with actors working in costume, without scripts.

constructive evaluations of the work of others—usually describing it as 'sensational' before offering his criticisms. He described *Sister Aimee* with the same word when talking about it to rock writers who tracked him down after the 1990s CD reissue of his three Elektra albums.

Ackles was at home in the workshop. Ever since he was a teenager, he had immersed himself in musical theatre—as a writer, performer, arranger, director, scene maker, and teacher. Even when his recording career started, he continued to contribute to his mother's church theatre group, The Geneva Players. Musical theatre was his métier, where he belonged, creatively. Not the man alone on stage performing, the focus of attention, but in the heart of or leading a collective creative endeavour. A rehearsal tape for one of the *Sister Aimee* readings records Ackles teaching parts to the cast, playing the piano with a flourish and singing each line with gusto—even when the melodies extend well beyond his comfortable range. His instructions are conversational and precise. Thirty-plus years after the tape was made, you can hear his brimming enthusiasm through the tape hiss.

A young singer, Stacy Sullivan, played the lead role in one of the *Sister Aimee* readings. While the first reading at least consisted of actors simply standing at music stands reading and singing their parts, the performance in which Sullivan took part, which came later, was closer to a staged rendition. There were costumes and planned stage entries and exits, and the scripts were memorised.

STACY SULLIVAN I got an audition for this musical called *Sister Aimee*, and it was for a staged reading. And I knew the people who were producing it—it was the LA theatre centre—and I went in and sang, and David was there, and he basically said, 'Well, you're completely wrong for this, but I like you, let's sing.' So, he sat down at the piano and started playing, and the passion that came through his fingers, and he started singing the role of Sister Aimee. Oh my gosh, it was absolutely thrilling. I was very young at the time, and I was doing lots of readings of musicals and I was very,

very busy but he started playing, and the sound that came out of him … I said, 'Are you a performer, you have an incredible voice?' And he looked at me slyly and said, 'I've done a little performing.'[26]

Whether Ackles ever arrived at what he considered a finished version of *Sister Aimee* isn't clear. Certainly, programme notes indicate he made changes between the first LEMTW reading in 1991 and a later one in 1995. The earlier version had twenty-three songs, the later twenty-six. Lyrically, these songs demonstrate Ackles's strength at telling stories through his characters, which was a feature of his recorded work, though obviously in the context of a musical each character contributes their parts to the main story, whereas in an album context the stories-in-song are self-contained vignettes. It indicates his commitment to the project that, in 1994, Ackles ploughed considerable resources into a studio demo of *Sister Aimee* songs, hiring established professional performers Judy Kaye, Richard White, Teri Ralston, and Jack Ritschel.*

Musically, there is a clear evolutionary link from *Sister Aimee* back to *American Gothic* and *Five & Dime*, with Ackles's melodies, chord structures and rhythms referencing a mix of church and stage music and a liberal dose of period-correct ragtime—while never sounding derivative of any genre. Many of the songs are delivered in the sort of speak-singing styles used in opera and musical theatre. *Sprechgesang* (spoken singing) and *Sprechstimme* (spoken voice) are terms sometimes used interchangeably for two distinct but related vocal techniques. In Sprechgesang pitches are sung, whereas Sprechstimme is more like rhythmic speech without pitches. Ackles deployed an approximation of these approaches from time to time across his recorded work. You hear a hint of it in 'Laissez-Faire', in the line 'the government takes all the cash and eats it or something'. To get a sense

* Judy Kaye (born 1948) is a Tony Award-winning stage singer and actress. She made her Broadway debut in *Grease* in the 1970s. Richard White (born 1953) is an actor and opera singer with extensive film, stage, and recording credits. Teri Ralston (born 1943) is an actress best-known for appearing in *Frasier*. Jack Ritschel (1931–2020) was a voice actor.

of what Ackles's musical theatre compositions sound like, imagine songs where that style is dominant or at least extensively used.

This and the other musical-theatre demos recorded in the late 1970s (*Allendor* and *La Bohème*) confirm that the muse didn't leave Ackles after *Five & Dime*, it just took him off in different directions. Possibly in the direction he'd always wanted to go anyway, toward a unique theatrical art song.

Sister Aimee finds Ackles emphasising the tension between McPherson the sincere woman of faith and McPherson the rather lonely middle-aged woman looking for human love, who has never got over the death of her first husband. He doesn't entertain the kidnap theory but has McPherson holed up with her lover, Kenneth Ormiston, for the weeks of her absence. Ackles deploys the caustic humour that surfaced from time to time throughout his recorded work in the voices of a chorus of reporters, forever lusting after a sensational headline:

When your day is just beginning,
No one wants to start depressed.
You want news about murder and sinning…
Complete with photo of victim undressed,
Blood on her chest, hole in her breast.
We tell America
What America wants to know.[27]

McPherson's life ended in a manner that's become sadly familiar in celebrity culture—the lonely overdose in a hotel room, which may or may not have been accidental. Ackles, though, gives her a kind of redemption. At the end of *Sister Aimee's* second and final act, as the last of the chorus of reporters leaves the stage, Aimee reappears upstage right. She is dressed in white. She hears a sound and sees her first husband, Robert, upstage left, also dressed in white:

Aimee and Robert begin to waltz—tentatively at first, then more and more joyously as the MUSIC BUILDS.

They are still waltzing as the curtain falls.

Sparks and the workshop supported Ackles in trying to get a full production of *Sister Aimee* underway but could not find a theatre willing to take it on. After Ackles's death, Janice asked Sparks if he could again help promote a production, and he tried, but once more nothing happened. So, as things stand, the big creative work of Ackles's later years, which occupied him for a decade or more, remains unheard and unseen, apart from the workshop readings.

JOHN SPARKS I remember it as a very, very fine piece of work. Thematically, as I recall, it was about her need to find meaning in her life beyond her work as an evangelist. She had an unhappy personal life. And that's what was interesting about the show. What I recall liking about the show was how he took what was essentially an icon and turned her into a human being that you got to know and empathise with ... it's a serious musical and given the right team of actors and music director there's plenty there that could be made into a very effective musical. The topic is very timely.[28]

Sparks worked closely with Ackles on *Sister Aimee*. His recollections differ from those of many others I spoke to for this book in that they emphasise Ackles's seriousness. Perhaps because Sparks was seeing Ackles engage with something that clearly meant a great deal to him.

JOHN SPARKS He had high language skills, both when he spoke and in what he wrote. He had ... I don't want to call it religious fervour, because I don't think it was. He had a sort of humanism about him that was extremely fixed. He had compassion, great compassion, and he was very serious about it. He knew how to laugh, but he was not a jovial person, he was a serious person. At least as I knew him. What stays with me whenever

I hear the name David Ackles is a combination of his seriousness and his talent, or ability, and the way he handled his frustration at wanting to get that show before a larger audience and his inability to do so. Because he was very invested in that story.[29]

—

By the time Ackles joined the Lehman Engel Musical Theatre Workshop in the 1980s, he and his family were living at Three Penny Farm, an old horse farm on a hilly six-acre plot in Tujunga, on the northern fringes of Los Angeles. The Tujunga settlement had started as a Little Landers utopian experiment in the early twentieth century, with settlers building their own houses on one-and-a-half-acre plots. It sounds somewhat like the boating Londoners claiming their plots on the banks of the River Loddon in Wargrave at around the same time.

While living in Tujunga, Ackles was an active member of All Saints Episcopal Church in Pasadena. The church had then, and still has, a strongly inclusive and socially activist stance. The rector in Ackles's final years, Ed Bacon, had encountered Martin Luther King by chance at an airport and prompted by that meeting had cultivated a theology of inclusion and universal compassion.

In 1993, while heavily involved in LEMTW and working on *Sister Aimee*, Ackles was diagnosed with lung cancer. He had surgery to remove part of his lung. The illness and Ackles's subsequent treatment weren't discussed at the workshop, and indeed, when Powell visited him in hospital, Ackles tried (and failed) to get him to go away. Ackles recovered well and got back to work. To celebrate his recovery, he and Janice rented a mansion in Pasadena and invited friends to a big party, with different types of music in each room.

CHAPTER TEN

YES, WE'LL GATHER AT THE RIVER

REISSUES AND PRESS INTERVIEWS • TEACHING AT USC • FINAL ILLNESS • *THERE IS A RIVER* COMPILED AND WITHDRAWN

"

You know we go on forever, don't you? Even when life ends, we still go on, all of us.

DAVID ACKLES, *SISTER AIMEE*

"

Shortly after his cancer treatment and twenty years after his last release, Ackles became a modest beneficiary of the CD reissue gold rush. Record labels had embraced the idea that there was money to be made by reissuing back-catalogue albums from even the dustiest, neglected corners of their archives, and Warners duly excavated Ackles's three Elektra albums.

There was a flutter of interest in the UK, and Ackles might, at that time, have made a return to recording and performing.* There were independent record companies that would have taken him, and he could have filled small theatres had he toured. But though he was pleased that the records at least were now available again, he didn't seem overly interested in reviving his recording career. Instead, he was focused on *Sister Aimee*, and he always mentioned it when he was interviewed about the albums' reappearance.

The reissues had all the hallmarks of a rushed job. There were no contextual liner notes, no bonus previously unreleased tracks, and the artwork simply shrank the album covers into the smaller format. Furthermore, the stereo image was inadvertently reversed. Even so, they introduced Ackles to a new audience and prompted a small, brief resurgence in attention. In the British music press, a few 'whatever happened to' features appeared alongside reviews of the reissues. The first of these was in *Q*, in June 1994, written by Martin Aston. For anyone, me included, who had loved Ackles's albums for some time but had no idea what happened to him, Aston's article was a revelation. In those days, you couldn't access a potted life story with a few clicks, and until reading the article I had no idea what had happened to Ackles after he stopped recording.

The British folk music community had nurtured an affection for Ackles since the release of his debut album in 1968. Ackles might not have been aware of this, as he expressed surprise when Ian Kearey interviewed

* A few years later, Tim Rose, a contemporary of Ackles to whom he was occasionally compared, re-emerged, having drifted out of music in the mid-70s, making new albums and touring Europe.

him for *Folk Roots* magazine.* Kearey, a musician himself and a member of The Oyster Band in the 80s, had long admired Ackles.

IAN KEAREY It must have been in 1970, when I was fifteen. A school friend played me his elder brother's copy of the first album. I was entranced and burst into tears listening to 'Down River'. We played it over and over that day, then I found a copy for myself, and then *Subway To The Country*. The songs, the voice, the arrangements were so moving and had a simplicity and profundity unlike anyone else at the time—there was a novelistic quality to them that reminded me of The Band, who I also adored: that whole-story-in-three-minutes thing.[1]

Kearey, in common with all other journalists who contacted Ackles for similar features around this time (me included) found him affable and helpful. He laughed a lot. Kearey's subsequent article summarised Ackles's life to date, with most attention given over to the four albums. A closing paragraph mentions the car accident, Ackles's first cancer diagnosis, and *Sister Aimee*. Not included in the piece is Ackles's answer to Kearey's question about why he chose Aimee Semple MacPherson as a subject. Ackles replied that her life was like a musical anyway—everything she did was for the public gaze, and she treated the church like a stage.

Kenny MacDonald wrote an interview piece for *Ptolemaic Terrascope*, which gave a more detailed account of Ackles's life since he stopped recording. In this and in the *Q* article, he talked of having conversations with Rob Dickens, then of Warners, about doing another album, but it sounds vague and speculative.

In all these articles, Ackles comes over as being pleased about and a little baffled by the interest in his recorded work. But it's apparent that his real interests are elsewhere. He talks about *Sister Aimee* and says he would

* Launched by the indefatigable folk musician, label proprietor, promoter, and journalist Ian A. Anderson (the A added to avoid confusion with Jethro Tull's frontman) in the late 70s, *Folk Roots* was the UK's leading folk, roots, and world music publication in the 1990s.

love to do more musical theatre. He sounds happy. MacDonald asked him to describe an average day:

DAVID ACKLES Well, in the morning I usually go to a gym where I'm a member, just to get the blood moving. I write songs. I work at my computer. I play the piano every day. In the afternoon I sometimes go for a hike in the hills around my home... I'm sitting here at my kitchen table talking to you and it's a beautiful sunny morning. The hills have some snow on them, it's lovely. I'm not despondent. Not in any way. I have a wonderful life.[2]

The car accident and the cancer treatment had taken an inevitable physical toll, but Ackles remained engaged and energetic. Photos from the time show a handsome smiling man, his hair still thick and now greying. He sometimes wore a moustache. Powell recalls walking across the grounds of USC with Ackles in excited, earnest conversation about their next project. After a while, Ackles stopped and said, 'Slow down, I've only got one lung.'[3]

Ackles turned sixty in 1997. His father Thomas died that year, but that marker of the inevitable march of time aside, it was as if life had come full circle for Ackles. Once again, he was at USC, enthusing about his next student musical theatre production, as he had forty years earlier. The most passionate and engaged of teachers, he was loved by students. His last creative project was directing a USC student production of *Threepenny Opera* in April 1997, with Jan Powell as musical director. When the USC newspaper interviewed him, he was articulate and overflowing with excitement.

DAVID ACKLES It's like being given a playpen and inviting a bunch of friends in to play. There are so few restrictions, as opposed to the commercial theatre, where you are answerable to whoever put up the money. Here you are responsible... to the educational standards of whatever institution you are working in and it's important to understand them and abide by them. The good side of it is you don't have the egos to deal with. You don't have the people who say, 'Well, this is the way we've always done it,' because these people have never done this before, so they are fresh to it, they are excited, they have energy and enthusiasm; there is not a diva in the cartload. I mean it is wonderful to work with these kids. Exciting people and so talented, I feel very lucky . . . I have regained the joy of directing. It's been about four years since I have directed. Directing is never less than satisfying. The pure joy of creating in this wonderful playpen is something that I have been missing, and boy, have I regained it.[4]

JAN POWELL The students loved him. They couldn't get enough of David. Therefore, he could get their best work out of them. And I said, 'There's only two ways you can do the show: you can be licensed to do it just with a piano, or you can be licensed to do it with the original orchestrations—Weill's original band, which is a nine-piece band. And he said, 'Oh, I'm getting the best players for you. We're having the nine-piece band.' . . . David did it right. He did anything, he did it meticulously.[5]

After *The Threepenny Opera*, Ackles and Powell planned to stage *Chicago*. Both had seen the original Bob Fosse Broadway production in 1975. But it never happened. Ackles's cancer returned. I didn't know this when, on April 24, 1998, about a year after *The Threepenny Opera*, I cold-called Ackles at his Tujunga home. Kenny MacDonald, who had interviewed him for *Ptolemaic Terrascope* in 1994, had given me his number. I was planning to write a 'Buried Treasure' feature for *Mojo*. Ackles was friendly and gracious.

DAVID ACKLES Well, I am as well as can be expected. I have lung cancer and I'm under treatment for it and the consequences of that—as anybody who's been through it will tell you—are not pleasant, but they're doable.[6]

Fittingly, the last bit of press coverage Ackles got in his life was in the UK. In January 1999, the *New Musical Express* recommended his debut album in a 'Respect Overdue' feature, which revisited 'yesterday's obscure classics'. It emphasised Ackles's near invisibility at the time, saying that a web search in those early days of the internet came up with almost nothing.

Ackles died on March 2, 1999, shortly after his sixty-second birthday. He was survived by his mother, Queenie. When Ackles knew his life was almost over, he chose the music he wanted for his memorial service and asked Janice to ask Jan Powell to act as musical director. The service was held on March 20, a Saturday, at Ackles's church, All Saints Episcopal in Pasadena. Ed Bacon delivered the homily.

The service opened with a two-piano arrangement of Kurt Weill's overture from *The Threepenny Opera* and the nineteenth-century hymn 'Shall We Gather At The River'. With those two choices, Ackles summed up his musical life: the stage music, the hymns, and the river motif.

STACY SULLIVAN And somebody got up and read a letter from Bernie Taupin. And I looked at the people next to me and said, 'Bernie Taupin? How did David know Bernie Taupin?' He never once mentioned he had four albums on Elektra and Columbia. It was astonishing that he had never mentioned this career.[7]

In addition to the hymns sung by the congregation, there were six Ackles songs, performed by friends and former students, including Sullivan. Two of these were from his recorded works—'Be My Friend' and 'Family Band'. The other four were later compositions, drawn from Ackles's various theatre projects. Janice sent Powell Ackles's own piano and vocal arrangements. The service closed with a Powell arrangement of the old gospel tune, 'I'll Fly Away':

Some glad morning when this life is o'er,
I'll fly away;
To a home on God's celestial shore,
I'll fly away (I'll fly away).

—

In death as in life, Ackles got more attention in British media than American. On hearing of Ackles's passing, John Peel played 'Sonny Come Home' on BBC Radio 1.* It was most likely Ackles's first mainstream airplay since Phil Collins chose 'Down River' as one of his *Desert Island Discs* in 1993.

The *Los Angeles Times* published a short, misguided obituary that over-egged a misspent youth angle and repeated an error from a 1968 feature, that Ackles had done time in five prisons. It then published a correction after Ackles's younger sister Kim explained that the only time Ackles had been in jail was as part of a USC choir singing for inmates.[8] In 1973, Ackles had said that the incorrect *Los Angeles Times* article prompted more media interview requests than anything else in his career. All of which he had to turn down when explaining that the article was full of fabrications.

This and many other obituaries regurgitated the press release Elektra put out with the first album, which romanticised Ackles's various temporary jobs in early adulthood and his role in the *Rusty* films. One obituary likened Ackles's life to a Jim Thompson novel, because of a handful of temporary jobs he did shortly after university. It's a cautionary tale for PR departments everywhere. That crafted persona disproportionately emphasising minor details became indelibly written into Ackles's public story when his life was summed up in print.

As well as the expected coverage in heritage rock magazines like *Mojo*, British broadsheets including the *Independent* and the *Guardian* published obituaries. The most informative of these was written by Brian Mathieson for the *Independent*.[9] Indeed, it became a template for other obituaries. Mathieson had launched an Ackles fan website in 1998, which, for many years, was the only source of reliable, detailed information online. The *Guardian*'s obituary, by Christopher Hawtree, repeated the Los Angeles

* Ackles's albums were retained among John Peel's twenty-six-thousand-strong collection until the DJ's death in 2004.

jail error and judged *American Gothic* the equal of The Band and superior to most Springsteen.[10] A week later, the *Guardian* ran a lucid, reflective evaluation by Jonathan Romney. Ackles, Romney pointed out, simply wasn't working in the American pop tradition but came from somewhere else entirely. He praised Ackles's first album especially and noted that even he, a fan, had never seen nor heard *Five & Dime*.

Reading these short summations of a life of creative work, you realise again how obscure Ackles had become. The writers couldn't afford to assume readers had any prior knowledge of him at all. In the May issue of *Record Collector*, then the British music publication most prone to excavating forgotten corners of rock history, I was allowed a couple of pages to summarise Ackles's recording career. A few months later, *Ptolemaic Terrascope* published a longer piece, combining a career overview and an interview. This was planned when Ackles was alive, before I understood that he was terminally ill—but it became an obituary. The interview drew on the call I made to Ackles in 1998, and a subsequent exchange of emails that lasted until early 1999.* This experience of speaking to Ackles briefly toward the end of his life mirrors that of other writers who interviewed him a few years earlier, when the Elektra albums were reissued. He was good-humoured, accommodating, and modest. With hindsight, it is poignant to read his enthusiasm for *Sister Aimee*:

DAVID ACKLES Well, at the moment I'm expecting that I will someday—and I hope rather soon—get a production of a musical I have been working on for a number of years, based on a year and a half in the life of Aimee McPherson, who is someone I'm sure completely unknown to anyone, but who was an evangelist in the 1920s who led a rather scandalous life, and I think there are a lot of interesting parallels between that time and this, and I wanted to explore that.[11]

---

* At the time, this was the longest feature on David Ackles since the days when he was an active recording artist. It formed the basis of my chapter about Ackles in my book *American Troubadours* (2001).

After that brief flurry of posthumous interest, Ackles was relegated again to the footnotes. An occasionally mentioned curiosity. The streaming age was a long way off, and although the CD reissue boom continued, it was a time when it was hard to locate obscure music from the past unless it was put in front of you—by virtue of coverage in *Mojo* or *Record Collector*, for example, or a reissue campaign. Or, as was usually the case, the two going hand in hand. For Ackles, this didn't happen in any methodical way. There were low-key reissues of the Elektra albums in 2002. In 2004, the Australian label Raven reissued *Five & Dime*—the first time the album was available in any form outside the US. Every now and then Ackles's name would crop up. In 2008, Elvis Costello interviewed Elton John on his talk show, *Spectacle*. They talked about Ackles with palpable reverence and affection and performed a duet of 'Down River'. Then, in his 2015 memoir, *Unfaithful Music And Disappearing Ink*, Costello once again lauded Ackles as a formative influence. Elton John's 2020 autobiography retold the Troubadour story, describing it as ridiculous that he should headline over Ackles. *American Gothic* made it into the 2005 book *1001 Albums You Must Hear Before You Die*. But these were isolated incidents. There was no real sense of a growing awareness, a rising profile. Crucially, there seemed to be hardly any contemporary artists latching on to Ackles as an influence. His few champions were near contemporaries, who had loved the records first time around.

This might have changed in 2007, when Rhino announced an Ackles box set. Titled *There Is A River*, it collected Ackles's three Elektra albums with several rare and previously unreleased tracks. Under the guidance of producer Andy Zax, *There Is A River* got as close to release as it is possible to get without being released. It was compiled and mastered (properly this time), and the cover and booklet were designed, incorporating erudite and heartfelt liner notes by Bernie Taupin and Elvis Costello. And—probably—actually manufactured. It was announced in release schedules, and adverts began to appear in the British music press. David Cavanagh published a thoughtful review in *Uncut*. Like the reviewers of 1972, he reached for comparisons and tried to capture the elusive essence of Ackles's music:

> *American Gothic* is arranged in a spectacular variety of styles, from boater-and-cane 'show tunes' to blissful country rock. The album's peaks are numerous, with narratives both surreal ('Ballad Of The Ship Of State') and poignant ('Waiting For The Moving Van'). The sheer musical scope (clarinets, trombones, pedal-steel guitar, Appalachian fiddles) implies a union of Sondheim, Nesmith and The Band. The ten-minute climax, 'Montana Song', in which a troubled urbanite ventures to a remote rural location to research his ancestors is a shattering experience in sounds and words.[12]

Then, abruptly, and without explanation, *There Is A River* was withdrawn. It was never reinstated in the release schedules and remains unreleased to this day. Occasionally, advance promo copies appear for sale on eBay.

I was working at Jawbone Press—publishers of this book—at the time. We had signed a book about Elektra Records, *Becoming Elektra*, by Mick Houghton. Elektra founder Jac Holzman was involved and visited the office several times. He and I spoke about Ackles, who Holzman regarded as a great talent. Mick Houghton gave me a promo CD-R of *There Is A River*. Through conversations at that time and subsequent research for this book, it seems that *There Is A River* was withdrawn at the last minute largely over a dispute about the ownership of one of the previously unreleased songs. Had it been released, Ackles would be better known now.

There were nine previously unreleased or rare songs on *There Is A River*, plus the 'Subway To The Country' interview from the promo single. Alongside the various outtakes and alternate versions described in earlier chapters sits a curio, 'Hold Me In Your World'. Recorded on June 28, 1971, this was a co-write with Michael Small, a proposed theme for the Jane Fonda and Donald Sutherland film *Klute*. Small was a film composer who, in the 70s, specialised in thriller soundtracks. Other credits include

Marathon Man and *The Stepford Wives*. 'Hold Me In Your Arms' is a demo for piano, guitar, and bass, with Ackles delivering a smooth, controlled vocal without his usual rasp and in a higher-than-normal register. You'd be forgiven for thinking it was someone else singing. It's a decent song that proves Ackles could collaborate, and another 'might have been' moment. The song wasn't used, and a few months later, Ackles was off to England to make *American Gothic*.

In July 2016, the actor and singer Stacy Sullivan debuted her one-woman show, *A Night At The Troubadour: Presenting Elton John And David Ackles*, at the Metropolitan Room in New York. Directed by Mark Nadler with accompaniment by pianist Yasuhiko Fukuoka, Sullivan's show focuses—as the title suggests—on Elton John's 1970 breakthrough residency at the Troubadour, with Ackles as support act, and begins with her singing a fragment of 'Your Song'.

> **STACY SULLIVAN** Imagine it's August 25th, 1970, the Troubadour, a legendary rock club in Los Angeles. If you can, try to imagine you don't know what song I'm singing because you've never heard it… even though it was probably played at your wedding, and your daughter's wedding. (I'll probably be singing it at my daughter's wedding.)
>
> After the opening act, this young British kid comes out, sits down at the piano, and opens his set with this song… that he has written.[13]

But what starts out as an apparently straight retelling of that defining moment in Elton John's career quickly becomes more about the 'opening act'.

STACY SULLIVAN This night at the Troubadour is legendary. It's the night that introduces Elton John to the world. Every important person in the music industry is there. A couple of days before the concert, Elton John is scheduled to be the OPENING ACT … for David Ackles. Who?

Now, Elton happens to be a huge fan of this guy David Ackles. But at the last minute, the record executives switch it, and David Ackles is now the OPENING ACT for this unknown kid! David Ackles has never heard of Elton John. He says to his wife, Janice, 'I hope this kid's good!' The kid is good … but so is David Ackles.

Tonight, I'd like to introduce you … to David Ackles, with the help of Elton John. Aside from 'Your Song', I'm going to sing three other Elton John songs for you tonight. You'll recognise them. All of the others are by David Ackles. Starting with this one.[14]

With that about turn, *A Night At The Troubadour* reveals itself as something of a trojan horse, with Ackles's songs outnumbering Elton's three to one. Through the course of the performance, Sullivan presents a retrospective of most of Ackles's songwriting career, interpreting songs from all four albums and beyond, right through to 'Your Face, Your Smile', from the unproduced 1980s musical *Prince Jack*. Sullivan had first heard this sung at Ackles's memorial. The show becomes less about Elton John and more an introduction to Ackles against the backdrop of Elton John's leap into stardom.

A Night At The Troubadour was warmly received, critically. Stephen Holden wrote about *American Gothic* for *Rolling Stone* back in 1972. Writing in the *New York Times* in 2016, he started his review by asking who remembered David Ackles and called Sullivan's performance and acting a tour de force. 'Among the many gifted, half-forgotten singer-songwriters from the period who merit rediscovery, none are more deserving than Mr. Ackles, whose complicated story-songs are realistic, often bleak but compassionate tableaus of life in the American heartland.'[15]

David Hadju, writing in the *Nation*, praised Sullivan's exceptional sensitivity and interpretive skill. The critical attention focused as much on Ackles's short career as Sullivan's performance, which is what she intended. 'Ackles's songs, by contrast, tell dramatic, but not melodramatic, little stories about real-seeming people... musically, the songs defy categorization, with the melodic cadences of theater music and the rhythms of pop.'[16]

Not only did *A Night At The Troubadour* introduce new audiences to Ackles, it also got him—indirectly—more critical attention in his homeland than he'd had since 1973. The other notable thing about the show is the presentation and setting. More theatrical performance than gig, it's the sort of thing Ackles himself, never at home in a rock club, would have felt comfortable with.

—

Times change. Times change, I know. The house where Ackles recorded *Five & Dime* in 1973 was reported lost in the 2025 Los Angeles wildfires. The big money has moved into the once bohemian enclave on the banks of the River Loddon. Farthings was renovated in 2015 and the following year sold for £1.5 million. Shortly after, a planning application to demolish and replace it was approved. I visited Wargrave and located a few people who used to live there in the 1970s, before things changed. They all remembered Farthings. Some remembered Colonel Blaber and his ducks. But nobody remembered David Ackles, who lived so happily for the best part of a year in the wooden house on brick stilts, preparing his masterpiece.

DAVID ACKLES We had this lovely house in the country and a lovely, lovely life, and I was just not able to put it together to make a career there, so I had to come back to the States. And that worked out too.[17]

EPILOGUE

TRIBUTARIES

“

David was the opposite of pretension. David was always congenial. David was always genuine. Never phoney. Never sucked up to anybody. Always polite to everybody. I don't exaggerate when I say he was probably the most dignified person I ever met. In a completely unpretentious way. David could do anything. He was like the renaissance man.

DOUGLAS GRAHAM[1]

”

Through decades of listening to David Ackles's albums, and especially when writing and researching this book, I've found myself wondering not just why they under-achieved commercially when released, but also why Ackles hasn't retrospectively and posthumously acquired cult status. There are no definitive answers to questions like that, but two things keep coming back. One is about how the music business is set up. The other has to do with Ackles's music.

The 'lost genius rediscovered' narrative is perpetually potent. It appeals on multiple levels, the most obvious being that it points us toward great work that we didn't know about before. Music to listen to, books to read, films to watch. And there's more. It also offers us, the audience, a sense of being in the know. As if we've been granted a sort of gnostic insight into a mystery and can now partake in some rarefied communion. The narrative tends to lose its appeal when too many people 'find' the lost genius. Further still, for anyone who writes, or composes, or performs, or paints, it holds out evidence of the tantalising prospect that talent will out in the end. That maybe, just maybe, the unpublished novels and demo tapes and unseen paintings and commercial failures will—one day—be exhumed and elevated to their rightful place. We tell ourselves the value of the work is in the doing of it and how it turns out. But we all want external validation as well. And what better than the proving-the-doubters-wrong validation of seeing your work suddenly in demand, after years of languishing in obscurity?

And then there are the agents of the rediscovery. The people who claim to have found again the artist or work once lost. Like Howard Carter breaking into Tutankhamun's tomb, they get to enjoy the anticipatory thrill of the chase and the revelatory moment itself. And then bathe in reflected glory and acquire a stake—sometimes literally—in the rediscovered work.

I admit I have always been drawn to the narrative myself. For all the above reasons. I know the genuine thrill, like a sudden unbidden mystical experience, of hearing or reading something previously unknown to me (and apparently almost everyone else) that connects. Maybe the day before I'd never heard of that artist, and here they are, right now, enriching my life. Speaking to me. Once experienced, that shock of grace becomes addictive. Finding a used copy of the first David Ackles album in a shop in North London, early in 1985, was one of those moments—an especially powerful one.

But I've become uncomfortable with the idea, too. When does the idea of the lost genius become problematic? Maybe the rediscovered artist isn't a genius, even if they're very good. Is it their story we elevate, at the expense of the work itself?

The thing about the lost genius narrative is that we seem to need some tragedy thrown in to make the paradigm work. It's rarely enough that someone did good work that got ignored or overlooked, was forgotten for a while, and was then rediscovered. We want some kind of loss or suffering or damage as well. There are examples of this in most fields, including science and sport. But, most of all, the creative arts. All forms have their own examples. Literature has John Kennedy Toole, for example, who took his own life aged thirty-one, in despair at not getting published. Some years later, his mother brought the manuscript of Toole's novel *A Confederacy Of Dunces* to the attention of the novelist Walker Percy, who ushered the book into print in 1980. Twelve years after his death, Toole won the Pulitzer Prize for Fiction. Then there's Van Gogh. And Frances Farmer. But it seems to me that since the second half of the twentieth century, popular music has constructed a disproportionate share of myths of troubled, tragic figures who never got their due.

There are many variants of the proposition. Toole's is at the far end of the spectrum. You could say he wasn't really lost because he'd never been found in the first place. And his story had the most tragic of ends—suicide—and the most dramatic of postscripts—being published to huge acclaim, big sales and a major literary award.

Singer-songwriter Connie Converse is a recently popular exemplar. Writing quirkily intelligent, literate songs on an acoustic guitar in the 1950s, her sole known public performance was a TV show from which only a few still photographs survive. There were no records, no reviews, no tours, no career at all. Converse drifted out of music and into academia, before packing her belongings into a VW Beetle and vanishing at the age of fifty. She was forgotten by everyone apart from her family and a few friends until a gradually burgeoning interest in her work through the twenty-first century culminated in her songs being released for the first time, and a biography.* But how much of the attention is an interest in her songs, and how much a fascination with her vanishing act?

Nick Drake's story is a case study in how far this can go. It ends at a similar point to Toole's, with mass public and critical admiration and big sales, though it starts from a different place, sitting closer to the middle of the continuum. A public school and Cambridge-educated golden

* Howard Fishman's *To Anyone Who Ever Asks: The Life, Music And Mystery Of Connie Converse* (Wildfire, 2023) is a work of extraordinary, painstaking research.

boy from a privileged background, Drake began a career and—by his reckoning—failed. But his work was at least in the public domain when he died. Drake made three impeccable albums for Island Records between 1969 and 1972. He had his admirers at the time, but the records sold poorly, and Drake slipped into depression before dying of an overdose in November 1974 (the suicide verdict is disputed by some). The process of 'rediscovering' Drake began a few months after his death, with Nick Kent's obituary published in the *New Musical Express*. Thereafter, a sequence of events enhanced Drake's posthumous status and sales by increments. The *Fruit Tree* box set in 1979. The Dream Academy including a dedication to Drake on the sleeve of the 1985 hit single 'Life In A Northern Town'. Patrick Humphries's biography in 1997. A BBC Radio 2 documentary in 1998. This emerging recognition achieved critical mass in 1999, a quarter of a century after Drake's death, when BBC television broadcast a documentary and one of Drake's songs was used in a Volkswagen commercial. By then, Drake had become an archetype of the doomed romantic poet/hero, and he was feted by a subsequent generation of musicians, including Kate Bush, Paul Weller, and Peter Buck of R.E.M. Now, expensive vinyl re-pressings of Drake's albums can be found in supermarkets alongside canonical works by the likes of Led Zeppelin, Michael Jackson, and ABBA.

On the fiftieth anniversary of Drake's death, Rob Chapman, writing in *The Quietus*, argued that Drake's music was now eclipsed by a reductionist myth that emphasised his depression. Little attention is paid to the finely honed craft in his guitar playing, for example. 'Unfortunately, this is not the Drake that most people like to hear about,' Chapman writes. 'Instead, they fixate on the psychological malaise and black-eyed dog depression he ultimately succumbed to.'[2]

Drake's rediscovery gathered impetus with the rise of the CD reissue in the late 1980s and 1990s, which offered a second chance to tens of thousands of artists. Digital resurrection for music that had languished in an analogue purgatory for decades. Around then, I started writing reviews for magazines that explored the intricate, arcane byways of music history. There was a sort of inverted snobbery at play. Not for us the big-name artists and hit records, but rather the commercial failures, the eccentrics, the might-have-beens. Preferably with a good story attached. And that's the crux of the matter. The story.

In those days you would get sent a physical review copy with a paper press release folded into the CD box. Before long the tone and content of those press releases became familiar. Here is someone you've never heard of who is at least as good as Scott Walker/The Raincoats/Big Star/Young Marble Giants (insert appropriate name here). The trick was to find a comparator that still retained a cult allure and yet was known and widely accepted into a sort of unwritten non-mainstream canon. Then, hopefully, there'd be the 'story'. Preferably tragic. There were multiple variants. Collapse of the record company the week after initial release. Victim of crime. Drug-related decline. Mental health problems. Car or aircraft or motorbike accident. Getting lost in a controlling cult. Suicide.

The problems with this approach became apparent to me quite quickly. First, the music hardly ever lived up to the comparator. That orchestrally backed male singer from 1968? He didn't really sound much like Scott Walker and was nowhere near as good. Second, the story often competed with the music and even eclipsed it. Sometimes, it was as if the record was being reissued *because* of the story surrounding the artist, rather than the music. A later instance of this tension is the strange case of Lewis (Randall A. Wulff, also known as Lewis Baloue and Randy Duke). A Canadian musician who apparently worked as a stockbroker when he self-released music in the early 1980s, his recordings were completely overlooked until two of his albums were reissued in 2014. His story was irresistible. A tall, blond, handsome, seemingly wealthy, white-suited man driving a white Mercedes convertible, reputed to live in an apartment with all-white furniture. The multiple names. Bounced cheques. A vagueness about origins and family. Then the leads dry up until Lewis is sighted by chance, decades later, by a representative of a record company in search of him, sitting in a café. Magnificently, he is still dressed in white. He gives his blessing to the reissues of his albums but declines any payment. He grants one interview, during which he brushes off direct questions and regales the interviewer with impossible-to-confirm anecdotes. And then he is gone. Almost like a ghost.

As lost genius narratives go, it's an exceptional one. Except for the nagging yet essential question—is Lewis a genius? That's where things get tricky. I can't be alone in feeling just a little underwhelmed on hearing the music. Not that it's bad. I think it's good in its way. Intriguing and mysterious. I've enjoyed listening to it. It's just nowhere near as good and mysterious and intriguing as the story, if such a comparison can be made. And by the time it reaches our ears, the two—the music and the story—can't be separated. To me, the albums sound exactly like what they are—self-made vanity projects from the early 80s, by a promising singer who delivers his lines in a murmur like a hybrid of Bryan Ferry and Tim Hardin. Far better than most self-released records. Some decent but underdeveloped songs. Music with merits and engaging features that cries out for more work, discipline, a producer. Music falling well short of greatness, retrospectively elevated above and beyond its natural status on the back of a dazzling creation myth. I might have enjoyed it more were it not for the distorting prism of the story. I feel much the same about Connie Converse. I like the songs, but I can't help but wonder if there would have been the same level of interest if it was just the songs and no mysterious disappearance. It's as if the work itself is twisted out of shape by the weight of the myth constructed on it.

Tracey Thorn published an article prompted by a 2024 book about Lawrence, from Felt.[3] A band I like a great deal. Her point was that elevating the Lawrences of the world to genius status is perhaps misguided. I think that's right. It's an honour too liberally bestowed. Even if an artist is good and we like them, the word genius is thrown about too casually. It means exceptional. It has almost supernatural connotations. The genius seems to be a cut above the rest of us mere mortals. We can call Bob Dylan a genius, maybe. The songs pouring out of him. But let's be a little more reticent with our use of the term.

In the context of the music business, none of this is a surprise. The popularity of the lost genius story in music is an entirely predictable and natural by-product of an industry set up to promote not just music, but persona and image. Almost all stars combine natural ability, hard-earned craft, and something that can be shaped into an identity. The market demands it. So, when some promising music is unearthed from an archive, the business—whatever level it's functioning at, from micro-indie label to international entertainment conglomerate—becomes susceptible to the same market forces. It feels the need to amplify or create and develop and burnish an identity. And in the case of an artist no longer around, or so long out of the game as to be forgotten, this identity often takes the form of an intriguing back story.

So prevalent and established is the notion that it finds its way into fiction. Tom Cox's novel *Villager* (2022) demonstrates an acute awareness of the phenomenon. In the novel, R.J. McKendree, an obscure Californian folk singer, makes a vanishingly rare album, *Wallflower*, while living in Devon, in the west of England, in 1968. It's preceded by a garage band apprenticeship and a handful of later and even rarer recordings. Much of what we learn about McKendree in the novel comes from an incomplete, unpublished biography written by a fading music journalist. Cox, a music writer himself, is obviously well acquainted with the deployment of the lost genius tropes in the repackaging of once-forgotten music. He neatly dissects why McKendree doesn't quite measure up by showing that while he qualifies on some counts—the esoteric records deeply loved by a few—in others he fails.

> In some ways, perhaps part of the problem for McKendree, and part of the reason he has still not been reappraised in the way a Nick Drake or even a Judee Sill has, is that his story doesn't follow a traditional rock tragedy narrative. He did not die in his twenties

> and was not a suicide. He failed at all points to be a major abuser of drugs. He part-vanished rather than totally vanished, only part gave up making music.[4]

You could insert Ackles for McKendree in that paragraph.

British singer-songwriter Bill Fay is an unusual variant of the warping effect of the market's need for a story. Fay made two excellent albums in 1970 and 1971, which attracted little critical notice and hardly sold when released. They were then forgotten until reissued on CD in 1998. For once, the music lived up to the press release. Here was somebody quite the equal of the artists he was compared to, who included Nick Drake, Ray Davies, and Syd Barrett. But as almost nothing was known about Fay, legends emerged to fill the vacuum. That he had drifted into a dark version of the post-hippie twilight. This seemingly on account of him looking a bit wild on the cover of his second album. When located, Fay, a modest and retiring man, explained that nothing odd or tragic had happened at all. It was all a lot more prosaic. A lot of people had wild hair in 1971. And the photo was taken at the end of a long day in the studio. There really wasn't much of a story, apart from that Fay had stopped making records because he had been unable to get a record deal. He hadn't left the music business, he said. The music business had left him. And he had lived quietly ever since. A normal, humble life in North London.

When artists get rediscovered in the context of the lost genius paradigm, whether posthumously or after languishing in obscurity, saying that the story counts and it sometimes confuses is not the same as saying they are undeserving of the attention, necessarily. It's not that every artist who is delivered to us in this way is, by default, *not* very good, and just a beneficiary of a marketing ploy. Nick Drake created a small body of exceptional work. What heights might he have reached if he'd lived longer? Even so, you wonder if the light of posthumous glory might have burned just a tiny bit dimmer if there was no intrigue. See also Roky Erickson, Arthur Lee, Karen Dalton. It is now almost impossible to listen to the music without a knowledge of the backstories. Because—more often than not—the stories are the vehicles that delivered the music to us. Which becomes a problem when, as Chapman argues about Drake, the stories are oversimplified, or one theme is emphasised at the expense of others.

Where does all this leave David Ackles and his posthumous reputation? How does he shape up in the lost genius stakes—allowing for the caveat that the word genius is over-used, and really we should be saying lost talent or similar? If you take it as given—as I do—that he *was* a hugely talented artist, then why did his recording career stall and why has he not yet been substantially reappraised? How does his career trajectory compare with other artists of similarly obvious talent active at the same time, who also got lost?

Judee Sill was born Judith Lynne Sill on October 7, 1944. She spent her first years in Oakland, California, where her father, Milford Sill—who imported exotic animals for films—owned a bar. It was here that Sill learned to play the piano. Sill's father died when she was eight, and her mother soon remarried, to Tom & Jerry animator Kenneth Muse. Sill's relationship with her stepfather was strained, and at school she fell in with a group of fellow teenage rebels. She took part in a series of armed robberies, leading to a spell in reform school that failed to reform her, where she was the church organist. After her mother died in 1964, Sill slid into a life marked by periods of drug addiction, sex work, and crime.

Following a spell in prison and the death of her brother, Sill began writing songs and soon found influential admirers. The prodigiously talented singer, pianist, and guitarist toured supporting Graham Nash and David Crosby, Tom Paxton, Gordon Lightfoot, and Cat Stevens. Her song 'Lady-O' was a minor hit for The Turtles in 1969. David Geffen signed her, and in September 1971 Sill released her eponymous debut album, the first release for his label, Asylum. It was a beguiling, baroque triumph of Bach-like precision, Sill's layered vocals delivering lyrics of cryptic Christian mysticism and redemptive longing. The album did not sell well, but Sill seemed to be creeping up on commercial success. She featured on the front cover of *Rolling Stone*, toured the UK supporting Roy Harper, and appeared on BBC television's *Old Grey Whistle Test* twice.

Sill's second album, *Heart Food*, was released on Asylum in March 1973. Elaborately and ambitiously arranged and orchestrated by Sill herself, and with her lyrics' mystical tendencies resolving into something like orthodoxy on 'When The Bridegroom Comes', it was admired critically but again sold poorly. Sill's association with Asylum came to an end, and though she continued to write songs and began sessions for a third album at Mike Nesmith's studio, there would be no more Judee Sill records released in her lifetime. Years later, her small body of work provides incontrovertible evidence of a rich, deep well of talent. In 1978, a stray, belated review of *Heart Food* concluded, 'If she never is heard from again, she's created something of value right here, and it's a genuine shame that the only place you can find this masterpiece is in the odd deletion rack at virtually next to nothing prices. Wherever you are, come back.'[5]

She never did. After a few years of car accidents, declining health, and continued struggles with drug addiction, Sill died of an overdose on November 23, 1979. She had slipped so far into obscurity that no obituaries were published. The coroner ruled her death a suicide, on account of a note found near her body—a conclusion challenged by some friends, who thought the writings were most likely a journal entry or song lyrics.

Sill's two albums were all but forgotten for years, making the lonely journey from the deletion racks to second-hand stores. I first heard of them in the mid-1980s, shortly after coming across David Ackles's records. The Scottish singer-songwriter Jackie Leven, then not long out of Doll By Doll, recommended her. This was in response to me saying I liked Tim Hardin. (Both Leven and Hardin score 'lost genius' points, incidentally). At the time, I was working at the Record & Tape Exchange in Notting Hill Gate, London. I found Sill's albums easily enough, languishing in the bargain basement for a pittance. At first, I didn't get Leven's Tim Hardin comparison. But in time I did. It's something to do with the artist's total immersion in the spirit of their music.

Sill's life reads like a personification of the hippie counterculture gone wrong. She died young, alone and forgotten. But just a few years earlier, the press coverage around her debut album betrays clear attempts to package her chaotic life into a convenient rebel myth, the sort that the rock music industry thrives on. And signs, too, that Sill might have gone along with it. Though how knowingly it is impossible to say. Certainly, she was willing to talk about some of the more challenging aspects of her early life in interviews. But a certain damaged volatility and downright strangeness couldn't be contained in the myth. She said her biggest influence was Pythagoras. She railed in interviews against having to support rock bands, pleading with audiences to buy her album to deliver her from that particular evil. And, eventually, she insulted her benefactor, David Geffen, in public.

It took a while for Sill's posthumous rehabilitation to gather force, and—unlike Drake—she remains a music enthusiast's choice, not a household name. But the sequence of events is familiar. The lovingly curated reissues and issues of previously unreleased material from 2005 onward. A BBC Radio 4 show in 2014. A few cover versions of her songs. A documentary film in 2022.

Sill is an interesting comparator for Ackles. There are striking similarities and glaring differences in their stories. Both were supremely gifted piano-playing singer-songwriters operating in the booming Los Angeles music business at about the same time. Both were often described as folk artists in the absence of a more fitting description. Both had early life connections with Hollywood. Both were respected—even revered—by their peers. Both attracted critical acclaim during their careers. Both had the musical ability to perform to the highest standard yet struggled to translate their evident talent to rock audiences in a live setting. Both failed to sell many records and fell out of the music business shortly after their final releases in 1973. There was something hard to categorise about them. They were concerned with faith and spiritual things.

Unlike Sill, though, Ackles did not have a troubled adolescence before his music career, and he had a good life when the spotlight's glare moved on. A happy marriage and family, lots of friends, success in other ventures apart from music, a comfortable standard of living. There was the car crash and a relatively early death. But the car crash didn't kill or disable him, and you can't say he died young, just younger than anyone might have wished. It was still a good life. Though there was loss and pain, as there are in all lives, his story is not a tragedy. When his albums were reissued in the 1990s and a few journalists approached him for interviews, he was at pains to point out that things had been good for him.

The reappraisal of Judee Sill and Bill Fay's re-emergence were aided by the support of younger musicians who championed them and in doing so introduced their music to a new audience. David Tibet of Current 93 released several Fay albums on his own label. Jeff Tweedy of Wilco is another of Fay's cheerleaders, covering his songs and even coaxing the retiring British singer onto the stage at a Wilco show in London. Composer, singer-songwriter, instrumentalist, producer, and one-time Sonic Youth member Jim O'Rourke is another Fay enthusiast. And he mixed Judee Sill's third album *Dreams Come True* when it got a belated and posthumous first release in 2005. O'Rourke is perhaps the only contemporary musician sometimes operating in the rock world (albeit from the fringes of it) who champions Ackles, often mentioning him as one of his favourite artists. He hears in Ackles the conventions of serious art song.

JIM O'ROURKE 'Midnight Carousel' was one I liked as it reminded me of Charles Ives … it was the beginning of me stopping listening to pop and listening to more jazz and classical music. There's one Charles Ives song called 'The Cage' … even now I can still hear comparisons between that and something like 'Midnight Carousel'. I'd never heard a songwriter who was referencing this whole other area of music.[6]

And it's this very characteristic of Ackles's work, this distance from pop convention, that makes it harder for audiences now to engage.

JIM O'ROURKE Judee Sill's and Bill Fay's music is much easier to listen to for a lot of people, and fills in more of the checkboxes for what people are looking for in an undiscovered songwriter… I can understand that Ackles might be a step too far for them… his vocal melodies are not really from the pop tradition… they're more from the *Sprechgesang* and *Sprechstimme*, Weill style. And if your ear is used to that, that's not a problem. Judee Sill's melodies all come from Bach, it's all counterpoint—people are more used to that. I can see that it [Ackles's music] might seem a bit alien to the ear.[7]

Ackles, then, is very much like Cox's fictional lost hero, McKendree. He ticks some lost genius boxes. But not all of them. This is one reason why his reputation continues to hover a degree or two below cult figure status. Halfway through the research and writing of this book, I was very provisionally approached by a film production company looking for subjects. Briefly, a Netflix documentary seemed like a tantalising possibility. The conversation quickly stalled, though. Much as I would like Ackles's music to be explored in a documentary and to reach a wider audience, I was relieved in a way that it came to nothing. Maybe I'm doing the film company a disservice, but I think the story they wanted just wasn't there. It's been tempting, too, when writing this book, to try to locate Ackles's career with at least some reference to the lost genius coordinates. But that would be a distorting error, and I hope I've avoided it. Even if, in doing so, I've disappointed some readers and scuppered my chances of selling the rights to a film company.

It's easy to get drawn in. To think that somebody like Ackles only counts if he gets that retrospective reappraisal. And the only way to get the reappraisal is to squeeze him into a narrative that doesn't work. What if the reappraisal never happens? What if this book has no impact at all on Ackles's posthumous reputation because it doesn't tell the story that we all seem to want? That's not important. What's important is that David Ackles lived a good life and made some great records. If that's to the detriment of his posthumous reputation in an industry conditioned to thrive on stories of dissolute, collapsing lives, so be it. When viewed in the context of the lost genius paradigm as it's applied in rock music, Ackles is the wrong way around. If you're looking for anguish and self-destruction, you won't find it. The music trumps the story we've been primed to think of as a badge of authenticity. The more you suffer and the more you fall apart, the more 'real' your art is. Ackles doesn't fit into that. He lived an interesting life and made an enduring impression on people who knew him and his small audience. Without exception, everyone I spoke to when researching this book said he was a good man. Intelligent, talented, serious about his work. Cheerful, friendly, generous, good-humoured.

BERNIE TAUPIN I know it sounds odd, but I learnt a lot about decency from him, because he did have such a positive outlook all the time ... he was just a really great positive force. I benefitted from it.[8]

Nobody had anything bad to say about him, which is almost unheard of in an industry consumed by vanity and ego. But when it comes to rock history, it seems we prefer stories of despair and desolation. Though most of us would choose to live Ackles's life over Sill's, or Drake's, or Roky Erickson's, we have an insatiable thirst for the darker aspects of their stories. We want our tragedy and drama once removed.

This is the posthumous expression of one reason why Ackles didn't make it in the first place. His back story is intriguing, but it became obvious early on in his recording career that he wasn't really the sort of person you could package as a rock star. He was an anomaly. An Anglophile American. A theatre writer in the rock world. A Christian whose best friends were atheists. An optimistic man who made often dark, intense music. He was too old.

BERNIE TAUPIN It's not just that his music was different; he was different. David had a robust, Midwestern outdoorsy, open-range campfire character. When everyone else was West Coast cool or East Coast artsy, David seemed almost Paul Bunyan by comparison.[9]

And just as Ackles couldn't be conveniently packaged when active, so he resists easy categorisation now. And this, I contend, is one reason why he has yet to be posthumously canonised. There have been flurries of interest, but they've come to nothing. When his albums were reissued when he was still alive, there were a few 'where are they now?' magazine features. I wrote two of them myself. But so far, these brief ebbs and flows of interest have not accumulated into any sort of rising tide. Had Rhino Records released *There Is A River* in 2007, Ackles's name might now be a little better known. But maybe not much.

There is another reason why Ackles's albums have not yet benefitted from widespread reappraisal. His music will always be an acquired taste. And maybe not widely acquired. This is the main reason why he didn't sell a lot of records when active. The musical unfamiliarity and lyrical particularity of many of the songs, which read like mini film treatments or short stories, render them unsuitable for generic use. It's no accident that the cover versions tailed off the further Ackles progressed down his singular musical road.

It isn't right to describe Ackles as ahead of his time, or behind the times, or even out of time. It's more that there was no niche in the music business to accommodate his chosen metier when he was active. There still isn't now. He was a musical theatre writer influenced by the rock music of his day (to an extent), protestant hymns, classical music, and a bit of jazz and country. The musical theatre influence—his first love—dominated by the time he recorded his big statement, *American Gothic*. But as much as this approach disqualified him from rock stardom, it wouldn't have worked on Broadway or the West End, either. His mature music was a peculiar, unique hybrid—extreme, intense, idiosyncratic—with no natural home.

In England, at least, we have a romantic attachment to glorious failure, especially when it resolves in some kind of redemption. While writing this book, it's been tempting at times to try to fit Ackles into that arc as much as the lost genius one, but to do either would be a misrepresentation. Our culture conditions us to measure the value of art in the currencies of fame and money. By those measures, Ackles was a chronic underachiever. A talent that failed to deliver on its promise. But if we measure art in other ways—by a correlation between intent and outcome, by its capacity to move an audiencc (cven if small), by originality—Ackles was a successful artist. Resoundingly so.

APPENDIX ONE

THE CANTERBURY HOUSE RECORDINGS

TAPE 1

The Canterbury House archive held at Bentley Historical Library holds one audio recording of David Ackles, a cassette listed as tape number 12. There is no date and no other information written on the cassette.

There is music on both sides of the cassette, with a total running time of about one hour and thirty-five minutes. Both sides are dominated by songs from the first two albums, with all ten songs from *David Ackles* and five out of the eight on *Subway To The Country* included. Ackles also performs other songs that never got a commercial release. Session records indicate that Ackles attempted to record these unreleased songs in 1968 and 1969.

There are multiple obvious edits in the cassette, especially on side two, which indicates that the recordings were most likely dubbed from another source. This was probably a quarter-inch tape, as the recording booth at the venue held a reel-to-reel tape machine. It is unlikely that the recording was made direct to cassette.

Across both sides of the cassette, we hear five songs performed twice. While Ackles himself explains in the recording why he is playing 'Down River' for the second time that night (it's an audience encore request, and he says he doesn't have any more songs), it seems unlikely that he would play so many songs twice in one night.

There are some sound variations. To my ears, the piano sounds louder and a little out of tune on side two, while the vocal level fluctuates on some songs on side one. All of this points to the likelihood that tape number 12 was compiled from recordings of several Ackles sets, possibly spread across more than one of his residencies.

Given the provenance of the songs Ackles performs, both released and unreleased, it then becomes likely that this cassette is compiled from recordings of one or both of his first two Canterbury House residencies, in November 1968 and March 1969. Reviews of the first 1970 show mentioned two songs that would appear on *American Gothic*, but neither are featured on the cassette. The audience response appears warm throughout, with applause particularly spirited for 'Be My Friend' and 'Inmates Of The Institution'.

SIDE 1 (48:27)

1. 'Since You've Been Gone' (unreleased song)
A bluesy, jazzy ballad that shares something of the atmosphere of 'Woman River' (*Subway To The Country*). It is listed and crossed out on a quarter-inch tape box marked 'David Ackles Demo 20 Dec 1968' that belonged to David Anderle.

Ackles speaks after audience applause: 'Thank you, thank you.'

2. 'Road To Cairo'
Ackles speaks after audience applause: 'All right … gee … sounds like you don't care that you lost that game today [audience laughter] … yeah … funny thing.'

3. 'Where Is Canaan' (unreleased song)
A scathing social-comment song with Old Testament references (Canaan and Babylon), an early example of Ackles's dramatic musical-theatre style that matured on *American Gothic*. This is also listed and crossed out on the 'David Ackles Demo 20 Dec 1968' tape box.

4. 'Such A Woman'*
Assuming this version was recorded in 1968 or '69, this was then an unreleased song. Ackles recorded it for *Subway To The Country*, though it wasn't included on the album. He then re-recorded it for *Five & Dime*.

5. 'Sonny, Come Home'
Ackles speaks after audience applause. Words indistinct.

6. 'Lotus Man'*
This performance sounds less confident than all the others on the cassette. The vocals are sometimes hesitant, and the tuning drifts in places. Ackles changes the melody and phrasing for the phrase 'while the other world decays' and ends the song at that point on a crescendo.

Ackles speaks after audience applause: 'That song comes from living in San Francisco for too long. This next song came from living in Scotland for too long.'

7. 'His Name Is Andrew'
A brief smattering of applause when Ackles starts singing indicates that part of the audience was already familiar with this song.

8. 'Be My Friend'
Ackles begins this song underneath continuing applause for 'His Name Is Andrew'. Both this and the second version of the song on the cassette end after the last repeat of the words 'be my friend', with no extended instrumental coda.

Ackles speaks over prolonged audience applause: 'Thank you very much. It's not that cold.' There is a possible edit in the tape here. Ackles often ended his sets with 'Be My Friend', and there is a moment's silence at this point, before the next song.

9. 'Mainline Saloon'
Ackles speaks over audience applause: 'Thank you.' Edit in tape (applause cuts out abruptly).

10. 'That's No Reason To Cry'
11. 'Cabin On The Mountain'*

12. 'Blue Ribbons'*
Edit in tape. Applause cut off after one second.

*In these songs Ackles's voice is quiet in places, as if he is singing off-mic.

SIDE 2 (46:24)
1. 'Old Shoes'
An unreleased studio recording of this song survives in outtakes from sessions for the first album.

2. 'Inmates Of The Institution'
Ackles speaks after spirited audience applause, cheering and whistling: 'Thank you very much.'

3. 'Down River'
Edit in tape. Ackles speaks: 'I make a little list of songs that I'd like to sing. And they don't always correspond to songs you'd like to hear [laughs] so let me play [indistinct].'

4. 'Laissez-Faire'
The audience laughs when Ackles sings the line 'The government takes all the cash and eats it or something'. Edit in tape.

5. 'What A Happy Day'
Edit in tape. Ackles speaks over the introduction to the next song: 'This one you've already heard.'

6. 'Such A Woman'
Edit in tape.

7. 'When Love Is Gone'
Ackles speaks after audience applause: 'Last night I was accused . . . it was pointed out to me ... by various people that I sing very unhappy songs. So today I spent all afternoon trying to remember a happy song. [audience laughter] I don't know if I remembered it or not.'

8. 'In The Morning'
Unfinished backing tracks of this song survive in outtakes from sessions for the first album. Ackles's spoken introduction indicates it was not a regular feature in his live set.

9. 'His Name Is Andrew'

10. 'Be My Friend'
Edit in tape.

11. 'Inmates Of The Institution'
Edit in tape. Ackles speaks: 'Thank you very much [indistinct voice from audience]. How do you think I feel? You are really, really lovely people, and if I had known that Ann Arbor were here, I think I'd have been here all my life [audience laughter]. You're really nice [audience laughter]. Hey, don't knock it if it makes you this way. Um. You've heard all the stuff that I've got. Anything? [indistinct calls from audience] I'm sorry. Volume wins.'

12. 'Down River'
Slower than usual. Ackles's voice breaks with hoarseness in the final phrases.

TAPE 2

The second known recording of Ackles performing at Canterbury House is a reel-to-reel tape owned by Jim Friedrich, who worked at the venue. Friedrich's tape is a copy dubbed at 3.75 inches per second made from a Canterbury House recording that is now lost, of an Ackles performance on February 15, 1970. This was a Sunday, the third night of a three-night residency. The piano is panned to the right of the stereo spectrum, Ackles's voice to the left. Although there is evidence of at least one clear edit, this is much closer to a record of an Ackles concert than the Bentley Historical Library tape, with between song pauses, chatter, and audience interaction largely intact. Ackles sounds comfortable, playing and singing with panache and joking with the audience between songs. Judging by Ackles's remarks and the audience reactions, some of his comments were accompanied by gestures and comic facial expressions.

The song choices indicate that this recording is later than the Bentley tape, which was dominated by songs from the first two albums. Here, there are five songs from *David Ackles*, six from *Subway To The Country*, four that would later appear on *American Gothic*, and one that turned up on *Five & Dime*. Amid these recognisable songs from the Ackles catalogue are a pair of unreleased Ackles compositions and three cover versions. Ackles's between song patter indicates that he may have performed a fifth *American Gothic* song, which has been edited from the tape.

Unknown announcer: 'Evening. Welcome to Canterbury House. It's truly a pleasure to bring David Ackles back again this year. And—uh—nice crowd here tonight … ought to be a good night … will you all welcome Elektra recording artist and nice person and great musician et cetera … David Ackles.' [audience applause]

Ackles: 'One of the great dreams of my life is to one day wear a swallow-tailed coat and have a standard grand and walk out and do one of those [Ackles and audience laugh] … it just never has worked out. The direction of the directory is vastly important to the quality of my performance. At base I'm an obscurantist. You'll get used to that after a while. It won't bother you at all.'

1. 'American Gothic'
Ackles opens the set with a then unreleased song.

Ackles: 'There he is folks, your favourite musical polemicist striking again. I recognise some faces from previous meetings, and I really wish that I had written about twenty new songs for the weekend. But I haven't. So I should tell you that upfront in case you were harbouring secret hopes … parallel to my own. But I haven't. It's just the old songs.' Plays piano chords and continues speaking, words obscured.

2. 'That's No Reason To Cry'
Delivered softly, ending with a brief, gentle piano improvisation.

Ackles: 'I have a feeling that this piano is slanted more than it was on previous occasions, as I feel that I'm really [goes off mic, speech becomes unclear, some audience laughter]. Oh, that's a vast improvement. Vast. Vastly improved.'

3. 'Laissez-Faire'
Slower and more relaxed compared to the recorded version.

4. 'Inmates Of The Institution'
Ackles: 'I think the next time I come [unclear] a couple of young ladies to sort of sit around and between songs they can get up and shake tambourines or something. I can kind of back off from what I just did and start what I'm going to do. It's a problem. On television sets you can just switch channels [unclear—audience laughs]. Well, they only last for four minutes. Okay, this being Sunday night, it's the Sunday night song [more audience laughter]. No, no, not that one.'

5. 'Family Band'
The audience clap when Ackles starts playing, indicating familiarity with the song, even though it was unreleased at the time. As this was the last night of a three-night residency, the audience familiarity and a subsequent remark indicate Ackles played it on the previous two nights. After the song, the audiences reacts with louder and more prolonged applause compared to the reaction to the previous four songs.

Ackles: 'And don't I wish I had ten more, just like that. No [audience laughs] … anything but that. Yes, those of you who were here before know that that is a true story [something unclear, off mic].'

6. 'Road To Cairo'
Ackles: 'It's really funny, I've been singing essentially the same eighteen songs—twenty songs actually, I added two—the whole weekend, and that's the first time I've ever sung that song this weekend. That's what happens with old songs. They just get old. Play 'em once in a while … that's about it.'

7. 'Old Man' (possible title)
An unreleased song. The applause is faded down after the song and then back up again. This might indicate an edit, although Ackles's subsequent remark suggests otherwise.

Ackles: 'Anyway, now that I've done a song about an old man, I'll do the only song I have about children. It's only fair, after all. It's my security blanket in disguise. Did anyone watch the *Peanuts* show this afternoon? It was called Come Back Snoopy or something like that. Snoopy ran away [unclear, audience laughter] . . . the baseball player, right? Oh boy. At least Lucy's upfront about it. But she's gonna—she could deal with that. She's neat. But ... aah ... what a state. I felt bad about the whole thing [audience laughter] but I'm getting over it. I'll be okay.'

8. 'What A Happy Day'
Ackles: 'I'm sorry for all these lengthy pauses that work their way into evenings. There are times when I'm actually articulate and make myself understood by waitresses and bellhops and people like that. This is more of a [unclear]. This next song is a little ditty ... is intended to make you rise up as a body and go out and form civilian boards of review over police actions. It was written as a result of several deaths in Los Angeles, brought on by the police, of people who were innocent of anything. There are only two in the song but there are others of which you should be aware. One was a guy leaning over into his glove compartment when he was stopped for a ticket to get his car registration, and he got shot. Then there were two kids who were up in Griffith Park and they had jumped over the fence of the merry-go-round which is there, and the policeman who was coming by in his car—it was late at night and they had no business being there, except that it's a toy for children and they were children—I don't think it much matters whether it's day or night. They don't grow up at night and the carousel doesn't go away. So, the policeman came by and called to them to stop, and they were scared and they ran away, and he fired a shot—he says he fired into the air twice before he fired at them, and he killed one of them, and then there are these that are in the song.'

9. 'The Boys In Blue'
An unreleased song. As Ackles's introduction indicates, this is a strident protest song, delivered with intensity.

Ackles: 'I lose touch [unclear] bear with me. This is kind of ... I feel a little weird about tonight. A little. In that you're acting a lot less like an audience than most audiences and I tend to respond as if you're all just sitting around, which is what you're doing. It reduces it all to its reality, which is that you're all sitting around, I'm sitting over here—which is only three feet, you know—and I'm playing and singing. It's all kind of silly, isn't it? I mean, it's nice, I like it and I'm glad you're here. And that's why some of the songs that require a little more theatre, let's say—are harder to do. I'm sitting in a living room—it just doesn't work [audience laughter]. Maybe this next one will be more fun, as it's a living room song. Here's a song about a living room [audience laughter]—it's not that at all. Now this is a song about Montana, but it's long and drawn out and sort of relaxed.'

Ackles appears to be introducing 'Montana Song', later the centrepiece of *American Gothic*, at this point. There is documentary evidence that Ackles had already cut a demo of the song by this date. But there's an edit in the tape, and we don't hear 'Montana Song.'

10. 'Subway To The Country'
Ackles sings the verses slowly and softly compared to the recorded version, thus emphasising the dynamic contrast with the swelling 'your daddy, he's going to try ... ' sections.

11. 'Main Line Saloon'
Ackles: 'Did the dog leave? I used to have a cat, long time ago, who drove me nuts. Every time I'd sit down at the piano, he'd crawl up next to me and dig his claws into my shoulder in an attempt to get me to stop. But not to be discouraged, I ignored it. He died [audience laughter]. [Unclear] and death came to a cat named Chaucer.'

12. 'Candy Man'
Ackles: 'I feel like we've come down to the loyal few, at the end of a long winter. What is that mess? Someone has chewed up a Styrofoam cup and left it.'

Audience member: 'The dog did it.'

Ackles: Did the dog do that? That dog is a [unclear]. Did he swallow it? You all sat around and watched that dog eat a cup, and nobody did a thing.'

Audience member: 'My dog [audience laughter].'

Ackles: '[Unclear] ... the house lights up a little. It's just not fair, that you can see me and I'm up here and can't see you. Just this blank wall of darkness. But I can see you now. So watch it! I can see.'

13. 'One Night Stand'
The fourth as-yet unreleased song that later appeared on *American Gothic*. Applause is faded after the song, indicating an edit.

Ackles: 'Between now and the next time, when I come back, I'm going to take lessons to gratefully accept applause. I think there's a lesson there that I haven't quite picked up on. I really appreciate it, though, but I really have a hard time dealing with it. Well? Hmm. I feel like, something else. I'm going to do these things from the first set again. No one requested these ... I'm just going to do them anyway.

14. 'Family Band'
The audience can be heard singing along, and there is loud and prolonged applause and cheering when the song ends.

Ackles: 'That's the nicest kind of surprise I've had all week. You all know [unclear] that I played first, and next time I come back I expect you all to sing that, too. Gee, while I'm in that vein ...'

Audience member: 'David. "Be My Friend"?'

Ackles: 'I'll sing that last.'

Audience member: '"Down River"?'

Ackles: 'Let me play "Cabin" first.'

15. 'Cabin In The Mountain'
Ackles: 'Thank you. I just had a picture flash across my mind. Which was, *Abandon all polemics, ye who enter here* ... [unclear] warn you. It was for me, that was the sign.' (Ackles is probably referring to a famous quote from Dante's *Inferno*, sometimes translated as 'Abandon all hope ye who enter here.')

16. 'Such A Woman'
Although this song wasn't released until Ackles's final album, *Five & Dime*, it must have been a favourite of his, as he performed it throughout his career.

Ackles: 'This very next song was requested ... it just struck me as kind of weird that anyone would want to hear it. This particular song. I play it a lot, but I do that sort of thing. I sit down and play songs I know people don't enjoy. And it isn't that I don't want to entertain or anything like that. I do, and I really want people—you, not just people, you—to enjoy what I do or I wouldn't be here. I write songs for people to hear [unclear, makes a sound like popping his cheek with his finger] but I just want you to be aware of that, that I understand when you don't enjoy a song. I really do, and that absolutely . . . that's more valid than sitting back and saying it's all terrible or it's all wonderful. And I think the tendency in music lately has been to go, *So and so: fantastic. So and so: terrible*, and there are things you can hear in what people do and if you're not enjoying it you should just make that known to other people and you know? You may be right. All of that person's stuff is not good. All of that person's stuff is not bad. Aah—shut up, David [audience laughs].'

17. 'His Name Is Andrew'
Ackles introduces multiple small changes in phrasing, speak-singing some lines, and often singing behind the beat. Allowing a few seconds silence after the last chord dies away, Ackles begins the next song without a spoken introduction.

18. 'Be My Friend'
Ackles: 'Thank you very much. [Prolonged audience applause, which fades, indicating edit.] This has really been a very nice evening, all of it, I really did enjoy it [unclear] and I wish that I had some knockout positive songs to send you off, away. But I don't. I know it's terrible, and stupid and awful but . . .'

Audience member: 'Play the church song again.'

Ackles: 'Yes, I was going to say, do you mind if we all . . . [drowned out by applause]. Let's all sing the first part together . . . [unclear] . . . it's a good song.'

19. 'Family Band'
The audience sings along, and after the song finishes, applauds and cheers.

Ackles: 'Now you know as well as I do that I don't have another song . . .'

Audience member: 'Can you play a hymn?'

Ackles: 'Uh huh . . . that's not a particularly good idea. Well, what shall we do?'

There follows banter between Ackles and members of the audience as they suggest hymns he could sing. Ackles demurs and says that he doesn't know the hymns, only the chords. He then begins improvising on the piano and gradually moves into 'What A Friend We Have In Jesus' followed by 'In The Garden', encouraging the audience to sing along, to cover for his unfamiliarity with the lyrics. He joins in with some lines. ('What A Friend We Have In Jesus', with words by Joseph M. Scriven and music by Charles Crozat Converse, dated from the late nineteenth century. 'In The Garden', by C. Austin Miles, is from 1912. Both are popular evangelical gospel hymns.)

After a particularly florid piano run Ackles quips, 'Baptist piano. That's what that's called.' The set closes with a similar sing along on the country standard 'The Green Green Grass Of Home'.

APPENDIX TWO

UNRELEASED SONGS

In an email sent on October 18, 1998, Ackles wrote in response to my question 'do you have any unreleased material in the vaults that might get released one day':

> Stuff in the vaults? You bet! A lot of it is with demo singers, some just me and the piano, a few with full orchestra. As with any performer, there are cuts which just didn't fit the concept when the album was put together. These few still don't make up a coherent collection of songs, but maybe one day…

This is a list of all of David Ackles's unreleased songs that I'm aware of, in rough chronological order, according to the information I have. It does not include alternate versions of released songs. I know it is incomplete. For example, I haven't been able to track down any of the songs Ackles wrote in the period after being dropped by Columbia, when he was still working as a staff songwriter for Warner Bros (some of these might be the material recorded with demo singers Ackles mentioned). Therefore, nothing from those years is listed unless some of those songs cropped up in later musical theatre projects of or were developed from earlier songs not included on the four albums and listed here.

I have heard some of the following songs—as studio outtakes, fly-on-the-wall rehearsal captures, or live recordings. The others I know of from musical theatre scripts, session records, and other documents. With each song I list the source and a date if known, and sometimes a few descriptive notes.

THE ELEKTRA PERIOD

• 'Happy Birthday World' (AFM session records, January 11, 1968)
I haven't heard any evidence of this song, but it is listed in the same run of sessions as the next four.

• 'In The Morning' (Elektra outtake / AFM session records, January 12, 1968 / Canterbury House cassette, likely 1968/69)
This is a lighter, upbeat song by Ackles's standards. The Elektra outtake does not have a vocal. Ackles performed it at Canterbury House in response to a request for a more upbeat song. The chorus strikes an optimistic note:

> *Step out in the morning*
> *and you'll find a new love*
> *waiting in the morning*
> *see the dew dress and lilac glove*
> *In the morning.*

• 'It's Me, It's Me' (Elektra outtake / AFM session records, January 12, 1968)
Another faster song, with no vocal on the Elektra outtake. Much of the song is on a two-chord pattern.

• 'We Are Not Ready' (Elektra outtake / AFM session records, January 16, 1968)
Starting off a little like an accelerated 'Stand By Me', this is another medium-to-fast-

tempo number. What are presumably the verses are restrained, while the choruses swell dynamically. Slows down into a dramatic ending. No vocal.

• 'Old Shoes' (Elektra outtake / AFM session records, January 16, 1968 / Canterbury House cassette, likely 1968/69)
A slow, simple blues shuffle, with a vocal, recorded during sessions for *David Ackles*. This was included on the abandoned *There Is A River* box set.

• 'The Grave Of God' (Elektra outtake, 1968)
Also slated for *There Is A River*, lyrically 'Grave of God' explores similar themes to 'His Name Is Andrew'. Slow, with a picked electric guitar, organ, and bass.

• 'Since You've Been Gone' (David Anderle archive, December 20, 1968 / Canterbury House cassette, 1968/69)
This song is listed (and crossed out) on the back of a box of a quarter-inch tape reel kept by David Anderle, with 'David Ackles demo' written on the front of the box. It can also be heard as a live recording from Canterbury House. The Anderle tape reel includes several songs that were later included on *Subway To The Country*.

A first-person bluesy lament that features one of Ackles's favoured plot devices—the narrator trying to persuade himself of something that we, the audience, know isn't true.

My friends all try to tell me
Leave that girl alone
She ain't coming home
But they don't see they just don't see
You've got to find yourself
And when you find yourself
You'll find me.

• 'Where Is Canaan' (David Anderle archive, December 20, 1968 / Canterbury House cassette, 1968/69)
Again, listed and crossed out on the Anderle tape box, and included in the first Canterbury House live recording.

Lyrically, musically, and in terms of general atmosphere, this bears a faint resemblance to 'His Name Is Andrew' and the darker songs on *American Gothic*. Ackles references Biblical place names (Canaan, Babylon) in a gloomy lyric of alienation:

Lord I'm so tired of living among strangers
in Babylon
I can't go on
You don't care.

• 'Hello Woman' (David Anderle archive, December 20, 1968)
Listed, but not crossed out, on the Anderle tape box (see above).

• 'Was It Only Yesterday' (David Anderle archive, December 20, 1968)
Again, listed but not crossed out on the Anderle tape box.

• 'Theme To The Way We Live Now' (1969)
On November 29, 1969, the *Press & Sun Bulletin* reported that Ackles was writing the theme song to the movie *The Way We Live Now*, though the film does not include a song by Ackles.

• 'Old Man' (Possible title. Jim Friedrich reel-to-reel tape of an Ackles live performance at

Canterbury House, February 15, 1970)
An old man is teased by children:

Like a flower in the snow
At first it pleases him
As some sign of life
In the coldness of his day today, today.

Fast, pent-up, restrained piano arpeggios in the verse break out into bouncy honky-tonk rhythms in the chorus.

• 'The Boys In Blue' (Possible title. Jim Friedrich reel-to-reel tape of an Ackles live performance at Canterbury House, February 15, 1970)
Ackles's most direct protest song, deploying a similar device to 'Blues For Billie Whitecloud', choosing a deliberately bright, singalong idiom to throw the dismal subject matter into sharp relief:

It's good to know how the boys in blue
Are watching out for me and you
Just remember they're human too
When you're having fun and you have a gun
What's a mistake or two?

• 'Hold Me In Your World' (June 28, 1971)
A proposed (and unused) theme for the movie *Klute*, co-written by David Ackles and Michael Small and included on the unreleased *There Is A River*. A ballad with a simple acoustic guitar, piano, and bass arrangement.

• 'There Is A River' (Elektra outtake, March 1972)
A rousing, hymn-like song with piano, brass, percussion, and a Salvation Army choir. One of two complete songs recorded during the *American Gothic* sessions but left off the album.

• 'I'm Only Passing Through' (Elektra outtake, March 1972)
The second *American Gothic* outtake, an acoustic country-rock-style song. Both this and 'There Is A River' were included in the *There Is A River* box set.

POST-RECORDING CAREER, MUSICAL THEATRE PERIOD: LA BOHÈME

In the late 70s, Ackles and Douglas Graham were commissioned to create a contemporary resetting of Puccini's *La Bohème*, which was eventually abandoned after they fell out with the producer. At least four songs were completed and recorded in some form, as Ackles included a cassette demo of them with a letter to Joseph Papp at New York's Public Theater, dated October 7, 1984. In the letter, he describes the songs as 'based on the Puccini score'. They are:

• 'Waiting In Line'
A complex six-minute song that moves from abstract sung/spoken sections with characters trading remarks to a rousing pop chorus. Ackles overlays his voice to create three-part harmonies, giving a decent impression of what a staged performance with a full cast might sound like.

• 'Xmas Rag'
Again, Ackles takes multiple sung and spoken vocal parts in a song that starts off merging rattling ragtime piano with churchy choral choruses. References to Dickens's *A Christmas Carol* underline the seasonal flavour. As things progress, it all becomes strange, with references

to uncles giving unsuitable Christmas presents and unexpected art-song melodic twists and chord changes.

• 'Mississippi Small Talk'
Ackles voices a character harking back to small-town life in Moline, Illinois (close to Rock Island, where Ackles was born). Shorn of the dialogue, it's a delicate and exquisite ballad.

• 'Country Home'
As the title suggests, a country-style song. This and 'Mississippi Small Talk' are the equal of anything on Ackles's four albums.

ALLENDOR / PRINCE JACK
(Script and four-song demo cassette, mid-70s to mid-80s / New York Public Library)
Ackles spent some years working on a musical adaptation of *The Little Lame Prince And His Travelling Cloak* by Dinah Craik. His project was first titled *Allendor* and then *Prince Jack.* Douglas Graham recalls helping Ackles record some songs from this project in a medieval style, with piano, nylon-string guitar, and lute, at Bruce Langhorne's studio. This was sometime in the 1970s, a few years after *Five & Dime.*

When Ackles approached the Public Theater, New York, in 1984, his primary purpose was to propose a production of *Allendor / Prince Jack.* By 1985, Ackles had a full script of this project complete featuring twenty songs (listed below). During these interactions, Ackles sent a cassette with what he described as 'sketches' of four of those songs: 'Without Words', 'Other Boys', 'A-Hunting A La King', and 'Friends', all roughly two minutes long. These are not the Graham/Langhorne recordings.

• 'This Is It!'
• 'Christening Day'

• 'Your Face, Your Smile'
Stacy Sullivan covered 'Your Face, Your Smile', a love song from a father to a child, on her album *At The Beginning.*

• 'A Proper Name'
• 'For All Good Things'
• 'Laudes Regiae'
• 'We Bid You, Welcome'
• 'How Delicious To Be A King'
• 'Growing Up Inside'
• 'Happy Twelfth Jubilee, Orfred The Good'
• 'Anyone But You'
• 'In The Business'

• 'Friends' (fourth song on the Public Theater demo)
A novelty ditty. You can imagine one of Ackles's performing forbears in the music hall singing it.

• 'Without Words' (first song on the Public Theater demo)
This is a short, sweet ballad that would have fitted comfortably on *Five & Dime.*

• 'And A Little More'
• 'I'm A Falcon, I'm A Lark'

• 'A-Hunting A La King' (third song on the Public Theater demo)
Referencing Shakespeare ('hey nonny nonny') and jugs of mead to conjure up an Olde English atmosphere, Ackles adopts an indeterminate Dick Van Dyke-style accent to voice a servant's speaking part.

• 'Duty'

• 'Other Boys' (second song on the Public Theater demo)
Written in the voice of the boy at the centre of the story and comprising a list of things 'other boys' can do that he can't (run, jump, climb a tree, and so on). 'In the whole wide world, I'm the only boy who never learned to spit.'

• 'Before The Dawn'

SISTER AIMEE

Ackles was working on the musical *Sister Aimee* by 1988, though he might have started some time earlier. He kept working on the project until close to the end of his life. There were several iterations of the script and songs in that time. This list of songs with the associated notes is compiled from multiple sources: programme notes for 1991 and 1995 readings; a full script from 1991; a fragmentary rehearsal cassette recording for the 1991 reading; and a studio-recorded demo cassette from 1994 featuring singers/actors Judy Kaye, Richard White, Teri Ralston, and Jack Ritschel.

• 'Aimee's Answer'

• 'Welcome To Angelus Temple'
A rousing fanfare of a song in 3/4 time, sung by the temple choir (the chorus). 'Each person has a home here 'neath the dome here.'

• 'Suffer The Heathens'
Sung by Aimee with the choir supporting. Fast ragtime-influenced sections morph into multiple time changes and pauses. Toward the end, the song slows as Aimee sings a reverie to the spirit of her deceased first husband, Robert. 'Why did you die?'

• 'Kneel and Pray'
A straightforward hymn that sounds like it could have come out of an early twentieth-century evangelical hymnal. Slow, with a repeated verse/bridge/chorus structure.

• 'Forever' (parts 1 and 2)
A slow duet between Aimee and her lover, Kenneth Ormiston. In part 2, Kenneth takes Aimee to the cottage where the couple hide out during Aimee's supposed kidnapping. 'From now on there's no more Sister Aimee, can you blame me?' Structurally complex, with no obvious verse/chorus structure, 'Forever' needs male and female voices with wide ranges.

• 'Minnie's Daughter'
Minnie is Aimee's mother (Minnie Kennedy), here addressing her daughter, who she doesn't understand. 'Who taught you how, it sure wasn't me?'

• 'America Wants To Know' (parts 1 and 2)

• 'Aren't We Lucky'
'Aren't we lucky to be living in the Golden State?' Jaunty, sarcastic, Jazz Age satire. Harmony ensemble singing with sung/spoken sections.

• 'Every Face I See'
An intense, slowly building ballad with Aimee unburdening herself to Emma Shaffer, her devoted secretary.

• 'Drowned'
• 'I'm On Top'
• 'This Waltz Is Your Waltz'
• 'Dance With Me'
• 'Minnie Responds'

• 'Hymn To The Sea'
A choral lament, with a repeated refrain of 'Oh sea, give up thy dead'.

• 'Here's To Aimee'
'Our ninety-point headline queen.'

• 'Santuaridad'

• 'Ave Mater Dei'
Choral. Sorrowful and slow, as if from a Latin Mass.

• 'Waiting To Say Hello'
• 'The Healing'

• 'One Of The People'
Written for the William Randolph Hearst character, the newspaper tycoon and inspiration for Orson Welles's *Citizen Kane*. On the demo, the song is performed by Jack Ritschel, who played Hearst in the 1992 film *Chaplin*. Ackles himself interjects briefly, as Hearst's butler Jensen. Mid-paced, with syncopated piano.

• 'Here With You'
Another spare ballad duet with Aimee and Kenneth. Aimee struggles to balance her love of Kenneth with her commitment to her work. 'Millions of people need me.'

APPENDIX THREE

THE SUBWAY TO THE COUNTRY INTERVIEW

'David Ackles About Subway To The Country' / 'Subway To The Country' (Elektra DA-1, 1970)
The A-side of this seven-inch promo single has David Ackles talking about living in New York and his inspirations for 'Subway To The Country'. The B-side is the song itself.

DAVID ACKLES There was a time, you know, when I lived in New York. That's a kind of a bummer experience. It can be—I don't think it necessarily has to be—depends on how much you're willing to live the life of the New Yorker—and subdue your own natural longings for the natural life. Unfortunately, I never could quite adjust to it, and this last time I was back there was in the capacity of a performer and I was … hate to say stuck, but that's what I felt, for six weeks in New York, and it just finally got to me that the main problem with New York is that you can't get out of it, that you are really stuck there. And I was talking with a friend of mine who the year before that had been teaching in elementary school, and she had the kids drawing a winter scene, that I guess was the assignment or something, and several of the kids came back with just all grey, because for them that was what winter was, this grey stuff that came down out of the sky. And it really hit me that here are some kids, probably eight or nine years old, who've never seen snow the way it really is. It's snow after it's already come through the city, and all of their experiences are filtered through the city. So, consequently, they have no ... they're totally out of touch with the reality of the earth they're living on. So, how can we expect that that generation, coming up out of New York, out of Philadelphia, out of any major city in the East, is going to be deeply concerned about the earth they're living on? We can't expect that, because for them the bad air, the bad water the lack of sunlight are natural conditions. And there's a kind of tragedy in that. So that, plus the human thing, of kids ought to have a place to go where they can be kids. And the place to do that is in the country. And so I wrote this 'Subway To The Country'—at least it was the result of all of that, and, uh, it pretty much sums up what I've wanted to do musically for a long time, too. And that I think finally I can say just something as simply as possible.

INTERVIEWER Why the two little boys in the song, was there any particular reason for that?

DAVID ACKLES Well [*clears throat*], it's because while I was there I spent a lot of time in Central Park. I don't know, well, Central Park and Battery Park, because somehow they both—at least you're not absolutely surrounded with the city, and yet you are, it's very much a city park. And I was always seeing groups of little boys, either playing hooky or just there, or whatever. And they were fulfilling a lot of dreams and imaginings of childhood. And all I could think was, *Yeah, but given better tools, who could these kids be?* And there's a kind of poignance in thinking in terms of them being your own kids—if they were my sons, would this be the kind of life I would wish for them? And it wouldn't be.

ACKNOWLEDGEMENTS

I first spoke to Janice Vogel Ackles about her husband's career more than twenty-five years ago. In the years since we have spoken many times and exchanged dozens of emails. This book would not have been possible without her support, generosity, and insight. I am indebted to her.

Janice introduced me to several people close to David who were similarly free-handed and supportive. I had two lengthy conversations with Douglas Graham, followed by many emails. Douglas lived in Wargrave, England, with David in late 1971 and helped produce David's last album, *Five & Dime*. David and Douglas collaborated on several musical and scriptwriting projects thereafter. Douglas provided much detail about the home recording of *Five & Dime* and life in Wargrave, when Ackles was preparing *American Gothic*. Steve Spellman and David were close friends from teenage years until David's death. Without him I would not have known of David's failed attempt to crack Broadway in the months immediately after leaving university. David's younger sister Kim Nixon provided information about the Ackles family that I would not have been able to find anywhere else.

Jim Friedrich met David when he played at Canterbury House, Ann Arbor. The two became friends and remained in touch. Jim allowed me to hear a live tape he holds of David performing at Canterbury House, which is the most complete record of David Ackles the live performer that I'm aware of. Thanks too to Jim's sister, Marilyn Robertson, for use of her photo of David performing at Jim's ordination service.

Several fellow music writers and researchers went above and beyond any conceivable call of duty. I have been talking to Brian Mathieson about David Ackles since the late 1990s, when he launched his Ackles fansite. Brian has been a constant encouragement during the writing of this book. Richie Unterberger and Mick Houghton shared helpful unpublished interview material. Richie viewed an archive television performance that I could not see remotely and provided detailed notes. Justin Rivers sent me old reviews of *Five & Dime* that I hadn't seen before. Adam James Smith provided information from his research into the *Colour Me Pop* television programme. Nuno Robles copied for me the original transcript of John Tobler's lengthy interview with David Ackles, conducted in 1973. Nick Warburton helped me navigate the intricate network of relationships around the Elektra supergroup, Rhinoceros, members of which played on David's first album before Rhinoceros formed.

Several people enabled me to access invaluable archive material. Producer Andy Zax shared a wealth of previously unreleased recordings from the Elektra era, which he unearthed when preparing the aborted *There Is A River* box set. Hearing these outtakes and studio chatter helped me to gain a far richer understanding of David's approach than I would have got simply listening to the records. Peter Charlton delved into the British Music Hall society archives and located information about the rich performing history on the maternal side of David's family, which had such an influence on him. Peter Delaney at the Wargrave Local History Society provided detail about the peculiar character of the corner of England where David lived when preparing and recording *American Gothic*. Caitlin Moriarty at the Bentley Historical Library was extraordinarily helpful in unearthing documents about and live recordings of David's appearances at Canterbury House. Similarly helpful was Rose Doylemason, of the American Federation of Musicians Local 47, who located multiple records for David's many Los Angeles recording sessions.

Bernie Taupin met David in 1970 and the two became close. He went on to produce *American Gothic*. Bernie sent me a written account summing up his perceptions of David and their work together, which he enlarged on in a subsequent call. Damon Lyon Shaw was *American Gothic*'s engineer. In many emails he provided technical detail about the album sessions. Damon, Bernie and Janice were in the studio everyday with David as he recorded *American Gothic* back in March 1972. Taken together, their complimentary recollections paint a detailed picture of the making of David's masterwork. I'm grateful for their insights.

I referred to many books when researching *Down River*. Two stand out as particularly helpful. Jeremy Harding's memoir *Mother Country* is essential reading for anyone wanting to get a sense of life in the community of ramshackle dwellings on the banks of the River Loddon, in Wargrave, where Ackles lived when making *American Gothic*. Howard Massey's *The Great British Recording Studios* takes you into IBC studios in London, where that album was recorded.

John Sparks, Jan Powell, Ken Stone, and Stacy Sullivan all knew Ackles in the latter part of his life, when he was working on his last major creative project, *Sister Aimee*. Their observations cast light on a project that I had previously only heard mention of. Furthermore, Ken provided a recording of Ackles rehearsing singers for a workshop performance of *Sister Aimee*, as well as programmes and other documents. Stacy sent me the script of her show about Ackles and Elton John, *A Night At The Troubadour*, and a demo cassette of songs from *Sister Aimee*.

For information and encouragement, thanks also to Jon Boden, Tom Cox, Doug Hastings, Barney Hoskyns, Ian Kearey, Jon Keliehor, Jon Klages, Mark Leviton, Tim McAlmont, Phil McMullen, Jim O'Rourke, Mike Ross, Lynda Rutherford, Phil Smee, Pat Thomas, Dean Torrence, John Tobler, Steve Turner and Craig Woodson.

Thank you to my agent Matthew Hamilton, for taking *Down River* to Tom Seabrook and Nigel Osborne at Jawbone Press. A sort of homecoming.

Finally, and most of all, thank you to Madeleine.

I don't think I've forgotten anyone, but if I have, I apologise. Any mistakes are mine.

BIBLIOGRAPHY

BOOKS

Elvis Costello, *Unfaithful Music & Disappearing Ink* (Viking, 2015)

Tom Cox, *Villager* (Unbound, 2022)

Tom Davies, *The Reporter's Tale* (Berwyn Mountain Press, 2009)

Howard Fishman, *To Anyone Who Ever Asks: The Life, Music, And Mystery Of Connie Converse* (Wildfire, 2023)

Rosemary Gray and Sue Griffiths, *The Book Of Wargrave: History And Reminiscences Of The People Of Wargrave* (Wargrave Local History Society, 1986)

Jeremy Harding, *Mother Country* (Faber, 2006)

Phil Hardy and Dave Laing, *The Encyclopedia Of Rock Volume 2: From Liverpool To San Francisco* (Panther, 1976)

Jac Holzman and Gavan Daws, *Follow The Music: The Life And High Times Of Elektra Records In The Great Years Of American Pop Culture* (FirstMedia, 1998)

Barney Hoskyns, *Hotel California: Singer-Songwriters And Cocaine Cowboys In The LA Canyons, 1967–1976* (Fourth Estate, 2005)

Mick Houghton, *Becoming Elektra: The True Story Of Jac Holzman's Visionary Record Label* (Jawbone, 2010)

Jerome K. Jerome, *Three Men In A Boat* (1889)

Elton John, *Me* (Pan 2020)

Howard Massey, *The Great British Recording Studios* (Rowman & Littlefield, 2015)

Gerald Newman & Joe Bivona, *Elton John: Behind The Spotlights And Sequins* (NEL, 1976)

Clive Selwood, *All The Moves (But None Of The Licks): Secrets Of The Record Business* (Peter Owen, 2003)

Adam James Smith, *Colour Me Pop—A Guide To The Pioneering BBC2 Music Show* (unpublished manuscript)

Jacques Vassal, *Electric Children: Roots And Branches Of Modern Folk-Rock* (Taplinger, 1976)

NEWSPAPERS AND MAGAZINES

Albuquerque Journal, Baltimore Sun, Beat Instrumental, Billboard, Capitol Journal, Cash Box, Chicago Tribune, Citizen News, Classic Rock, College Report, Creem, Croydon Advertiser, Daily Trojan, Democrat & Chronicle, Detroit Free Press, Disc & Music Echo, The Era, Fat Angel, Guardian, Hartford Courant, High Fidelity, Hit Parader, Hot Wacks, Independent, International Times, Los Angeles Free Press, Los Angeles Times, Melody Maker, Mercury (Pottstown), Michigan Daily, Mid-Lothian Journal, Montreal Gazette, The Nation, New Musical Express, New Statesman, New York Times, Philadelphia Inquirer, Phonograph, Phonograph Record, Post-Crescent, Press & Sun Bulletin, Ptolemaic Terrascope, Quad City Times, Rolling Stone, San Antonio Express & News, San Francisco Examiner, Sounds, The Stage, The Sunday Times, The Tidings, Times-Herald Newport News, Time Out, Uncut, Valley News, Valley Times, Vanity Fair, Village Voice, Zig Zag.

ENDNOTES

CHAPTER 1

1 Email to author, October 19, 1998
2 Email to author, November 11, 2022
3 *Mid-Lothian Journal*, December 27, 1907
4 *The Era*/*The Stage*, December 12, 1908
5 *The Stage*, October 8, 1914
6 *Time Out*, May 19, 1972
7 Author's interview, April 24, 1998
8 Author's interview, July 1, 2000
9 *Los Angeles Times*, May 22, 1955
10 Email to author, November 11, 2022
11 Email to author, November 11, 2022
12 Tobler, 1973 (via Robles)
13 *Ptolemaic Terrascope*, February 1994
14 Tobler, 1973 (via Robles)
15 *Valley Times*, March 1, 1960
16 *Beat Instrumental*, November 1968
17 *The Tidings*, March 6, 1964
18 *College Report*, broadcast May 24, 1964
19 *Los Angeles Times*, June 3, 1967
20 *Los Angeles Times*, August 6, 1962
21 *Los Angeles Times*, June 6, 1965

CHAPTER 2

1 Jac Holzman and Gavan Daws, *Follow The Music*
2 *Rolling Stone*, June 22, 1968
3 Jac Holzman and Gavan Daws, *Follow The Music*
4 Tobler, 1973 (via Robles)
5 *Evening Standard*, September 21, 1968
6 Email to author, October 18, 2024
7 Richie Unterberger, interview with Janice Ackles, 2002
8 Richie Unterberger, interview with David Anderle, June 24, 2002
9 Mick Houghton, previously unpublished interview with Jac Holzman c. 2007, conducted during research for *Becoming Elektra*
10 *Hit Parader*, July 1970
11 *Cash Box*, July 20, 1968
12 www.rhinoceros-group.com/dailyflash.htm, accessed January 6, 2025
13 Author's interview, March 16, 2023
14 Richie Unterberger, interview with David Anderle, June 24, 2002
15 Author's interview, April 3, 2023
16 Richie Unterberger, interview with David Anderle, June 24, 2002
17 Tobler, 1973 (via Robles)
18 Author's interview, April 24, 1998
19 Richie Unterberger, interview with David Anderle, June 24, 2002

CHAPTER 3

1 Author's interview, April 24, 1998
2 Tobler 1973 (via Robles)
3 *Melody Maker*, October 5, 1968
4 Interview segment of NRK TV performance, August 29, 1968
5 *Disc & Music Echo*, October 5, 1968
6 NRK TV, August 29, 1968
7 Author's interview, July 1, 2000
8 *The Daily Trojan*, April 10, 1997
9 NRK TV, August 29, 1968
10 Author's interview, April 24, 1998
11 Author's interview, April 24, 1998
12 *Los Angeles Times*, July 7, 1968
13 *Albuquerque Journal*, October 3, 1968
14 *Post-Crescent*, Appleton, Wisconsin, August 11, 1968

15 *Disc & Music Echo*, October 5, 1968
16 *Beat Instrumental*, November 1968
17 *Evening Standard*, September 21, 1968
18 *Hartford Courant*, October 8, 1968
19 Clive Selwood, *All The Moves (But None Of The Licks)*
20 Mick Houghton, previously unpublished interview with Clive Selwood, conducted during research for *Becoming Elektra*
21 peel.fandom.com/wiki/18_September_1968, accessed August 22, 2023
22 Adam James Smith, *Colour Me Pop*
23 Author's interview, September 17, 2024
24 Adam James Smith, *Colour Me Pop*
25 *Croydon Advertiser*, October 10, 1968
26 *Beat Instrumental*, November 1968
27 peel.fandom.com/wiki/29_September_1968, accessed August 22, 2023
28 peel.fandom.com/wiki/27_October_1968, accessed August 22, 2023
29 Author's interview, April 18, 2024
30 Mick Houghton, *Becoming Elektra*
31 Richie Unterberger, interview with Janice Ackles, 2002

CHAPTER 4

1 *Rolling Stone*, July 28, 2018
2 Email to author, March 2, 2023
3 *Express & News* (San Antonio, Texas), June 15, 1969
4 Author's interview, November 22, 2022
5 *New York Times*, December 16, 1969
6 *Cash Box*, December 20, 1969
7 *Billboard*, December 27, 1969
8 Tobler, 1973 (via Robles)
9 Telephone call with author, April 3, 2023
10 Author's interview, January 19, 2024
11 Tobler, 1973 (via Robles)
12 Tobler, 1973 (via Robles)
13 *Hit Parader*, July 1970
14 *Melody Maker*, September 23, 1972
15 Author's interview, December 10, 2024

CHAPTER 5

1 *Cash Box*, January 17, 1970
2 *Village Voice*, January 8, 1970
3 *Chicago Tribune*, February 15, 1970
4 *Zig Zag*, February 1970
5 *International Times*, February 12, 1970
6 *Times-Herald Newport News*, February 21, 1970
7 *Michigan Daily*, February 18, 1970
8 Richie Unterberger, interview with Janice Ackles, 2002
9 *Michigan Daily*, December 1970
10 *New Musical Express*, January 17, 1970
11 Author's interview, November 14, 2022
12 *Hit Parader*, July 1970
13 Email to author, March 7, 2023
14 Author's interview, December 10, 2024
15 *Cash Box*, October 31, 1970
16 Bernie Taupin, unpublished essay for liner notes to *There Is A River*
17 Author's interview, December 10, 2024
18 Author's interview, November 22, 2022
19 Author's interview, December 9, 2024
20 Jac Holzman and Gavan Daws, *Follow The Music*
21 www.eltonjohn.com/stories/troubadour-50, accessed October 29, 2024
22 Johnny Black, *Classic Rock*, August 25, 2023
23 Elton John, *Guardian*, October 15, 2024
24 Gerald Newman & Joe Bivona, *Elton John*
25 Author's interview, November 13, 2022
26 Author's interview, November 14, 2022
27 Author's interview, November 14, 2022
28 *Phonograph Record*, September 1970
29 *San Francisco Examiner*, September 2, 1970

30 *Capitol Journal*, January 7, 1971
31 *Los Angeles Times*, March 27, 1971

CHAPTER 6

1 Tobler 1973 (via Robles)
2 Bernie Taupin, previously unpublished writing
3 Interview with Richie Unterberger, 2002
4 Mick Houghton, previously unpublished interview with Jac Holzman c. 2008, conducted during research for *Becoming Elektra*
5 *Cash Box*, September 15, 1971
6 Author's interview, November 22, 2022
7 Rosemary Gray and Sue Griffiths (eds), *Book Of Wargrave*
8 Jeremy Harding, email to author, August 2, 2024
9 Peter Delaney, secretary, Wargrave Local History Society, email to author, November 23, 2022
10 Author's interview, November 29, 2022
11 Author's interview, December 10, 2024
12 *Rolling Stone*, August 31, 1972
13 Tobler 1973 (via Robles)
14 Tobler 1973 (via Robles)
15 Author's interview, November 22, 2022
16 Email to author, January 6, 2024
17 Author's interview, April 24, 1998
18 Author's interview, February 8, 2022
19 Howard Massey, *The Great British Recording Studios*
20 Author's interview, April 24, 1998
21 Author's interview, December 10, 2024
22 Author's interview, December 10, 2024
23 Bernie Taupin, previously unpublished writing
24 Email to author, February 22, 2023
25 Email to author, February 22, 2023
26 *Baltimore Sun*, August 13, 1972

CHAPTER 7

1 Author's interview, November 23, 2024
2 Back cover notes to *American Gothic*, 1972
3 *Time Out*, May 19, 1972
4 Author's interview, December 10, 2024
5 Interview with Richie Unterberger, 2002
6 *Sounds*, April 1, 1972
7 Author's interview, September 28, 2023
8 *Rolling Stone*, August 31, 1972
9 Email to author, January 6, 2024
10 *Los Angeles Free Press*, volume 9, number 20, May 19, 1972
11 *Los Angeles Free Press*, volume 9, number 20, May 19, 1972
12 *Detroit Free Press*, June 25, 1972
13 *Democrat & Chronicle*, September 24, 1972
14 *Rolling Stone*, September 14, 1972
15 *Sunday Times*, June 18, 1972
16 *Melody Maker*, June 17, 1972
17 *Melody Maker*, February 16, 1974 (drawn from an interview conducted in 1973)
18 *Montreal Gazette*, September 9, 1972
19 *Creem*, October 1972
20 *Phonograph Record*, October 1972
21 Mike Davenport, *Valley News*, September 1, 1972
22 Author's interview, December 10, 2024
23 *Phonograph Record*, October 1972
24 *Phonograph Record*, October 1972
25 *Baltimore Sun*, August 13, 1972
26 *Philadelphia Inquirer*, October 30, 1972
27 *Melody Maker*, September 23, 1972

CHAPTER 8

1 *Melody Maker*, February 16, 1974
2 *Ptolemaic Terrascope*, 1994
3 Mick Houghton, previously unpublished with Jac Holzman c. 2008, conducted during research for *Becoming Elektra*

4 Author's interview April 24, 1998
5 Author's interview November 22, 2022
6 Author's interview, August 14, 2003
7 Author's interview, November 22, 2022
8 Author's interview, November 22, 2022
9 Email to author, October 4, 2023
10 Tobler 1973 (via Robles)
11 Author's interview, November 22, 2022
12 Author's interview, August 14, 2003
13 Author's interview, November 29, 2022
14 Author's interview, November 29, 2022
15 *Q*, June 1994
16 Mick Houghton, *Becoming Elektra*
17 Author's interview, November 22, 2022
18 Author's interview, August 14, 2003
19 Tobler 1973 (via Robles)
20 *Rolling Stone*, November 22, 1973; *Variety*, November 28, 1973; *Billboard*, October 20, 1973; *Los Angeles Free Press*, November 9, 1973
21 Tobler 1973 (via Robles)
22 Jim O'Rourke, *Essential Tremors* podcast, August 5, 2024
23 Tobler 1973 (via Robles)
24 *Melody Maker*, February 16, 1974
25 Author's interview, November 22, 2022
26 Tobler 1973 (via Robles)
27 Tom Davies, *The Reporter's Tale*
28 Tobler 1973 (via Robles)
29 Author's interview, August 14, 2003
30 Tobler 1973 (via Robles)
31 Author's interview, August 14, 2003
32 Author's interview, November 29, 2022

CHAPTER 9

1 Author's interview, August 14, 2003
2 Author's interview, December 10, 2024
3 Author's interview, November 29, 2022
4 *The Mercury*, Pottstown, November 20, 1976
5 *Ptolemaic Terrascope*, 1994
6 *Q*, June 1994
7 Author's interview, November 14, 2022
8 Author's interview, November 22, 2022
9 Author's interview, November 29, 2022
10 Author's interview, April 24, 1998
11 *Q*, June 1994
12 Letter from David Ackles to Joe Papp, October 7, 1984, Joseph Papp New York Festival Shakespeare Collection, Billy Rose Theatre Collection, The New York Public Library
13 Letter from Linda Miller to Joe Papp, September 17, 1984, Joseph Papp New York Festival Shakespeare Collection, Billy Rose Theatre Collection, The New York Public Library
14 Letter from David Ackles to Joe Papp, as above
15 Letter from David Ackles to Joe Papp, as above
16 Letter from David Ackles to Joe Papp, as above
17 Notes by Gail Papp in Ackles correspondence file, Joseph Papp New York Festival Shakespeare Collection, Billy Rose Theatre Collection, New York Public Library
18 Letter from David Ackles to Gail Papp, April 11, 1985, Joseph Papp New York Festival Shakespeare Collection, Billy Rose Theatre Collection, The New York Public Library
19 *Q*, June 1994
20 Author's interview, September 5, 2024
21 Author's interview, September 17, 2024
22 Author's interview, September 5, 2024
23 Author's interview, September 5, 2024
24 Author's interview, September 17, 2024
25 Letter from Ken Stone to David Ackles, June 17, 1991

26 Author's interview, September 11, 2023

27 David Ackles, *Sister Aimee*, unpublished manuscript 1991

28 Author's interview, September 17, 2024

29 Author's interview, September 17, 2024

CHAPTER 10

1 Email to author, September 12, 2024

2 *Ptolemaic Terrascope*, June 1994

3 Author's interview, September 5, 2024

4 *Daily Trojan*, April 10, 1997

5 Author's interview, September 17, 2024

6 Author's interview, April 24, 1998

7 Author's interview, September 11, 2023

8 *Los Angeles Times*, March 10, 1999

9 *Independent*, March 15, 1999

10 *Guardian*, March 19, 1999

11 Author's interview, April 24, 1988

12 David Cavanagh, *Uncut*, July 2007

13 Stacy Sullivan, *A Night At The Troubadour: Presenting Elton John And David Ackles*, 2016

14 Stacy Sullivan, *A Night At The Troubadour: Presenting Elton John And David Ackles*, 2016

15 Stephen Holden, *New York Times*, July 15, 2016

16 David Hadju, *The Nation*, July 20, 2016

17 Author's interview, April 24, 1998

EPILOGUE

1 Author's interview, November 22, 2022

2 Rob Chapman, 'Beyond The Black-Eyed Dog: Why Nick Drake Deserves More Than "Indiefication"', *The Quietus*, November 25, 2023

3 Tracy Thorn, 'We Can't All Be Geniuses', *New Statesman*, October 16, 2024

4 Tom Cox, *Villager* (Unbound, 2022)

5 Sandy Robertson, *Sounds*, 22 April 1978

6 Author's interview, November 23, 2024

7 Author's interview, November 23, 2024

8 Author's interview, December 10, 2024

9 Bernie Taupin, previously unpublished writing

INDEX

ALSO AVAILABLE FROM JAWBONE PRESS

Riot On Sunset Strip: Rock'n'roll's Last Stand In Hollywood Domenic Priore

Million Dollar Bash: Bob Dylan, The Band, And The Basement Tapes Sid Griffin

Jack Bruce Composing Himself: The Authorised Biography Harry Shapiro

Seasons They Change: The Story Of Acid And Psychedelic Folk Jeanette Leech

The Resurrection Of Johnny Cash: Hurt, Redemption, And American Recordings Graeme Thomson

What's Exactly The Matter With Me? Memoirs Of A Life In Music P.F. Sloan and S.E. Feinberg

Lee, Myself & I: Inside The Very Special World Of Lee Hazlewood Wyndham Wallace

Adventures Of A Waterboy Mike Scott

Becoming Elektra: The Incredible True Story Of Jac Holzman's Visionary Record Label Mick Houghton

What's Big And Purple And Lives In The Ocean? The Moby Grape Story Cam Cobb

Relax Baby Be Cool: The Artistry & Audacity Of Serge Gainsbourg Jeremy Allen

Renegade Snares: The Resistance & Resilience Of Drum & Bass Ben Murphy and Carl Loben

Southern Man: Music And Mayhem In The American South Alan Walden with S.E. Feinberg

Frank & Co: Conversations With Frank Zappa 1977–1993 Co de Kloet

Holy Ghost: The Life & Death Of Free Jazz Pioneer Albert Ayler Richard Koloda

Conform To Deform: The Weird & Wonderful World Of Some Bizzare Wesley Doyle

Happy Forever: My Musical Adventures With The Turtles, Frank Zappa, T. Rex, Flo & Eddie, And More Mark Volman with John Cody

Absolute Beginner: Memoirs Of The World's Best Least-Known Guitarist Kevin Armstrong

Revolutionary Spirit: A Post-Punk Exorcism Paul Simpson

Chopping Wood: Thoughts & Stories Of A Legendary American Folksinger Pete Seeger with David Bernz

Through The Crack In The Wall: The Secret History Of Josef K Johnnie Johnstone

Forever Changes: The Authorized Biography Of Arthur Lee & Love John Einarson

I Wouldn't Say It If It Wasn't True: A Memoir Of Life, Music, And The Dream Syndicate Steve Wynn

Jazz Revolutionary: The Life & Music Of Eric Dolphy Jonathon Grasse

Down On The Corner: Adventures In Busking & Street Music Cary Baker

Gliders Over Hollywood: Airships, Airplay, And The Art Of Rock Promotion Paul Rappaport

Decade Of Dissent: How 1960s Bob Dylan Changed The World Sean Egan

Doing Time: Comedians Talk Stand-Up JT Habersaat